SOFTWARE ENGINEERING:
A BEGINNER'S GUIDE

SOFTWARE ENGINEERING
A Beginner's Guide

Roger S. Pressman, Ph.D.

President, R.S. Pressman & Associates, Inc.
and
Adjunct Professor of Computer Engineering
University of Bridgeport

McGraw-Hill Book Company

New York St. Louis San Francisco Auckland Bogota´ Caracas
Colorado Springs Hamburg Lisbon London Madrid Milan
Montreal New Delhi Oklahoma City Panama Paris San Juan
São Paulo Singapore Sydney Tokyo Toronto

67890 HAN HAN 932

ISBN 0-07-050790-2

This book was set in Times Roman. The editor was Karen M. Jackson; the
cover was designed by Joseph Gillians; the production supervisor was Louise
Karam. Edwards Brothers was printer and binder.

Library of Congress Cataloging-in-Publication Data

Pressman, Roger S.
    Software engineering.

    Includes bibliographies.
    1. Software engineering.   I. Title.
QA76.758.P74   1988   005.1   87-35396
ISBN 0-07-050790-2

ABOUT THE AUTHOR

Roger S. Pressman is a nationally recognized consultant and author in software engineering. He received a B.S.E. (cum laude) from the University of Connecticut, an M.S. from the University of Bridgeport and a Ph.D. in engineering from the University of Connecticut, and has nearly 20 years of industry experience, holding both technical and management positions with responsibility for the development of software for engineered products and systems.

As an industry practitioner and manager, Dr. Pressman worked on the development of CAD/CAM systems for advanced engineering and manufacturing in aerospace applications. He has also held positions with responsibility for scientific and systems programming.

In addition to his industry experience, Dr. Pressman was Bullard Associate Professor of Computer Engineering at the University of Bridgeport. He was also Director of the University's Computer-Aided Design and Manufacturing Center, one of the first such centers established in the United States. He remains at the University as an adjunct Associate Professor of Computer Science and Computer Engineering where his research interests include software engineering methods and metrics, software reusability, and applications of computer graphics to software engineering.

Dr. Pressman is President of R.S. Pressman & Associates, Inc., a consulting firm specializing in software engineering methods and training. He serves as principal consultant and specializes in helping companies establish effective software engineering practices.

Dr. Pressman is author of many technical papers, is a regular contributor to industry newsletters, and is author of four books. His book, *Software Engineering: A Practitioner's Approach* (McGraw-Hill, second edition, 1987), is the world's most widely used software engineering textbook. Another recent book, *Making Software Engineering Happen*, is the first to address the critical management problems associated with implementing software engineering technology. Dr. Pressman is a member of the ACM, IEEE, and Tau Beta Pi, Phi Kappa Phi, Eta Kappa Nu, and Pi Tau Sigma.

To Mathew and Michael

TABLE OF CONTENTS

CHAPTER 5   CODING THE PROGRAM ... 161

PREFACE

When the concept of software engineering was first proposed in the late 1960s, it seemed like a radical idea. After all, programming was more like an art form than an engineering discipline, and software was often little more than an afterthought.

Today, nearly everyone recognizes that software is the driving force behind high technology systems. Yet we continue to encounter problems with the *process* through which software is developed. Software developers (whether undergraduate students or wizened veterans) struggle to build high quality programs that meet their customers' needs. Programs are often delivered behind schedule, are sometimes unreliable, and are frequently difficult to modify. But as the application of a *software engineering* discipline grows, things are beginning to change.

Software engineering is applied regularly when large software projects are undertaken in industry. Whether the application is a banking system or a robot, aircraft avionics or medical instrumentation, a disciplined approach to software development is a *must*. However, misconceptions about the applicability of software engineering abound. Because most software engineering is conducted for major industry projects, many people still believe that an engineering approach to software is applicable only for very large programs. Nothing could be further from the truth!

If it is applied intelligently and modified to best accommodate the application, a software engineering approach is applicable to programs of any size. Methods that enable us to analyze a problem, design a solid solution, code it effectively, and test it thoroughly are equally valuable to a university student working on a two-week homework assignment and a practicing software engineer building a new computer-based system. In fact, the sooner software engineering methods are learned, the more effective one becomes at solving software problems.

The objective of *Software Engineering: A Beginner's Guide* is to provide a step-by-step introduction to software engineering at a level of detail that can be easily applied by first- or second-year undergraduate students or entry-level industry professionals. The book is not intended as a comprehensive treatment of the subject, but rather as a "guide book" for software engineering, presenting the subject as a series of steps and principles that the student can apply to successfully complete any software project. In fact, the steps can be organized as a checklist that can be used by both student and instructor to ensure that all important software engineering activities have been accomplished

Software Engineering: A Beginner's Guide is designed so that it may be used as a supplementary text for any introductory programming course or as the primary text for an introductory software engineering course. Because the book is programming language independent, it can be used effectively regardless of the programming language that is used for instruction. The book can also be be used for any course that requires software project work in which the instructor demands application of software engineering principles.

It is important to note that a software engineering approach in no way diminishes the student's creative ability. In fact, by providing a systematic, rational approach to problem representation, solution, and implementation, *Software Engineering: A Beginner's Guide* can serve to enhance creativity by eliminating much of the confusion, false starts and frustration that often accompany software development.

The design of *Software Engineering: A Beginner's Guide* differs somewhat from that of a typical textbook. Each chapter (with the exception of the first) presents a major activity in the software engineering process. System engineering, problem analysis, design, coding, testing, and maintenance are presented as a series of "how to" steps. Within a chapter, a software engineering activity is described with a series of steps, substeps, principles and concepts that are set off from explanatory text. A single approach (methodology) rather than a survey of alternatives is presented so that the student will have an effective template for applying the discipline. The book also contains three appendixes: (1) a checklist of all steps presented in the book that can be used to track project work, (2) an introduction to software quality assurance techniques that emphasizes formal technical reviews, and (3) a complete example that illustrates the application of all software engineering steps.

The evolution of this book began with the completion of the second edition of *Software Engineering: A Practitioner's Approach*

(SEPA)—a more comprehensive treatment of software engineering technology. SEPA has been adopted widely for use in upper-level university courses and for professional training/reference. Although *Software Engineering: A Beginner's Guide* and SEPA are entirely different in size, form, and style, this book borrows liberally from its predecessor. Explanatory discussions, examples, and many figures have been excised, reworked, and reorganized for this introductory text.

The author of any book on software engineering is remiss if he or she does not acknowledge the hundreds of regular contributors to the literature. These educators, researchers, and industry practitioners have influenced my perception of software engineering and have undoubtedly molded the substance of *Software Engineering: A Beginner's Guide* . I would also like to express my thanks to the reviewers of this book: John Beider, University of Scranton; Robert Glass, University of Seattle; and Allen Tucker, Colgate University. Their constructive criticism and suggestions have been invaluable. Finally, my years as a Professor at the University of Bridgeport have given me important insight into the way undergraduate students best absorb and apply new concepts. The approach taken in this book owes much to the students who have attended my courses in software engineering and related topics.

Writing a book, while at the same time juggling classroom teaching and a successful consulting practice, presents many substantial challenges. My family—Barbara, Mathew, and Michael—provide me with the support to meet those challenges. For that, my love and thanks.

Roger S. Pressman

SOFTWARE ENGINEERING:
A BEGINNER'S GUIDE

CHAPTER 1

THE ROLE OF SOFTWARE

A few years ago, one of the largest companies in the world—an industrial giant that manufactures high technology products that range from CAT scanners to gas turbine engines—conducted a study to assess those technologies expected to have the greatest impact on the company for the remainder of the twentieth century. The resultant list of 24 important technologies (e.g., microelectronics, materials science, genetic engineering) contained few surprises. However, the study did uncover one rather startling fact.

The successful implementation of 18 of the 24 critical technologies was impossible without the development of computer software: software to assist engineers in performing analyses that enable a particular technology to be applied properly; software to be integrated into the manufacturing processes that transform the technology into practical products; software to be placed directly into products that bring the technology to the marketplace; software to aid management in making effective business decisions about the technology. In short, software was pivotal in nearly every aspect of the company's business.

Software is a driving force. Its impact goes far beyond newer and more powerful computers. It has become the pivotal element of the information age. We can no longer live without it!

Yet, building computer-based systems remains a significant challenge, and software is often the primary stumbling block. We create programs that don't function properly, programs that do work but don't do what we really want, programs that can't be easily changed or corrected when errors are found, programs that are delivered for use months or even years too late.

A front page article in *The Wall Street Journal* summed up the most ominous elements of the situation when it stated:

The tiniest software bug can fell the mightiest machine—often with disastrous consequences. During the past five years, software defects have killed sailors, maimed patients, wounded corporations and threatened to cause the government securities market to collapse. Such problems are likely to grow as industry and the military rely on software to run systems of phenomenal complexity ... .[*]

The problems that we associate with software have many causes. The growing complexity of modern computer-based systems often results in software that challenges the ability of even the most expert developer. We lack a comprehensive library of software "building blocks" that would enable us to create programs more easily. We build software in a business climate that demands more function, at lower cost in less time. But many software development problems can be traced to the early history of *programming*. In the early days (circa 1960), programming was an art form in which each programmer created software in an ad hoc fashion. We understood relatively little about problem analysis, program design, or testing—but we did know how to apply assembly language, FORTRAN, or COBOL to describe a program. In most cases one person had responsibility for creating and maintaining a computer program. You built it, you got it to work, and you stayed around to fix it or extend it as time passed. Today, things are much different.

As computer-based systems have become more complex, the demands placed on software have grown exponentially. One person cannot possibly create all software necessary for a large data base management system, a sophisticated personal computer application, or an automated manufacturing cell. John Musa[**] characterizes the problem in this way: "Imagine writing a large book, but instead of three

[*] Davis, B., "As Complexity Rises, Tiny Flaws in Software Pose a Growing Threat," *The Wall Street Journal*, vol. CCIX, No. 19, January 28, 1987, p.1.

[**] Musa, J., et al., *Software Reliability*, McGraw-Hill, 1987.

authors you have three hundred and they're all writing a few paragraphs—try putting it together and getting it to make sense."

Teams of software developers must often work together to meet tight deadlines. "Buggy" programs, once accepted as a *fait accompli*, can no longer be tolerated in systems that oversee power plants, control commercial aircraft, or monitor patients in an intensive care unit.

The artist's culture established for programming during the early days does not accommodate the demands of modern software development. A more disciplined approach—an approach called *software engineering*—must be applied.

Over the past two decades, software developers around the world have come to the realization that software is a product that can be engineered in much the same way as other more conventional products. That is, to develop high quality, industry-grade computer programs, we must take an engineering approach to their development. We must apply a discipline that encompasses procedures, methods, and tools that enable us to control the process through which software is developed, apply a technology that is rational and uniform, and integrate automation in a fashion that enhances human skills.

We've also learned something else. Many of the software engineering techniques that are applicable to large software projects can be effectively applied to any software development effort—no matter how small. Methods that enable us to analyze a problem, design a solid solution, implement the solution effectively, and thoroughly test it are available to all of us. Helping you to understand and apply these methods is what this book is about.

WHAT IS SOFTWARE?

Twenty years ago, less than 1 percent of the general public could have intelligently described what "computer software" meant. Today, most professionals and many members of the public at large feel that they understand software. But do they?

A textbook description of software might take the following form:

Software: (1) instructions (computer programs) that when executed within a digital computer provide desired function and performance, (2) data structures that enable the programs to adequately manipulate information, and (3) documents that describe the operation and use of the programs.

There is no question that other, more complete definitions could be offered. But formal definitions will do little to help us. We have to understand the characteristics of software before we can appreciate the proper approach for developing it.

Software Characteristics

To gain an understanding of software (and ultimately an understanding of software engineering), it is important to examine the characteristics of software that make it different from other things that human beings build. When hardware is built, the human creative process (analysis, design, construction, and testing) is ultimately translated into physical form. If we build a new computer, our initial sketches, formal design drawings, and breadboarded prototype evolve into a physical product (VLSI chips, circuit boards, power supplies, etc.). Although software does take on a variety of physical forms, it is fundamentally a logical system element and has characteristics that are considerably different from those of hardware.

> ## Software is developed or engineered;
> ## it is not manufactured in a classical sense.

Although some similarities exist between software development and hardware manufacture, the two activities are fundamentally different. In both activities, high quality is achieved through good design, but the manufacturing phase for hardware can introduce quality problems (e.g., a machine that reproduces a hardware component loses calibration) that are nonexistent (or easily corrected) for software. Both activities are dependent on people, but the the relationship between people applied and work accomplished is entirely different. Increased output can be achieved in hardware manufacturing by adding more people. The opposite is often true for software. Adding people to a software project can increase the need for communication, and communication takes time. Both activities require the construction of a "product," but the approaches are different.

Software costs are concentrated in engineering while hardware costs are concentrated in manufacturing. Therefore, our focus for software should be on better engineering.

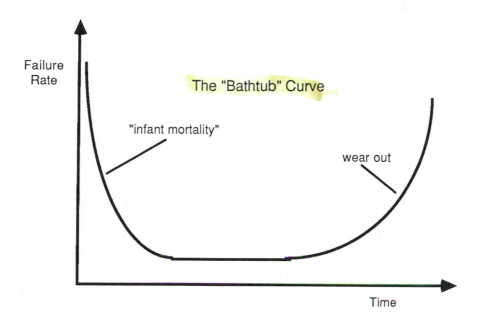

Figure 1.1 Failure Rate Curve for Hardware

Software doesn't wear out.

Figure 1.1 depicts failure rate as a function of time for hardware. This relationship, often called the "bathtub" curve, indicates that hardware exhibits relatively high failure rates early in its life (these failures are often attributable to design or manufacturing defects); defects are corrected, and failure rate drops to a steady state level for some period of time. As time passes, however, the failure rate rises again as hardware components suffer from the cumulative effects of dust, vibration, abuse, temperature extremes, and many other environmental maladies. Stated simply: the hardware begins to wear out.

Software is not susceptible to the environmental maladies that cause hardware to wear out. In theory, therefore, the failure rate curve for software should take the form shown in Figure 1.2. Undiscovered defects will cause high failure rates early in the life of a program. However, these are corrected (hopefully, without introducing other errors), and the curve flattens as shown. Figure 1.2 is a gross over–simplification of actual failure models for software. However, the

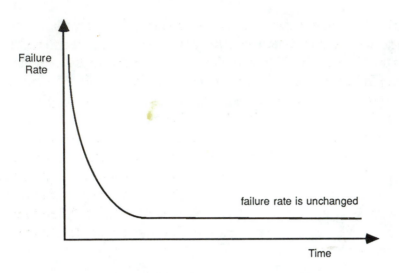

Figure 1.2 Idealized Failure Rate Curve for Software

implication is clear—software doesn't wear out, but it does *deteriorate!*

This seeming contradiction can best be explained by considering Figure 1.3. During its life, software will undergo change (maintenance). Changes occur because errors are corrected, the software is adapted to new computers or operating environments, or users request

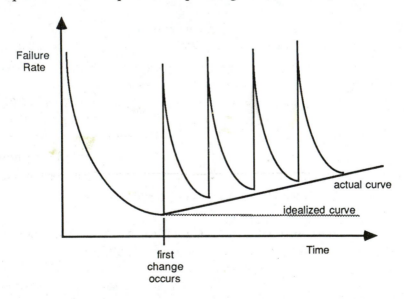

Figure 1.3 Actual Failure Rate Curve for Software

functional enhancements. As changes are made, it is likely that some new defects will be introduced, causing the failure rate curve to spike as shown in Figure 1.3. Before the curve can return to the original steady state failure rate, another change is requested, causing the curve to spike again. Slowly, the minimum failure rate level begins to rise—the software is deteriorating due to change.

Another aspect of wear illustrates the difference between hardware and software. When a hardware component wears out, it is replaced by a "spare part." There are no software spare parts. Every software failure indicates an error in design or in the process through which design was translated into machine-executable code. Therefore, software maintenance involves considerably more complexity than hardware maintenance.

Most software is custom built, rather than being assembled from existing components.

Consider the manner in which the control hardware for a microprocessor-based product is designed and built. The design engineer draws a simple schematic of the digital circuitry, does some fundamental analysis to ensure that proper function will be achieved, and then goes to the shelf where catalogs of digital components, called integrated circuits, exist. Each integrated circuit (often called an "IC" or a "chip") has a part number, a defined and validated function, a well-defined interface, and a standard set of integration guidelines. After each component is selected, it can be ordered off the shelf.

Sadly, software designers are not afforded the luxury described above. With few exceptions, there are no catalogs of software components.* It is possible to order off-the-shelf software, but only as a complete unit, not as components that can be reassembled into new programs.** Although much has been written about "software reuseability," little tangible success has been achieved to date.

---

   * Although "subroutine libraries" have been around for decades, their use is limited to specialized mathematical and data manipulation functions.

   ** New *object-oriented programming* techniques have resulted in libraries of "objects" that can be reassembled into new programs. These show considerable promise but are not yet widely used.

Software Application Areas

Software may be applied in any situation for which a prespecified set of procedural steps (i.e., an algorithm) has been defined (a notable exception to this rule is expert system software). Information content and determinacy are important factors in understanding the nature of a software application. Content refers to the meaning and form of incoming and outgoing information. For example, many business applications make use of highly structured input data (a data base) and produce formatted "reports." Software that controls an automated machine (e.g., a numerical control) accepts discrete data items with limited structure and produces individual machine commands in rapid succession.

Information indeterminacy refers to the predictability of the order and timing of input data for a program. An engineering analysis program accepts data that have a predefined order, executes the analysis algorithm(s) without interruption, and produces resultant data in report or graphical format. Such applications are determinate. A multiuser operating system, on the other hand, accepts inputs that have varied content and arbitrary timing, executes algorithms that can be interrupted by external conditions, and produces output that varies as a function of environment and time. Applications with these characteristics are indeterminate.

It is somewhat difficult to develop meaningful generic categories for software applications. As software complexity grows, neat compartmentalization disappears. The following software application areas indicate the breadth of software's impact:

System Software. System software is a collection of programs written to service other programs. Some system software (e.g., compilers, editors, and file management utilities) process complex but determinate information structures. Other systems applications (e.g., operating system components, drivers, telecommunications processors) process largely indeterminate data. In either case, the system software area is characterized by heavy interaction with computer hardware; heavy usage by multiple users; concurrent operation that requires scheduling, resource sharing, and sophisticated process management; complex data structures; and multiple external interfaces.

Real-Time Software. Software that measures/analyzes/controls real-world events as they occur is called *real-time software*. Elements of real-time software include a data gathering component that collects and formats information from an external environment, an analysis component that transforms information as required by the application, a control/output component that responds to the external environment, and a monitoring component that coordinates all other components so that real-time response (typically ranging from 1 millisecond to 1 minute) can be maintained. It should be noted that the term "real-time" differs from "interactive" or "timesharing." A real-time system must respond within strict time constraints. The response time of an interactive (or timesharing) system can normally be exceeded without disastrous results.

Business Software.   Business information processing is the largest single software application area. Discrete "systems" (e.g., payroll, accounts receivable/payable, inventory control) have evolved into management information system (MIS) software that accesses one or more large data bases containing business information. Applications in this area restructure existing data in a way that facilitates business operations or management decision making. In addition to conventional data processing applications, business software applications also encompass interactive computing (e.g., point-of-sale transaction processing).

Engineering and Scientific Software. Engineering and scientific software has been characterized by "number crunching" algorithms. Applications range from astronomy to volcanology, from automotive stress analysis to space shuttle orbital dynamics, and from molecular biology to automated manufacturing. However, new applications within the engineering/scientific area are moving away from conventional numerical algorithms. Computer-aided design, system simulation, and other interactive applications have begun to take on real-time and even system software characteristics.

Embedded Software. Intelligent products have become commonplace in nearly every consumer and industrial market. Embedded software resides in read-only memory and is used to control products and systems for the consumer and industrial markets. In most cases, embedded software takes on all of the characteristics described for the real-time category, with one important difference—embedded software never exists in a computer that is physically separated from the product or system that is being monitored/controlled; that is, if the product moves, the software moves with it. Embedded software can perform

very limited and esoteric functions (e.g., key pad control for a micro-
wave oven) or provide significant function and control capability
(e.g., digital functions in an automobile such as fuel control, dashboard displays, and braking systems).

Personal Computer Software. The personal computer (PC) software
market has burgeoned over the past decade. Word processing, desk-
top publishing, spreadsheets, computer graphics, entertainment, data
base management, personal and business financial applications, external network or data base access are only a few of hundreds of applications. In fact, personal computer software continues to represent some
of the most innovative human interface design of all software. The
characteristic that distinguishes personal computer software from programs developed for larger computers is the number of copies of the
programs in existence. Hundreds of thousands of copies of many
popular PC software applications are currently in use.

Artificial Intelligence Software. Artificial intelligence (AI) software
makes use of non-numerical algorithms to solve complex problems
that are not amenable to computation or straightforward analysis. Currently, the most active AI area is *expert systems,* also called knowl-
edge-based systems. However, other application areas for AI software
are pattern recognition (image and voice), theorem proving, robotics,
and game playing.

The Software Crisis

The phrase *software crisis* alludes to a set of problems that are encountered in the development of computer software. The problems
are not limited to software that "doesn't function properly." Rather,
the software crisis encompasses problems associated with how we develop software, how we maintain a growing volume of existing software, and how we can expect to keep pace with a growing demand for
more software. Although reference to a software crisis can be criti-
cized for being melodramatic, the phrase does serve a useful purpose
by encompassing real problems that are encountered in all areas of
software development.

Issues and Problems for the 1990s

The software crisis is characterized by many problems. Software engineers (and students who are learning to become software engineers)

struggle to properly analyze, design, code, and test programs. *"I've got so little time, I'd better begin coding"* has been the undoing of many practitioners. But what else can we do? How do we analyze a software problem? What aspects of design result in high quality programs? How should we go about the coding task? What is the most effective approach for testing computer programs? How should we build programs so that others can modify (maintain) them in the years ahead? The software crisis continues because too many of us still don't know the answers to these questions.

Technical issues and concerns are not the only ones that we encounter. Managers responsible for software development concentrate on the "bottom line" issues: (1) Schedule and cost estimates are often grossly inaccurate, (2) the "productivity" of software people hasn't kept pace with the demand for their services, and (3) the quality of software is sometimes less than adequate. Cost overruns of an order of magnitude have been experienced. Schedules slip by months or years. Little has been done to improve the productivity of software practitioners. Error rates for new programs cause customer dissatisfaction and lack of confidence.

We have presented the bad news first. Now for the good news. Each of the problems described above can be corrected. An engineering approach to the development of software, coupled with continuing improvement of techniques and tools, provides the key.

One problem (we could call it a fact of life) will remain. Software will absorb a larger and larger percentage of the overall development cost for computer-based systems. In the United States, we spend close to $80 billion each year on the development, acquisition, and maintenance of computer software. We had better take the problems associated with software development seriously.

SOFTWARE ENGINEERING PARADIGMS

The software crisis will not disappear overnight. Recognizing problems and their causes is the first step toward a solution. But solutions themselves must provide practical assistance to the software developer, improve software quality, and, finally, allow the "software world" to keep pace with the "hardware world."

There is no single best approach to a solution for the software crisis. However, by combining comprehensive methods for all phases in software development, better tools for automating these methods, more powerful building blocks for software implementation, better techniques for software quality assurance, and an overriding philosophy for coordination, control, and management, we can achieve a discipline for software development—a discipline called *software engineering*.

Software Engineering: A Definition

Software engineering has been defined as "the establishment and use of sound engineering principles in order to obtain economically software that is reliable and works efficiently on real machines." Although many more comprehensive definitions have been proposed, all reinforce the requirement for engineering discipline in software development.

Software engineering is an outgrowth of hardware and system engineering. It encompasses a set of three key elements—methods, tools, and procedures—that enable the manager to control the process of software development and provide the practitioner with a foundation for building high quality software in a productive manner. In the paragraphs that follow, we examine briefly each of these elements.

Software engineering methods provide the technical "how to's" for building software. Methods encompass a broad array of tasks that include: project planning and estimation; system and software requirements analysis; design of data structure, program architecture and algorithm procedure; coding; testing; and maintenance. Methods for software engineering often introduce a special language-oriented or graphical notation and introduce a set of criteria for software quality.

Software engineering tools provide automated or semiautomated support for methods. Today, tools exist to support each of the methods noted above. When tools are integrated so that information created by one tool can be used by another, a system for the support of software development, called *Computer-Aided Software Engineering* (CASE) is established. CASE combines software, hardware, and a software engineering data base (a data structure containing important information about analysis, design, coding, and testing) to create a software engineering environment that is analogous to CAD/CAE (computer-aided design/engineering) for hardware.

Software engineering procedures are the glue that holds the

methods and tools together and enables rational and timely development of computer software. Procedures define the sequence in which methods will be applied, the deliverables (documents, reports, forms, etc.) that are required, the controls that help assure quality and coordinate change, and the milestones that enable software managers to assess progress.

Software engineering comprises a set of steps that encompasses methods, tools and procedures discussed above. The ways in which these steps are applied are often referred to as *software engineering paradigms*. A paradigm for software engineering is chosen on the basis of the nature of the project and application, the methods and tools to be used, and the demands of the customer who has requested the software. Three paradigms have been widely discussed (and debated) and are described in the following sections.

The Classic Life Cycle

Figure 1.4 illustrates the classic life cycle paradigm for software engineering. Sometimes called the "waterfall model," the life cycle paradigm demands a systematic, sequential approach to software development that begins at the system level and progresses through analysis, design, coding, testing, and maintenance. Modeled after the

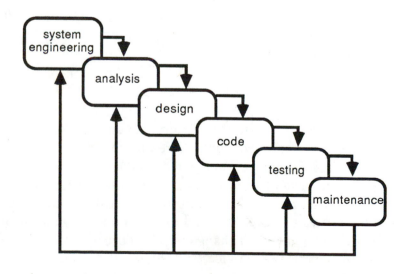

Figure 1.4   The Classic Life Cycle

conventional engineering cycle, the life cycle paradigm encompasses the following activities:

System Engineering and Analysis. Because software is always part of a larger system, work begins by establishing requirements for all system elements and then allocating some subset of these requirements to software. This system view is essential when software must interface with other elements such as hardware, people, and data bases. System engineering and analysis encompasses requirements gathering at the system level with a small amount of top-level design and analysis.

Software Requirements Analysis. The requirements gathering process is intensified and focused specifically on software. To understand the nature of the program(s) to be built, the software engineer ("analyst") must understand the information domain (described in Chapter 3) for the software, as well as required function, performance, and interfacing. Requirements for both the system and the software are documented and reviewed with the customer.

Design. Software design is actually a multistep process that focuses on three distinct attributes of the program: data structure, software architecture, and procedural detail. The design process translates requirements into a representation of the software that can be assessed for quality before coding begins. Like requirements, the design is documented.

Coding. The design must be translated into a machine-readable form. The coding step performs this task. If design is performed in a detailed manner, coding is a natural outgrowth that can be performed rather mechanically.

Testing. Once code has been generated, program testing begins. The testing process focuses on the logical internals of the software, assuring that all statements have been tested, and on the functional externals, that is, the conduct of tests to ensure that defined input will produce actual results that agree with required results.

Maintenance. Software will undoubtedly undergo change after it is delivered to the customer (a possible exception is embedded software). Change will occur because errors have been encountered, because the software must be adapted to accommodate changes in its external environment (e.g., a change required because of a new operating system or peripheral device), or because the customer requires functional or performance enhancements. Software maintenance reapplies each of the preceding life cycle steps to an existing program rather than a new one.

The classic life cycle is the oldest and the most widely used paradigm for software engineering. However, over the past few years, criticism of the paradigm has caused even active supporters to question its applicability in all situations. Among the problems that are sometimes encountered when the classic life cycle paradigm is applied are:

1. Real projects rarely follow the sequential flow that the model proposes. Iteration always occurs and creates problems in the application of the paradigm.

2. It is often difficult for the customer to state all requirements explicitly, up front. The classic life cycle requires this and has difficulty accommodating the natural uncertainty that exists at the beginning of many projects.

3. The customer must have patience. A working version of the program(s) will not be available until late in the project time span. A major blunder, if undetected until the working program is reviewed, can be disastrous.

Each of these problems is real. However, the classic life cycle paradigm has a definite and important place in software engineering work. It provides a template into which methods for analysis, design, coding, testing, and maintenance can be placed. In addition, we will see that the steps of the classic life cycle paradigm are very similar to the generic steps that are applicable to all software engineering paradigms. The classic life cycle remains the most widely used procedural model for software engineering. While it does have weaknesses, it is significantly better than a haphazard approach to software development.

Prototyping

Often, a customer has defined a set of general objectives for software but has not identified detailed input, processing, or output requirements. In other cases, the developer may be unsure of the efficiency of an algorithm, the adaptability of an operating system, or the form that human-machine interaction should take. In these and many other situations, a *prototyping* approach to software engineering may offer the best approach.

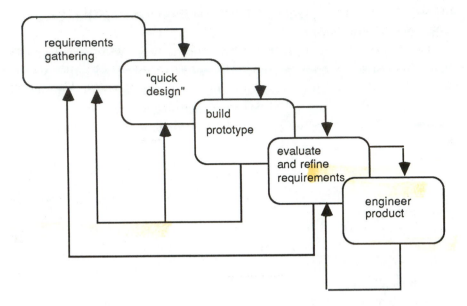

Figure 1.5   Prototyping

Prototyping is a process that enables the developer to create a model of the program that must be built. The model—or prototype—may be designed to depict one or more aspects of a human-machine interface, a sophisticated algorithm (whose results are as yet unclear), or a set of functional or performance requirements that are questionable. The model can take one of three forms:

Paper Prototype. This paper-and-ink model illustrates some aspect of the software and is usually used to represent human-machine interfaces. For example, a sequence of pictures can depict different screen interaction activities so that a potential user can understand how such interaction will occur.

Working Prototype. This model implements some subset of the function required of the desired software. The model is executed on a computer to provide a "feel" for the program to be developed.

An Existing Program. This model uses a fully operational program that performs part or all of the function desired but has other features that will be improved upon in the new development effort.

The sequence of events for the prototyping paradigm is illustrated in Figure 1.5. Like all approaches to software development, prototyping begins with requirements gathering. Developer and customer meet and define the overall objectives for the software, identify whatever requirements are known, and outline areas where further definition is mandatory. A "quick design" is then done. The quick design focuses on a representation of those aspects of the software that will be visible to the user (e.g., input approaches and output formats). The quick design leads to the construction of a prototype (remember that the prototype can be a paper model). The prototype is evaluated by the customer/user and is used to refine requirements for the software to be developed. A process of iteration occurs as the prototype is "tuned" to satisfy the customer's requirements, while at the same time enabling the developer to better understand what needs to be done. Ideally, the prototype serves as a mechanism for identifying software requirements. If a working prototype is built, the developer attempts to make use of existing program fragments or applies tools (e.g., report generators, window managers) that enable working programs to be generated quickly.

Like the classic life cycle, prototyping as a paradigm for software engineering can be problematic for the following reasons:

1. The customer sees what appears to be a working version of the software, unaware that the prototype is held together "with chewing gum and baling wire," unaware that in the rush to get it working we haven't considered overall software quality or long-term maintainability. When informed that the product must be rebuilt, the customer cries foul and demands that "a few fixes" be applied to make the prototype a working product. Too often, software development management relents.

2. The developer often makes implementation compromises in order to get a prototype working quickly. An inappropriate operating system or programming language may be used simply because it is available and known; an inefficient algorithm may be implemented simply to demonstrate capability. After a time, the developer may become familiar with these choices and forget all the reasons why they were inappropriate. The less than ideal choice has now become an integral part of the system.

Although problems can occur, prototyping is an effective paradigm for software engineering. The key is to define the rules of the game at the beginning; that is, the customer and developer must agree that the prototype is built to serve as a mechanism for defining requirements. It is then discarded (or reworked). The final version of the software is engineered with an eye toward quality and maintainability.

Fourth-Generation Techniques

The term *fourth-generation techniques* (4GT) encompasses a broad array of software tools that have one thing in common: each enables the software developer to specify some characteristic of software at a high level of abstraction. That is, the software developer specifies *what* the software is to accomplish rather than the implementation details associated with *how* it is to accomplish it. Software tools associated with fourth-generation techniques lead to programming language source code that is automatically generated based on the developer's specification.

Currently, a software development environment that supports the 4GT paradigm includes some or all of the following tools: nonprocedural languages for data base query, report generation, data manipulation, screen interaction and definition, code generation, high-level graphics capability, and/or spreadsheet capability. Each of these tools does exist, but only for very specific application domains. There is no 4GT environment available today that may be applied with equal facility to each of the software application categories described earlier in this chapter.

The 4GT paradigm for software engineering is depicted in Figure

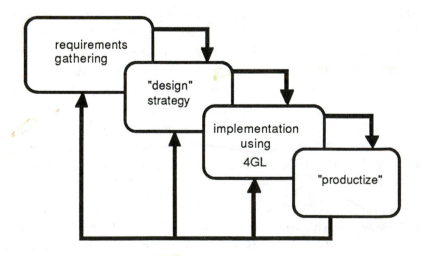

Figure 1.6   Fourth-Generation Techniques Paradigm

1.6. Like other paradigms, 4GT begins with a requirements gathering step. Ideally, the customer describes requirements. Using a 4GT, these are directly translated into an operational prototype. But this is unworkable. The customer may be unsure of what is required, may be ambiguous in specifying facts that are known and may be unable or unwilling to specify information in a manner that a 4GT tool can understand. In addition, current 4GT tools are not sophisticated enough to accommodate truly "natural" language and won't be for some time. At this time, the customer-developer dialogue described for other paradigms remains an essential part of the 4GT approach.

For small applications, it may be possible to move directly from the requirements gathering step to implementation using a non-procedural *fourth-generation language* (4GL). However, for larger efforts, it is necessary to develop a design strategy for the system, even if a 4GL is to be used.

The last step in Figure 1.6 contains the word "product." To transform a 4GT implementation into a product, the developer must conduct thorough testing, develop meaningful documentation, and perform all other "transition activities" that are required in other software engineering paradigms. In addition, the 4GT developed software must be built in a manner that enables maintenance to be performed expeditiously.

There has been much hyperbole and considerable debate surrounding the use of the 4GT paradigm. Proponents claim dramatic reduction in software development time and greatly improved productivity for people who build software. Opponents claim that current 4GT tools are not all that much easier to use than programming languages, that the resultant source code produced by such tools is "inefficient," and that the maintainability of large software systems developed using 4GT is open to question.

There is some merit in the claims of both sides. Although it is somewhat difficult to separate fact from fancy (few controlled studies have been done), it is reasonable to state that 4GT will be applied over an increasingly wider array of applications and that the level of sophistication of these techniques will increase over time.

Combining Paradigms

The software engineering paradigms discussed in the preceding sections are often described as *alternative* approaches to software

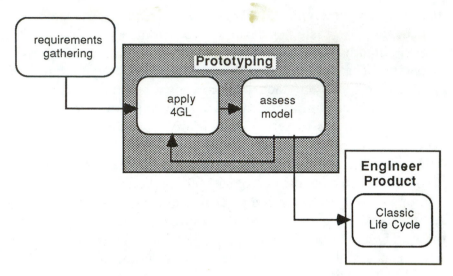

Figure 1.7   Combining Paradigms

engineering, rather than *complementary* approaches. In many cases, the paradigms can and should be combined so that the strengths of each can be achieved on a single project. An adversarial relationship need not exist!

Figure 1.7 illustrates one approach for combining the three paradigms during a single software development effort. In all cases, work begins with a requirements gathering step. The approach taken can follow the classic life cycle (system engineering and software requirements analysis) or can be the less formal problem definition used in prototyping. Regardless, customer-developer communication must occur.

The nature of the application will dictate the applicability of a prototyping approach. If the requirements for software function and performance are reasonably well understood, the specification approaches recommended by the classic life cycle paradigm may be applicable. On the other hand, if the software application demands heavy human-machine interaction or requires as yet unproved algorithms or output/control techniques, a prototype may be in order. In such cases, a fourth-generation language can sometimes be used to rapidly develop the prototype. Once the prototype has been evaluated and refined, the design and implementation steps of the classic life cycle can be applied to formally engineer the software.

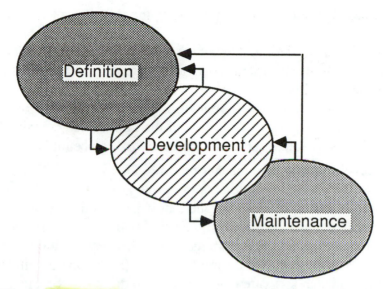

Figure 1.8 Generic Phases of the Software Engineering Process

There is no need to be dogmatic about the choice of paradigms for software engineering. The nature of the application should dictate the approach to be taken. By combining approaches, the whole can be greater than the sum of the parts.

A GENERIC VIEW OF SOFTWARE ENGINEERING

The software engineering process contains three generic phases (Figure 1.8) regardless of which software engineering paradigm is chosen. The three phases, *definition, development,* and *maintenance,* are encountered in all software development, regardless of application area, project size, or complexity.

The definition phase focuses on *what*. That is, during definition, the software engineer attempts to identify what information is to be processed, what function and performance are desired, what interfaces are to be established, what design constraints exist, and what validation criteria are required to define a successful system. The key requirements of the system and the software are identified. Although the methods applied during the definition phase will vary depending on which the software engineering paradigm (or combination of paradigms) is applied, three specific steps will occur in some form:

System Analysis. Already described in our discussion of the classic life cycle, system analysis defines the role of each element in a computer-based system, ultimately defining the role that software will play.

Software Project Planning. Once the scope of the software is determined, resources are allocated, costs are estimated, and work tasks and schedule are defined.

Requirements Analysis. The scope defined for the software provides direction, but a more detailed definition of the information domain and function of the software is necessary before work can begin.

The development phase focuses on *how*. That is, during development the software engineer attempts to define how data structure and software architecture are to be designed, how procedural details are to be implemented, how the design will be translated into a programming language (or non-procedural language), and how testing will be performed. The methods applied during the development phase will vary depending on which software engineering paradigm (or combination of paradigms) is applied. However, three specific steps will occur in some form:

Software Design. Design translates the requirements for the software into a set of representations (some graphical, others tabular or language-based) that describe data structure, architecture, and procedural detail.

Coding. Design representations must be translated into an artificial language (the language may be a conventional programming language or a non-procedural language used in the context of the 4GT paradigm) that results in instructions that can be executed by the computer. The coding step performs this translation.

Software Testing. Once the software is implemented in machine-executable form, it must be tested to uncover defects in function, logic, and implementation.

The maintenance phase focuses on *change* that is associated with error correction, adaptations required as the software's environment evolves, and changes due to enhancements brought about by changing customer requirements. The maintenance phase reapplies the steps of the definition and development phases, but does so in the context of existing software. Three types of change are encountered during the maintenance phase:

Correction. Even with the best quality assurance activities, it is likely that the customer will uncover defects in the software. *Corrective maintenance* changes the software to correct defects.

Adaptation. Over time, the original environment (e.g., CPU, operating system, peripherals) for which the software was developed is likely to change. *Adaptive maintenance* results in modification to the software to accommodate changes to its external environment.

Enhancement. As software is used, the customer/user will recognize additional functions that will provide benefits. *Perfective maintenance* extends the software beyond its original function requirements.

The phases and related steps described in our generic view of software engineering are complemented by a number of *umbrella activities*. Reviews are conducted to assure that quality is maintained as each step is completed. Documentation is developed and controlled to assure that complete information about the system and software will be available for later use. Change control is instituted so that changes can be approved and tracked.

In the classic life cycle paradigm, the phases and steps described in this section are explicitly defined. In the prototyping and 4GT paradigms, some of the steps are implied but not explicitly identified. The approach to each step may vary from paradigm to paradigm, but an overall approach that demands definition, development, and maintenance remains invariant. You can conduct each phase with discipline and well-defined methods, or you can muddle through each haphazardly. But you will perform them nonetheless.

In the remaining chapters of this book, you'll learn the individual steps that will enable you to apply software engineering to projects large and small. Rather than solving a software problem "by the seat of your pants," you'll have a proven set of steps that, if followed in a disciplined manner, will yield higher quality computer programs.

SUMMARY

Software has become the key element in the evolution of computer-based systems and products. Over the past four decades, software has evolved from a specialized problem-solving and information analysis tool to an industry in itself. But early "programming" culture and history have created a set of problems that persist today. Software has become a limiting factor in the evolution of computer-based systems.

Software engineering is a discipline that integrates methods, tools, and procedures for the development of computer software. A number of paradigms for software engineering have been proposed, each exhibiting strengths and weaknesses, but all having a series of generic phases in common. It is the steps of these generic phases and the methods that are applied within each step that comprise the remainder of this book.

WHAT THIS MEANS TO YOU

As a student who is just beginning the study of computer science and software engineering, it may be difficult to see what the "industry" problems and approaches discussed in this chapter have to do with your current situation. "I'll be working all by myself on small programs," you protest. "Do I really need to know about software engineering?" You do, and here's why.

Every program that you develop, no matter how small, should meet the requirements of a customer (in your current situation, the customer is your instructor). The requirements must be translated into a high quality computer program. Design accomplishes the translation and provides you with insight into the quality of your solution. Once the solution is coded (in Pascal, C or another high-level programming language), it should be thoroughly tested to ensure proper operation. Each of these activities is a software engineering step and is described in detail in one of the chapters that follow. When you understand them, you'll be one step closer to becoming a software professional.

FURTHER READINGS

Brooks, F., *The Mythical Man-Month*, Addison-Wesley, 1975.
Kidder, T., *The Soul of a New Machine*, Little-Brown, 1981.
Pressman, R.S., *Software Engineering: A Practitioner's Approach,* second edition, McGraw-Hill, 1987.

PROBLEMS AND POINTS TO PONDER

1.1 In many cases, it is software, not hardware, that differentiates new products. Select five products available in the consumer marketplace and indicate how software differentiates one company's version from another.

1.2 Provide a specific example of a program that resides in each software application category. Write a one-paragraph description of each example.

1.3 Find one or more examples of software "horror stories" (situations in which software has caused problems for an individual, a company, or government) written up in the popular press.

1.4 Describe a classic hardware development paradigm. How does it differ from the classic software life cycle?

1.5 How do system engineering and software engineering differ?

1.6 Suggest a situation in which prototyping would be a useful paradigm for software development. Can you cite examples in which prototyping is used for hardware development?

1.7 Why is software maintenance difficult? What characteristics of a computer program make it maintainable?

1.8 Do some research on fourth-generation techniques and provide an example of a "program" developed using these techniques.

1.9 Using the generic view of software engineering presented at the end of this chapter, develop a special paradigm that would be applicable to your classroom assignments.

1.10 How do you think a team software development project differs from a one-person project? How does software engineering provide support for a team project?

CHAPTER 2
UNDERSTANDING THE SYSTEM

As we make the slow (and often painful) transition into an information age, we often hear the phrase "high technology" used to describe both companies and their products. When "high technology" is used as an adjective, it almost always refers to the use of *computer-based systems*.

A computer-based system combines a group of *system elements* in a way that performs one or more functions to satisfy some explicit objective. Although there are many ways to represent a computer-based system, the most common approach depicts the system in terms of the following elements: software, hardware, people, information, documents, and procedures.

In this book, our attention will be focused on software and the engineering discipline for its development. But it is very important to note that software never stands by itself. Software must always be used in conjunction with hardware; it must interact (to varying degrees) with people; it often accesses organized sources of information; it should be documented; and it fits into a larger procedural model for the activities of the person or company that uses it. For these reasons, we must consider software in the context of a computer-based system. Before software engineering begins, we must apply a series

of system engineering steps so that the context for software is properly understood.

At this point you may object, "I don't create computer-based systems; I just design and build relatively small programs. This chapter
surely won't apply to me."

Don't be so sure! Even the smallest program can be viewed in a
system context.

For example, consider a small program for performing a numerical integration* of a function *f(x)*. Depending on the sophistication of
the integration algorithm, such a program can be created in less than
50 lines of Pascal or FORTRAN. Yet the program can be viewed in a
system context. The integration algorithm is contained in a text book
(document) and must be translated into a programming language using
a compiler (software). The program will execute on a computer
(hardware) that has specific system commands (software) for invoking the integration program. These must be documented (procedures)
for the user (a person) of the program. Input (information) must be
fed to the algorithm using a keyboard (hardware) or by accessing a
data file (information), and results (information) must be output on a
screen or printer (hardware).

Before a numerical integration program can be created (or acquired), each of the elements denoted in parentheses in the preceding
paragraph must be *identified* and *allocated*. The job of identification
and allocation is undertaken by a system engineer. Obviously, for a
program as simple as the one described in our example, system engineering will be reasonably straightforward—but it will occur. In fact,
the thoroughness with which system engineering is performed will
affect the completeness of the software solution.

The role of the system engineer is to identify and analyze the required function and performance of the system that is to be built and
then allocate this function and performance to each of the system elements shown in Figure 2.1. The process of *allocation* is pivotal to
system engineering. Once allocation has been completed, each system
element may be specified in a manner that lays a foundation for all the
work that is to follow.

In the case of software, function and performance allocated to

* Stated simply, numerical integration finds the area under the curve defined by
f(x) between bounding values *x=a* and *x=b*.

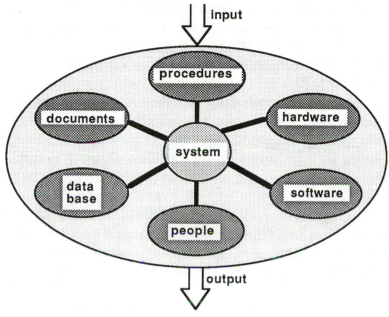

Figure 2.1 System Elements and Allocation

computer programs form the basis for all software engineering work. For this reason, it is important that we begin our step-by-step discussion of software engineering principles at the system level.

Develop or acquire a statement of system scope.

To understand the function and performance of a computer-based system we must begin with an overall *statement of scope*. The statement of scope identifies key system objectives and enables us to infer major system functions and important performance parameters. In some cases, the statement of scope is provided by the individual or entity (whom we shall call the "customer") who has requested development of a computer-based system. In the majority of cases, the system developer must work in conjunction with the customer to write a comprehensive statement of scope. Regardless of who writes the statement of scope, the following substeps should be accomplished.

Ask questions to understand overall system function.

Before the software engineering process can begin, we must understand the overall function of the computer-based system and software's role within the system. Ideally, a detailed description of system function is provided by the customer. In reality, the software engineer must pose a series of questions that help the customer to describe his or her needs in a concise and unambiguous fashion.

The initial set of questions should focus on output. What information or control does the system produce? What are the format, content, and structure of output data? Are they produced in report form, as graphical displays, or in some specialized format? Who makes use of the output data? What other systems use the output data? Answers to questions such as these help the software engineer to isolate the overall system objectives and provide an implicit indication of system function.

The second set of questions should focus on input. What information or control does the system accept as input? Are the input data provided through a human-machine interactive dialogue? What level of data validation is required? What format does the input take? Who provides the input?

The customer's response to output and input questions will often provide substantial information about system function. For example, if the customer indicates that "a histogram showing student average grades for each computer science course" is to be produced as output, we can infer that (1) a function that computes student grades will probably be required, (2) a function that produces histograms (graphic output) must be developed or acquired, and (3) data for more than one course must be accommodated.

The third set of questions is designed to refine our understanding of system function. The inferences derived from output and input questions are validated by probing the customer's perception of the operation of the system. Questions that attempt to clarify each inferred function are developed. The answers to these questions, coupled with earlier answers, lead to a written statement of scope.

Describe the overall system function.

A description of overall system function is often a paragraph that identifies the overall objectives for the computer-based system. The paragraph uses plain language to describe what function(s) the system is to accomplish and the information required and produced. For example, a statement of scope for the numerical integration program might read:

A system that uses numerical techniques to compute the integral of a function $f(x)$ between bounding values a and b is to be developed. Only functions of the form $f(x) = px^3 + qx^2 + rx + s$ are to be considered.

The statement of scope leaves many questions unanswered. Is the "system" to be computerized or manual? What level of accuracy is required? How are the function $f(x)$ and bounding values a and b described? How fast must the integration be performed?

As the statement of scope is refined (to provide answers to the preceding questions and others), two things happen: function is identified and analyzed, and the role of each system element is determined. For example, if only an approximation is required, speed is unimportant, and the method of implementation is inconsequential, the best allocation might be purely manual—graphical integration using paper and pencil. The appropriate system elements are a person, instructions (procedure), and a graphical representation of $f(x)$ on graph paper (information). On the other hand, if high accuracy is required and hundreds of integrations must be performed every minute, a computer-based solution is implied. In this case appropriate system elements would include hardware, software, people, documents, information, and procedures.

For very simple problems such as numerical integration, the process of identification, analysis, and allocation is often implicit. For more complex problems, however, we need a more systematic approach.

To begin our discussion of a systematic approach, we consider a more complicated problem: a computer-based system that enables an automobile (and its driver) to maintain constant speed while on the highway ("cruise control"). A statement of scope might be described initially in the following fashion:

The cruise control system will maintain constant automobile speed once it has been set by the driver. Speed will be maintained until the system is disabled or until the driver presses the brakes.

The above statement describes both the objective of the system and its overall function. It also indicates information required (a speed setting) and produced (maintenance of constant speed). However, many details have not been addressed. We have described the objective and overall function of the system at a high *level of abstraction*. That is, functional details have not yet been described, a specific delineation of input and output has not been identified, and implementation details have been omitted altogether. It is important to note, however, that these omissions are completely acceptable at this level. Our job is to develop a statement of scope—not to create a detailed design for the cruise control. That comes later.

For some readers, it may seem unnecessary and redundant to develop a statement of scope for a cruise control. By virtue of its name, cruise control implies a variety of functions and performance characteristics. In fact, our "understanding" of the function of a cruise control may cause as many problems as it solves.

Cruise control is a *procedural abstraction*. That is, the phrase "cruise control" implies a set of functions and performance characteristics to the knowledgeable reader. Using the procedural abstraction **cruise control**, we imply certain top-level system functions. However, we must be careful not to assume everyone who reads **cruise control** will necessarily interpret function, input and output, and implementation detail in exactly the same way. There are, of course, many different ways in which automobile cruise controls function and a variety of ways in which they are implemented. Therefore, the use of a procedural abstraction can be beneficial while at the same time being somewhat dangerous. The use of abstractions enables different people to communicate a concept in a concise manner. But abstractions can create problems because everyone participating in the communication assumes that their view of the system is the one that has been adopted by others.

It is for this reason that we must write it down. As a battle-hardened system engineer once said: "Everyone always agrees that the description of the system is correct, until someone decides to write it down."

A statement of overall system function can be developed in many different ways. However, it almost always pays to keep it very simple at the beginning. That is, the first statement or draft of overall system functions should be a simple sentence (a subject, a verb, and an object). For example, a statement of overall system function for the cruise control might be the following:

The cruise control system maintains automobile speed.

Subsequent iterations of this simple sentence can and will refine the subject, verb, and object to provide more detail and less ambiguity.

Our original statement of scope for the cruise control might represent the first iteration on the above simple sentence. However, as a first step, the simple sentence provides a mechanism for organizing our thoughts in a concise, yet effective, manner.

Identify key inputs and outputs.

Regardless of the area of application, every computer-based system is an *information transform*. That is, input data are transformed by the system to become output data. The next step in the creation of a statement of scope is a description of key inputs and outputs for the computer-based system. During the early stages of system engineering work, it is often useful to classify data transformed by the system into two broad generic categories: data items and control items. A *data item* is any system input or output that has information content and is transformed (i.e., modified, reorganized, computed, combined) by the software element of a computer-based system. In general, computational or combinatorial algorithms transform data items in one way or another. A *control item* generally implies the occurrence of a specific action or event or requests the initiation of a specific action or event.

To illustrate the difference between data items and control items, assume that the cruise control system allows the driver to key in the desired speed using a numeric key pad on the dashboard (beware human engineering problems!). The desired speed is a data item—that is, a system input that is processed by cruise control software and transformed into a boundary value for speed. To disengage the cruise control, the driver must depress the brakes or hit a **cruise-control-off** button. Either action causes a pulse to be read by the cruise control software. Because the pulse is not transformed (modified, reorganized, computed, combined) in any significant way but represents an *event* that causes an immediate change in the system function, it may be deemed a control item.

In many cases, the difference between data and control items is subtle. All control items are processed by software and transformed to some degree, and many legitimate data items may ultimately control system function in some way.

List all constraints that affect the system.

The specification and design of a computer-based system are constrained for many reasons:

- Economic concerns may limit both technical and human resources that can be applied to the problem.
- The characteristics of one system element may constrain the manner in which another system element is specified and subsequently designed.
- The environment into which the system will be placed may impose external constraints on the manner in which the system functions and the performance of the system.

To illustrate the manner in which constraints affect a system, let us consider a simple example:

A company involved in factory automation wants to develop an extremely low cost robot that can be applied for assembly operations in small manufacturing businesses. Preliminary market research indicates that cost must be kept to a minimum in order to penetrate this specialized market. In an effort to provide a low-cost robot control unit (RCU), a personal computer with a maximum address space of 512K bytes is chosen because of its low cost and overall reliability.

The choice of the personal computer hardware may place important design constraints on the RCU software. Control programs must be designed so that they will fit within the 512K addressable memory. Algorithms must be designed so that required performance to control the robot can be achieved within the hardware performance limitations of the personal computer. The choice of a programming language for implementation will be guided by those industry-proven languages that are available for the PC. The "standard" operating system available for the PC must be modified to accommodate specialized multitasking requirements of a robot controller.

Each of these constraints represents the effect of hardware on the software elements. However, the choice of hardware was itself dictated by economic constraints (i.e., low cost).

But why bother to list constraints? It appears that the hardware has already been chosen and there is very little that we can do about it. The software developers will just have to live with the environment that has been established for them.

It is important to recognize that such a fatalistic attitude can sometimes be counterproductive. Although the PC hardware (in our example) has already been selected, it may not be too late to "change our minds" if the constraints imposed on the software are so severe that (1) exorbitant amounts of time will be required to develop software, thereby increasing software development costs dramatically; (2) the ability to achieve required controller performance is at substantial risk; or (3) modifications to the standard operating system are not possible.

By listing constraints, we conduct an implicit review. Each constraint represents a potential problem in the development of one or more system elements. Unless this problem can be solved, the system engineer should take another look at the reasons for the constraint and attempt to characterize the system in a manner that will eliminate the constraint.

Some constraints, however, cannot be easily eliminated. For example, consider the developer of an automated teller machine (ATM) network for a large consumer bank. The network is composed of a number of different computers and associated software along with a data base, human operators, and substantial documentation and procedures. The processing capabilities of the hardware, the organization of the data base, the requirement imposed by untrained human "operators" (the bank's customers), and many other factors will dictate a set of constraints for this computer-based system. In addition, the nature of the application dictates its own *implicit constraints*:

1. The need for appropriate security that will protect the interests of the bank and its customers
2. The need for reliability that will assure that customers can interact with a teller machine in a manner that is problem free
3. The need for expandability that enables the network to grow as the bank's business grows
4. The need for extensibilty that will enable the bank to add additional features and functions to meet ever-growing competitive pressure

Each of these implicit constraints should be listed at this time. Each implies that certain system elements must have specific characteristics and in many cases perform specific functions.

Is a consideration of constraints applicable even to "small" problems? The answer is an unqalified "yes!" Reconsidering the numerical integration example discussed earlier, we see that the express and implied constraints imposed on the problem affect the usefulness of the system. The original statement of scope for the numerical integration indicates expressly that the functions to be integrated are limited to the form

$$f(x) = px^3 + qx^2 + rx + s$$

Obviously, we've precluded many useful functions and constrained the operation of the system. Analysis of the problem will also uncover implied constraints. For example, the customer may indicate that input to the program should be interactive, thereby constraining I/O and implying a human-friendly interaction protocol. Alternatively, further analysis might uncover the fact that the numerical integration must process 100,000 sets of bounding values in less than 100 milliseconds. This extremely high performance requirement would eliminate any human interaction and constrain the design of the system by demanding the use of specialized hardware and software.

Write a plain language paragraph.

If we have properly performed each of the steps associated with the development of a statement of scope for a computer-based system, we now have the following information committed to paper:

• A description of overall system function
• A listing of key input and output data items
• A listing of important system constraints

This information forms the basis for a plain language paragraph that describes the overall operation and characteristics of the system. The paragraph should be written in a manner that accurately and simply describes important system functions. It should contain references to important data and control items and the manner in which these items interact with key system functions. Because this paragraph is the essential input to the next series of system engineering steps, it should be developed with great care. In fact, it is often worthwhile to develop the paragraph iteratively. That is, we begin by writing a first draft, then let it "sit for a while," and return to write a second (and even a third) draft.

Each iteration (a better term might be *elaboration*) of the statement of scope eliminates ambiguity and provides more detail. To illustrate, consider the first draft statement of scope for the cruise control system (discussed earlier):

The cruise control system maintains automobile speed.

Although this draft of the statement of scope defines system objectives, it provides very little detail and must be elaborated upon. After discussions with the customer, we write:

The cruise control system will maintain constant automobile speed once it has been set by the driver. Speed will be maintained until the system is disabled or until the driver presses the brakes.

Better, but still relatively vague. We need to know what variation from constant speed is acceptable, what mechanism will be used to "set" the speed, what mechanism will be used to disable the system. In addition, we must determine any implicit requirements or constraints (e.g. safely features). Note, however, that we do not have to determine how the system will perform its function. That comes later. At this time, our focus is on stating the problem as explicitly as possible. A third draft follows:

The cruise control system will maintain automobile speed to within ± 3 miles per hour (mph) of a nominal speed value specified by the driver. The nominal speed value will be set by the driver in one of two ways: (1) by depressing a **set-speed** button while the auto is traveling at a speed equal to or greater than 45 mph, or (2) by keying in the desired speed using a key pad on the dashboard. Power train data will be monitored at 0.1 sec intervals and averaged once each second. The system will adjust speed once each second. The cruise control is automatically disabled when nominal speed falls below 45 mph. In addition the driver can disable the system by depressing the brake pedal or depressing a **cruise-control-off** button.

With each elaboration, more detail is provided and further questions surface. The remaining steps of the system engineering approach attempt to provide answers.

Isolate top-level processes and entities.

We have described a computer-based system as a set of interrelated elements that will accomplish a prespecified objective by performing a series of functions that transform information in some manner. Each system element performs or contributes to the performance of one or more processes that transform data to accomplish the function of the system. When we describe a system in this manner, we take a *process-oriented* point of view.

A computer-based system can also be viewed from an *object-oriented* perspective. That is, the system may be described by identifying *entities* (also called *objects*) that exist within the overall system environment. Each entity is an abstraction that contains both data and the processes required to manipulate the data. An entity represents any real-world object (e.g., a robot, an ATM) or specific subcomponents that comprise the object. Object-oriented methods (as they apply to software) are described in Chapter 3.

The substeps associated with the isolation of top-level processes and entities will allow us to describe the overall computer-based system. In essence, these steps refine the statement of scope and lay the groundwork for the allocation of function and performance to specific system elements.

Examine the statement of scope, and select entities.

Returning once more to the plain language paragraph that describes the overall statement of scope for the computer-based system, we can develop a relatively simple approach for the selection of entities.

1. The plain language paragraph that presents the system scope is reviewed to ensure that information is presented at a consistent level of detail. That is, the paragraph should not present both top-level functional descriptions and detailed implementation specifics.

2. Entities are determined by underlining each noun or noun clause and entering it in a simple table. Aliases should be noted.

3. Attributes of entities are identified by underlining all adjectives and then associating them with their respective entities (nouns).

As an example, we reconsider the low-cost industrial robot system discussed earlier in this chapter. The following plain language paragraph for the statement of scope has been developed for the robot:

C-R (cheap robot) 1000 is a low-cost industrial robot system that performs assembly operations. The robot is programmed using a teach-box mechanism that enables an operator to enter point locations for robot arm movement and articulation commands for gripping. Additional commands may be entered via a terminal using the ROBL robot programming language. Upon completion of programming, a complete ROBL program is stored in memory and interpreted by the robot control unit (RCU). The RCU reads all ROBL statements and decodes each statement. The RCU interpolates motion control coordinates for robot movement, produces control pulses that actuate the robot servosystem, and interprets feedback from servosystem sensors. The RCU terminal enables the operator to preview robot motion by simulating each ROBL statement and displaying the robot motion path on the screen.

It should be noted that the plain language paragraph is only one of a number of pieces of information that describe the C-R system. In addition to the above paragraph, key input and output are listed separately, performance characteristics must be defined, explicit and implicit system constraints are identified, and overall system function is described in more detail.

The above paragraph generates as many questions as it answers: How is the teach box used to program the robot? What is the structure of the ROBL language? What is the physical configuration of C-R? What performance characteristics are required? These and other questions are answered with supplementary information noted above or are more fully specified as later system engineering steps are undertaken.

Applying the three substeps that enable us to examine the statement of scope and identify entities, we note that the plain language paragraph is written at a consistent level of detail. Returning to the paragraph, all nouns and noun phrases (the possible entities) are underlined:

C-R (cheap robot) 1000 is a low-cost industrial <u>robot system</u> that performs <u>assembly operations</u>. The <u>robot</u> is programmed using a <u>teach-box mechanism</u> that enables an <u>operator</u> to enter <u>point locations</u> for <u>robot</u> <u>arm movement</u> and <u>articulation commands</u> for gripping. Additional <u>commands</u> may be entered via a <u>terminal</u> using the <u>ROBL robot programming language</u>. Upon completion of programming, a complete <u>ROBL program</u> is stored in <u>memory</u> and interpreted by the <u>robot control unit (RCU)</u>. The <u>RCU</u> reads all <u>ROBL statements</u> and decodes each <u>statement</u>. The <u>RCU</u> interpolates <u>motion control coordinates</u> for <u>robot movement</u>, produces <u>control pulses</u> that actuate the <u>robot servosystem</u>, and interprets <u>feedback</u> from <u>servosystem sensors</u>. The <u>RCU terminal</u> enables the <u>operator</u> to preview <u>robot motion</u> by simulating each <u>ROBL statement</u> and displaying the <u>robot motion path</u> on the <u>screen</u>.

Each of the entities noted above is entered in Table 2.1. Because we often use different terms to refer to the same entity, aliases are noted in the table. At this point the entity table is incomplete. The column marked *Allocation* will be completed during a later system engineering step.

Examine the statement of scope, and select processes.

The processes performed by a computer-based system are coupled directly to the system's overall function. We again return to the plain language paragraph that describes the overall statement of scope for the computer-based system. A relatively simple approach for the selection of processes can be stated in the following substeps:

Table 2.1 ENTITY TABLE

Entity name	Alias	Allocation
robot system		
assembly operations		
teach-box mechanism		
operator		
point locations		
robot arm movement		
articulation commands	commands	
commands		
terminal	RCU terminal	
ROBL	robot prog. lang.	
ROBL program		
memory		
RCU		
ROBL statements	statements	
motion control coordinates		
control pulses		
servosystem		
feedback		
servosystem sensors		
robot motion path	robot arm movements	
motion control coordinates		
screen	RCU terminal	

1. Processes are determined by underlining all verbs, verb phrases, and predicates (a verb phrase indicating a conditional test) and relating each process to the appropriate entity.
2. Attributes of processes are identified by underlining all adverbs and then associating them with their respective processes (verbs).

To illustrate, we continue the robot system example. This time, however, we underline "action" verbs (such as "read" or "compute") in an effort to define important system processes:

C-R (cheap robot) 1000 is a low-cost industrial robot system that performs assembly operations. The robot is programmed using a teach-box mechanism that enables an operator to enter point locations for robot arm movement and articulation commands for gripping. Additional commands may be entered via a terminal using the ROBL robot programming language. Upon completion of programming, a

Table 2.2 PROCESS TABLE

Process	Actor	Object
performs	robot system	assembly ops.
is programmed	robot system	
enables	teach box	operator
to enter	operator	pt. locations
may be entered	commands	
is stored	ROBL program	memory
interpreted	ROBL program	
	RCU	
reads	RCU	ROBL stmts.
decodes	RCU	ROBL stmts.
interpolates	RCU	motion coords.
produces	RCU	control pulses
actuates	RCU	servosystem
interprets	RCU	feedback
to preview	operator	motion path
simulating	ROBL stmts.	
displaying	motion path	

complete ROBL program is stored in memory and interpreted by the robot control unit (RCU). The RCU reads all ROBL statements and decodes each statement. The RCU interpolates motion control coordinates for robot movement, produces control pulses that actuate the robot servosystem, and interprets feedback from servosystem sensors. The RCU terminal enables the operator to preview robot motion by simulating each ROBL statement and displaying the robot motion path on the screen.

Each process underlined in the paragraph is entered into Table 2.2. The table indicates the process, the entity (called an *actor*) that invokes the process, and the entity (called an *object*) that is operated on by the process.

Tables 2.1 and 2.2 summarize all important entities and processes for a computer-based system. The *Process Table* (Table 2.2) may be used to relate entities and the processes that act upon them. However, care must be taken to ensure that the final version of the Process Table contains references to all objects that have been noted in the

Entity Table (Table 2.1), unless such entities lie outside the bounds of the system.

To accomplish this, a second pass must be taken through the paragraph describing system scope. Processes that are not stated explicitly must be inferred from the language of the paragraph. For example, the entity **robot arm movements** does not appear in Table 2.2. Arm movements occur as a result of point locations (**motion control coordinates**) that are represented as ROBL statements and are originally programmed via the teach box. The RCU invokes robot arm movement by sending appropriate control pulses to the robot servo-system. Therefore, an additional Process Table entry might be:

Process	Actor	Object
initiated by	robot arm movements	RCU

A similar analysis is performed for all entities that do not appear in Table 2.2.

Allocate processes and entities to physical system elements.

The allocation step forms the kernel of successful system engineering. We have collected and documented important information, defining all entities associated with the system and the processes that operate on each entity. We have described entities and associated processes without regard to the specific system element that will enable us to accomplish the implementation of a given object or process. That is, we have developed an *essential model* of the system—a model that describes entities and processing requirements without regard to their implementation.

The process of allocation moves us toward an *implementation model* of the system. At this stage, the implementation model does little more than identify how the work to be performed by the computer-based system will be partitioned among the candidate system elements. That is, the implementation model answers the following question: "What is the role of {software / hardware / people / data base / documentation / procedures} for this system?

The steps associated with allocation often result in a number of alternative solutions to a system problem. Each of the alternatives is evaluated, and ultimately a final system allocation is specified.

Develop a criterion list for allocation and prioritize.

The allocation process is driven by many parameters. Economics, past experience, the overall degree of risk, staff availability, and scheduling constraints are only some of the many factors that may influence the final allocation. In addition to these generic criteria, each system development project will have its own specific criteria. For example, the development of a computer-based system for aircraft avionics is driven by reliability and weight factors. In addition, an avionics system is custom designed to suit the characteristics of a specific aircraft and must have performance characteristics that result in safe operation of the aircraft. The need for reliability and high performance might result in redundant allocations in which a function allocated to software is "backed up" by a hardware subsystem.

It is important to note that criteria associated with allocation are often design constraints for the system. Therefore, the list of constraints that we prepared earlier can be reused during the assessment of alternative allocations for the computer-based system.

Propose at least two alternative allocations.

Someone once said: "If you can't solve a problem at least two different ways, it's likely that you don't really understand it!" We'll use this (admittedly debatable) attitude in our allocation of computer-based systems. That is, rather than proposing one solution (a "solution" is an allocation of system elements), we'll develop at least two and preferably more allocations in outline form. Then we'll apply the list of allocation criteria to each potential solution for the system, and finally we'll select the allocation that best meets the criteria that we have established.

To illustrate the process of allocation, we consider a small part of a factory automation system—a Conveyor Line Sorting System (CLSS). The following statement of scope for CLSS is used as a point of departure:

CLSS must be developed such that boxes moving along a conveyor line will be identified and sorted into one of six bins at the end of the line. The boxes will pass by a sorting station where they will be identified. Based on an identification number printed on the side of the box (an equivalent bar code is provided), the boxes will be shunted into the appropriate bins. Boxes pass in random order and are evenly spaced. The line is moving slowly.

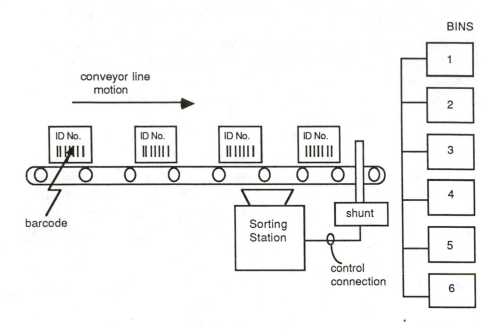

Figure 2.2   Schematic of the Conveyor Line Sorting System

CLSS is depicted schematically in Figure 2.2.

Before continuing, make a list of questions that you would ask the customer if you were the system engineer. The answers to these questions will help to identify appropriate allocation alternatives.

Among the many questions that should be asked and answered are the following:

1. How many different identification numbers must be processed, and what is their form?

2. What is the speed of the conveyor line in feet/second and what is the distance between boxes in feet?

3. How far is the sorting station from the bins?

4. How far apart are the bins?

5. What should happen if a box doesn't have an identification number or an incorrect number is present?

6. What happens when a bin fills to capacity?

7. Is information about box destination and bin contents to be

passed elsewhere in the factory automation system? Is real-time data acquisition required?

8. What error/failure rate is acceptable?

9. What pieces of the conveyor line system currently exist and are operational?

10. What schedule and budgetary constraints are imposed?

Note that the above questions focus on processes, entities, and performance, helping us to understand the system objectives and refine the statement of scope. The system engineer does not ask the customer *how* the task is to be implemented; rather, the engineer asks *what* is required.

Assuming reasonable answers, a number of alternative allocations are proposed. Note that function and performance are assigned to different generic system elements in each allocation.

Allocation 1. A sorting operator is trained and placed at the sorting station location. He or she reads the box and places it into an appropriate bin.

Allocation 1 represents a purely manual (but nevertheless effective) solution to the CLSS problem. The primary system element is people (the sorting operator). The person performs all sorting functions. Some documentation (in the form of a table relating identification number to bin location and procedural description for operator training) may be required. Therefore, this allocation uses only the people and documentation elements.

Allocation 2.   A bar code reader and controller are placed at the sorting station. Bar code output is passed to a programmable controller that controls a mechanical shunting mechanism. The shunt slides the box to the appropriate bin.

For allocation 2, hardware (bar code reader, programmable control, shunt hardware, etc.), software (for the bar code reader and programmable controller), and data base (a lookup table that relates box ID with bin location) elements are used to provide a fully automated solution. It is likely that each of these system elements will have corresponding manuals and other documentation, adding another generic system element.

Allocation 3.   A bar code reader and controller are placed at the sorting station. Bar code output is passed to a robot arm that grasps a box and moves it to the appropriate bin location.

Allocation 3 makes use of generic system elements and one *macro element* —the robot. Like allocation 2, this allocation uses hardware, software, a data base, and documentation as generic elements. The robot is a macro element of CLSS and itself contains a set of generic system elements.

From an examination of the three alternative allocations for CLSS, it should be obvious that the same function can be allocated to different system elements. In order to choose the most effective allocation, a set of allocation criteria should be applied to each alternative.

Apply criteria to assess viability of each allocation alternative.

Once a number of allocation alternatives have been developed, they must be assessed by applying the criteria for allocation described earlier. The following generic criteria govern the selection of a system configuration based on a specific allocation of function and performance to generic system elements:

Project Considerations. Can the configuration be built within pre-established cost and schedule bounds? What is the risk associated with cost and schedule estimates?

Business Considerations. Does the configuration represent the most profitable solution? Can it be marketed successfully? Will ultimate payoff justify development risk?

Technical Analysis. Does the technology exist to develop all elements of the system? Are function and performance assured? Can the configuration be adequately maintained? Do technical resources exist? What is the risk associated with the technology?

Manufacturing Evaluation. Are manufacturing facilities and equipment available? Is there a shortage of necessary components? Can quality assurance be adequately performed?

Human Issues. Are trained personnel available for development and manufacture? Do political problems exist? Does the customer understand what the system is to accomplish?

Environmental Interfaces. Does the proposed configuration properly interface with the system's external environment? Are machine-to-machine and human-to-machine communication handled in an intelligent manner?

Legal Considerations. Does this configuration introduce undue liability risk? Can proprietary aspects be adequately protected? Is there potential copyright or patent infringement?

It is important to note that the system engineer should also consider off-the-shelf solutions to the customer's problem. Does an equivalent system already exist? Can major parts of a solution be purchased from a third party?

The application of allocation criteria results in the selection of a specific system configuration and the specification of function and performance that are assigned (allocated) to hardware, software (and firmware), people, data bases, documentation, and procedures. Each system element addresses some aspect of the system's scope. The role of hardware engineering, software engineering, human engineering, and data base engineering is to refine scope and produce an operational system component that can be properly integrated with other system elements.

There is no question that the generic criteria noted above are not necessarily applicable to every problem that you will encounter. For example, manufacturing evaluation may be irrelevant for small systems that consist primarily of software. However, each of the other six criteria can be applied to software efforts of every size.

Select an allocation.

Although there are many ways to apply the allocation criteria and select one of the proposed alternatives, one of the more effective is to create a quantitative assessment by developing a grading scheme for all criteria and then weighting each criterion according to its overall priority and/or the importance to the implementation of the computer-based system. Using both a graded value and an associated weighting factor, Table 2.3 is developed.

Referring to the table, each criterion is weighted on a scale of 1 to 5, where 1 implies "of little importance" and 5 implies "of critical importance." The weight is used to assign priority to each of the criteria.

Each alternative is graded on a scale of 1 to 5, where 1 implies poor satisfaction of a criterion and 5 implies excellent satisfaction of a criterion. Grades are represented as two numbers separated by a slash. The first value is the raw grade assigned by the system engineer, while the second value represents the weighted grade (raw grade multiplied by the weight). For example, from Table 2.3, "early delivery"

Table 2.3 ALLOCATION CRITERIA ASSESSMENT

Criteria	Weight	Alternatives		
		1	2	3
Project/Business Considerations				
early delivery	4	5/20	2/ 8	2/ 8
cost -- development	2	5/10	3/ 6	2/ 4
cost -- continuing	5	1/ 5	5/25	4/25
degree of risk	3	5/15	4/12	2/ 9
Technical/Manufacturing Considerations				
technical elements exist	3	5/15	5/15	4/12
ease of maintenance	5	4/20	3/15	2/10
reliability	5	2/10	4/20	3/15
performance	4	1/ 4	5/20	4/16
availability of components	3	5/15	4/12	4/12
complexity of configuration	4	5/20	4/16	2/ 8
degree of technical risk	3	5/15	4/12	3/ 9
Human Issues				
training requirements	3	4/12	4/12	3/ 9
ease of interface	3	3/ 9	5/15	5/15
degree of acceptance	3	3/ 9	5/15	5/15
Environmental Interfaces				
ease of integration	4	5/20	4/16	3/12
ease of extension	4	1/ 4	4/16	4/16
portability	2	5/10	3/ 6	3/ 6
Weighted total		213	241	201

is considered to be quite important (weighted a 4). Alternative 1 meets this criterion very well, receiving a raw grade of five and a total grade (weight x raw grade) of 20. Note that alternative 2 has been rated at a lower level, receiving a raw grade of 2 and a total grade of 8.

If a decision on the allocation alternative were based only on the table (this is generally not recommended), allocation 2 would be chosen. In reality, intangible factors such as customer preference, past experience, or management policy might dictate another alternative.

Once an allocation has been selected, the system specification process begins. We have described an essential model of the system during earlier steps. By selecting a specific allocation, we begin the specification of an implementation model that continues throughout problem analysis and design.

Develop a refined statement of scope for each allocated system element.

Using all information gathered and documented during the steps already described in this chapter, we are now ready to describe each allocated system element. Processes and entities associated with hardware, software, people, data base, documents, and procedures are each described. In effect, we reapply earlier steps to develop a statement of scope for each system element.

But why bother documenting the scope of each element if our primary concern is software? In order to properly engineer software, we must understand how it *interfaces* with other system elements. When computer-based systems fail, they do so not because the software alone is flawed, but because the software doesn't work *in conjunction with* hardware or a data base or a human operator. To understand the role of computer programs, we must understand all system elements that affect those programs. For this reason we develop a statement of scope for each system element.

The process of elaboration described earlier in this chapter is now applied at the system element level. To illustrate, the statement of scope for the software element (for allocation 2) of the CLSS system might be:

CLSS software will receive input information from a bar code reader at time intervals that conform to the conveyor line speed. Bar code data will be decoded into box identification format. The software will do a look-up in a 1000 entry data base to determine proper bin location for the box currently at the reader (sorting station). A queue will be used to keep track of shunt positions for each box as it moves past the sorting station.

CLSS software will also receive input from a pulse tachometer that will be used to synchronize the control signal to the shunting mechanism. Depending on the number of pulses that are generated between the sorting station and the shunt, the software will produce a control signal to the shunt to properly position the box. ... and so on.

It should be noted that the above statement of scope for software incorporates a number of implementation details (e.g., 1000 entry data base, pulse tachometer) that are derived from other allocated elements of the system. Similar statements are developed for hardware, human activities, and other system elements.

Meet with the customer to review the allocation.

In their best-selling book, *In Search of Excellence*, Thomas Peters and Robert Waterman suggest that successful businesses should remain "close to the customer." That is, a business should respond to the demands of its customers if it is to succeed in the long run.

Most successful system engineers also live by this motto. To be successful, a computer-based system must satisfy the needs of its customers. To ensure that these needs are met, a review of all systems work should be done before we proceed to other steps.

For small projects in which software is the primary system element, the customer may be a colleague, a professor (in a university setting), another department (in a large company), or even yourself. Reviews may be informal, but the need to review remains. For larger computer-based systems, more formal reviews may be conducted at this point. But all focus on the same question: Have we specified what the "customer" wants? The following checklist covers other important areas of concern.

1. Have major functions been defined in a bounded and unambiguous fashion?
2. Are interfaces between system elements defined?
3. Have performance bounds been established for the system as a whole and for each element?
4. Have design constraints been established for each element?
5. Was the best alternative selected?
6. Is the solution technologically feasible?
7. Has a mechanism for system validation and verification been established?
8. Is there consistency among all system elements?

Recognize that iteration is likely.

The steps required to understand the system have been presented in a distinct sequence. Yet the process of system engineering is not necessarily sequential! Often, the system engineer must "take a number of passes" to properly define a function or its performance. If a review is conducted properly, changes to the specification for the system will be required. New technology may have just been introduced. A particularly onerous constraint may have to be modified. The customer may change his mind. For these and many other reasons, iteration is likely.

WHAT THIS MEANS TO YOU

The systems that you will work on as a student and early in your career are likely to be "software only." That is, the program will be the only system element that must be developed. It is important to note, however, that the discussion contained in this chapter is still useful in your work.

Even the simplest program can be viewed in a system context. People, documentation, procedures, data, and hardware will undoubtedly be considered to some degree.

If you're not careful, you'll fall prey to a compelling urge to get on with it—to begin coding the solution without bothering to think about the system. Too many students and many industry practitioners succumb to this urge and ultimately take an approach that might best be characterized as "ready, fire, aim." The steps presented within this chapter and the analysis steps presented in Chapter 3 provide you with a way to "aim" before you take your best shot at building high quality software that meets your customer's requirements.

FURTHER READINGS

Athey, T.H., *Systematic Systems Approach*, Prentice-Hall, 1982.
Blanchard, B.S. and W.J. Fabrycky, *Systems Engineering and Analysis*, Prentice-Hall, 1981.
Menamin, S. and J. Palmer, *Essential Systems Analysis*, Yourdon Press, 1985.
Weinberg, G., *An Introduction to General System Thinking*, Wiley-Interscience, 1976.
Weinberg, G., *On the Design of Stable Systems*, Wiley-Interscience, 1979.

PROBLEMS AND POINTS TO PONDER

2.1 Using each of the steps outlined in this chapter, develop a system description for each of the "software only" systems noted below. You should play the role of the customer when specific requirements must be specified. One or more plain language paragraphs should be produced as a result of your work.

a. A "grade book" system that enables professors to enter student numeric test and quiz grades, compute averages, and produce letter grades. The system is to be implemented on the university's mainframe computer.

b. A "date book" system that serves as a calendar for recording important appointments. This system is to be implemented on a personal computer.

c. An "address book" system that maintains a list of contacts, customers, acquaintances, with address, company, phone number, personal information, and category keywords for categorizing entries. The system should be interactive so that a name (or other characteristic) can be found through direct query. This system is to be implemented on a personal computer.

d. A system described by your instructor.

2.2 Provide five examples of procedural abstractions that you encounter in everyday life. Provide five examples of procedural abstractions that you have encountered in programming.

2.3 Provide three examples of data abstractions that you encounter in everyday life. Provide three examples of data abstractions that you have encountered in programming.

2.4 Develop entity and process tables for one or more of the systems described in problem 2.1.

2.5 Describe the process of allocation in your own words. Provide an example of allocation using any high technology system.

2.6 Using the steps described in this chapter, develop a system specification for a "desk-top publishing system." Use the best features of systems such as *PageMaker* or *ReadySetGo* as a guide for defining system requirements. Your work should include the development of a plain language paragraph, entity and process tables, and definition of allocation criteria.

CHAPTER 3
ANALYZING A PROBLEM

Developing computer software, whether the application is a classroom exercise or an industrial product, requires problem-solving skills. In this chapter, we focus on *problem analysis* —a software engineering activity that defines the problem that we are to solve in explicit terms and lays the foundation for the design of a solution.

Problem analysis begins with an overall understanding of a computer-based system. What is the overall system objective? How does software interact with other system elements? What constraints are imposed on software by other system elements? These and many other questions are addressed by the system engineering steps described in Chapter 2. If these steps have been assiduously applied, a statement of scope for both software and the system as a whole has been developed. The statement of scope for software (developed as part of a system specification in Chapter 2) becomes our point of departure for analysis and problem solving. The portion of the statement of scope that focuses on software is written from a system perspective. That is, software is described in a manner that enables the reader to understand the top-level functions and performance but does not contain detailed requirements. The software description does not contain sufficient information for the software engineer, and therefore the first step in problem analysis is to refine the software statement of scope to meet the needs of the software engineering process.

Refine and clarify software scope.

Using the statement of scope as a point of departure, software scope is refined by creating an input-process-output model. Software functions are refined to delineate major processes. The input and output for each process are specified.

In essence, the refinement of software scope reduces the *level of abstraction* with which software is described. To illustrate, consider an excerpt from the description of software for the digital dashboard of an automobile, described from the system perspective:

The digital dashboard software (DDS) will acquire speed and fuel consumption data from the drive train and fuel flow subsystems, respectively, perform calculations of instantaneous miles per hour and miles per gallon, and display these data digitally as shown in Figure .... In addition, DDS will alert the driver to ... .

The software engineer must refine and clarify this statement of scope. Phrases such as "acquire speed and fuel consumption data," "perform calculations," and "display these data digitally" must be refined and clarified before further work can be accomplished. Continuing the digital dashboard example, the first paragraph of the system level description might be expanded as follows:

Digital dashboard software (DDS) acquires automobile speed by reading a drive train rotation signal, converted from analog to digital format, at 0.1 second intervals. An average rotation reading is computed at 0.5 second intervals and speed in miles per hour is computed by applying physical parameters to convert rpm to mph. A speed display is updated two times per second. Fuel flow data are acquired from an analog sensor in the fuel line that measures flow rate. The analog value of flow rate is converted to digital format and is read by DDS. Flow rate (in milliliters per second) is read at 0.2 second intervals and converted into English units. Data obtained from the speed computation are combined with fuel flow rate data to compute average miles per gallon. Fuel consumption is displayed at 1.0 second intervals. The output format for speed and fuel consumption displays is shown in Figure ... .

Because the processing associated with DDS is time sensitive, the refined statement of scope for software contains a number of implied performance constraints (e.g. "flow rate is read at 0.2 second intervals"). However, the software engineer has not attempted to describe an implementation model for DDS. That is, the details associated with the precise implementation (e.g., the number of microprocessors to be used, the scaling to be applied for analog to digital conversion, and other physical specifications), although very important, are not described at this time. Problem analysis begins when the software scope is completed. The analysis steps that follow use software scope as a point of departure and culminate with a detailed *Software Specification* for the problem.

Identify objects and operations.

In Chapter 2, we introduced a system analysis approach that isolated processes and information entities for a computer-based system. We refine this approach for software and identify *objects* and their related *operations* (sometimes called *methods*). In the software context, an *object* may be viewed as a data structure (one or more data items organized in a specific fashion) and a collection of procedures that operate on the data structure. Using computer science terminology, an object is an abstraction that corresponds to some physical entity in the real world.

Objects and operations can be defined for any software application, enabling us to better understand algorithms and data structures created to accomplish software function. For example, among many potential objects for the digital dashboard software (DDS) are: **drive train rotation signal, flow rate, speed display,** and **fuel consumption display.** Among the DDS operations that are applied to these objects are: **read, convert, combine,** and **display**. In some cases, it is possible to categorize objects by defining a *class*. A class contains a description of attributes (data structure and procedural components) that can be shared by similar objects. For DDS, the objects **drive train rotation signal** and **flow rate** might be members of the class **analog signals.** All objects within this class would share a similar set of attributes (e.g., eight-bit format, scale factor) and similar operations (e.g., **convert**).

The use of an object-oriented approach to problem analysis is not limited to complex computer-based systems that combine many different elements. Even relatively simple software applications are amenable to this approach. To help illustrate, consider a computer graphics system that combines conventional display hardware and software to draw two-dimensional geometric primitives: polygons, splines, and conics. Using a mouse, an operator can move, rotate, scale, and color each of the geometric primitives that are created. All objects associated

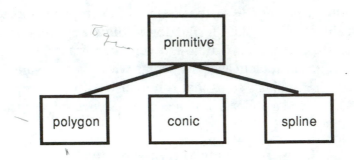

Figure 3.1 Class Hierarchy for Geometric Primitives

with the computer graphics system belong to a *class* of objects called **primitive**. Figure 3.1 illustrates a *class hierarchy* for geometric primitives. **Polygon, conic**, and **spline** each represent a *subclass* of objects that take on a set of characteristics that can be associated with each class. For example, all conics can be described using the relationship:

$$ax^2 + bxy + cy^2 + dx + ey + f = 0$$

Therefore, the class hierarchy can be expanded as shown in Figure 3.2. It is important to note that each of the subclasses (**conic, spline, polygon**) inherit all of the characteristics of graphics primitives (each can take on a color, can be rotated, etc.), but each may have individualized attributes as well. Each of the conic objects (**parabola, ellipse**, etc.) inherit the basic attributes of all conics (the attributes of their class or subclass).

We can also associate operations with classes, subclasses and specific objects. Considering the computer graphics system described above, the following operations can be defined:

create.primitive	creates a graphics primitive
set.position	sets the x,y position of an object
get.position	retrieves the x,y position of an object
set.orientation	sets the angle of rotation

and many others. During problem analysis, our first job is to identify objects and operations. Each is described in terms of the requirements necessary to satisfy the function and performance of the software. Later, during design, objects are translated into distinct data structures, and operations become procedures that operate on those data

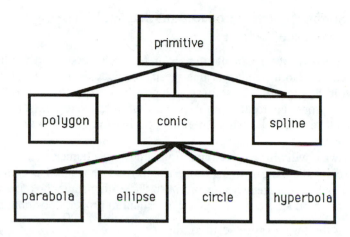

Figure 3.2   An Expanded Class Hierarchy

structures.* The steps that follow extend an approach introduced in Chapter 2 to identify objects and operations.

> *Identify objects and operations using the statement of software scope as a guide.*

The same approach is used to identify software objects and operations that was used (in Chapter 2) to identify system entities and processes. Restating the substeps for identifying system entities, but changing our focus to software:

1. The plain language paragraph that presents the software scope is reviewed to ensure that information is presented at a consistent level of detail. That is, the paragraph should not present both top-level functional descriptions and detailed implementation specifics.
2. Objects are determined by underlining each noun or noun phrase and entering it in a simple table. Aliases should be noted.
3. Attributes of objects are identified by underlining all adjectives and then associating them with their respective objects (nouns).

To illustrate the application of these substeps to a statement of software scope, we reconsider the description of software for the Convey-

---

* A relatively new software engineering approach, called *object-oriented programming,* makes use of special programming languages (e.g., Smalltalk or C++) to implement objects and operations. The definition of objects and operations is an important problem analysis activity, regardless of whether we intend to use object-oriented programming.

or Line Sorting System introduced in Chapter 2. The original software scope is reproduced below:

CLSS software will receive input information from a bar code reader at time intervals that conform to the conveyor line speed. Bar code data will be decoded into box identification format. The software will do a look-up in a 1000 entry data base to determine proper bin location for the box currently at the reader (sorting station). A queue will be used to keep track of shunt positions for each box as it moves past the sorting station.

CLSS software will also receive input from a pulse tachometer that will be used to synchronize the control signal to the shunting mechanism. Depending on the number of pulses that are generated between the sorting station and the shunt, the software will produce a control signal to the shunt to properly position the box ...

Applying the substeps described above:

CLSS software will receive input information from a bar code reader at time intervals that conform to the conveyor line speed. Bar code data will be decoded into box identification format. The software will do a look-up in a 1000 entry data base to determine proper bin location for the box currently at the reader (sorting station). A queue will be used to keep track of shunt positions for each box as it moves past the sorting station.

CLSS software will also receive input from a pulse tachometer that will be used to synchronize the control signal to the shunting mechanism. Depending on the number of pulses that are generated between the sorting station and the shunt, the software will produce a control signal to the shunt to properly position the box ...

A quick examination of the underlined nouns indicates that each represents either a *data item* (e.g., **bar code data**) that will be input, transformed, or output by the software; a *control item* (e.g., **control signal**) that is used to actuate, coordinate, or time a software function; a *data store* (e.g., **1000 entry data base**) that is used to store information for later use; a *data originator* (e.g., **bar code reader**) that is a source of information for the software, or a *data receiver* (e.g., **shunting mechanism**) that accepts information produced by the software. Each of these objects and their *aliases* (a different name referring to the same object) is entered in Table 3.1.

Returning to the substeps for identifying system processes introduced in Chapter 2, we state the following substeps for the identification of operations:

1. Operations are determined by underlining all verbs, verb phrases, and predicates (a verb phrase indicating a conditional test) and relating each operation to the appropriate object.

Table 3.1 OBJECT TABLE

Object Name	Alias	Type
bar code reader	reader	originator
time intervals		control item
conveyor line speed		data item
bar code data		data item
box identification format		data item
data base		data store
bin location		data item
FIFO list	User	data store
shunt positions	Request	data item
input		control item
pulse tachometer		originator
control signal		control item
shunting mechanism	shunt	receiver
number of pulses		data item

2. Attributes of operations are identified by underlining all adverbs and then associating them with their respective operation (verb).

Continuing with the CLSS example:

CLSS software will receive input information from a bar code reader at time intervals that conform to the conveyor line speed. Bar code data will be decoded into box identification format. The software will do a look-up in a 1000 entry data base to determine proper bin location for the box currently at the reader (sorting station). A queue will be used to keep track of shunt positions for each box as it moves past the sorting station.

CLSS software will also receive input from a pulse tachometer that will be used to synchronize the control signal to the shunting mechanism. Depending on the number of pulses that are generated between the sorting station and the shunt, the software will produce a control signal to the shunt to properly position the box ...

Some of the operations (verbs) noted in the paragraph refer to functions that are to be implemented directly by software (e.g., **receive, look up, produce**). These operations reside in what is called the *solution space* for this problem. Our goal will be to design and implement all objects and operations that reside in the solution space.

Other operations (e.g., **move, synchronize, position**) are part of what is called the *problem space* and refer to processes that are performed by other system elements (e.g., hardware, people). Only

Table 3.2 OPERATION TABLE

Operation	Object	Type
receive	information	data trans.
	bar code reader	
	input/pulse tach	
conform	time intervals	control trans.
	conveyor line speed	
decoded	bar code data	data trans.
	box ID format	
do a look-up	data base	data trans.
determine	bin location	data trans.
keep track	FIFO list	control trans.
produce	control signal	control trans.
generated	pulses	control trans.

solution space operations are entered in Table 3.2. For the CLSS statement of software scope, no significant operation attributes are noted.

Tables 3.1 and 3.2 enable us to isolate key data and control items and their origins or destinations, data stores, and important software functions. Each item and function shown in the tables can be further refined, and the analysis substeps described in this discussion reapplied recursively.

Use objects to identify information originators and receivers.

Information that is input to a program must be produced by an external object (e.g., a computer terminal, a human operator, a machine) and must be output to some external object. An object that produces information for use by the software is called an *originator* or *information source*, and an object the accepts information or control produced by the software is called a *receiver* or *information sink*.

It is important to identify originators and receivers because each will have an influence on the specification and design of the software. These external objects will often impose constraints on the function and performance of the software, as well as dictate the manner in which information is input and output from the system. Returning to the CLSS example, originators and receivers are identified in Table 3.1. The **pulse tachometer** emits a pulse each time a drive wheel on the conveyor line makes one revolution. This enables the CLSS software to synchronize itself with conveyor line movement. The **shunting mechanism** receives data and control signals from CLSS software that specify the bin location and activation commands required to shunt a box to the appropriate bin.

Use objects to identify data stores.

Many software applications make use of an object that stores data on either a temporary or permanent basis. In some cases, the data store is transient, existing only for the duration of a program execution (e.g., buffers, stacks, message pools). In other situations, a data store is maintained permanently (e.g., a permanent file or data base). Data stores have been identified in Table 3.1.

CLSS software maintains two data stores: (1) a part number bin location **data base** that contains information necessary to route the box to the appropriate bin and (2) a **queue** that "holds" bin locations for boxes that pass the bar code reader until they reach the shunting mechanism. Synchronization information is provided by the pulse tachometer.

The specification of data stores lays the groundwork for one important element of software design (called *data design* and discussed in Chapter 4). For this reason, these objects are identified at this time and represented in Table 3.1.

Use objects to identify data and control items.

Information flow (the movement of data or control items among various software-based functions) exists regardless of the software application area. According to the definition proposed in Chapter 2, a *data item* is any input or output that has information content and is transformed (i.e., modified, reorganized, computed, combined) by an algorithm implemented in software. A *control item* indicates the occurrence of a specific action or event. Alternatively, a control item can initiate a *control process* that results in a specific action or event.

By identifying data and control items, we prepare for the development of a *flow model* for the software (described later in this chapter). The flow model depicts objects and operations using sequential information transforms and is a mechanism that leads to effective *architectural design* (Chapter 4). Data and control items (objects) for the CLSS software are shown in Table 3.1.

> ## Use operations to identify data and control transformations.

A *data transformation* is an operation (a procedure implemented in software) that transforms input data items into output data items. Examples of data transformations are: an operation that computes payroll tax, an operation that performs two-dimensional rotation of a polygon, an operation that calculates stress in a cantilever beam, or an operation that does a global replacement of one text string with another. Data transformation operations form the basis for input-process-output models for software.

To illustrate the use of a data transformation, consider software for use in a standard cash register. One of many operations for the software computes sales tax for the purchase of consumer goods. This data transformation—we'll call it **compute tax**—accepts the data items **taxable total** and **tax rate** as input and produces the data item **sales tax** as output. The transformation takes the form:

$$\text{sales tax} = \text{taxable total} \times \text{tax rate}$$

Although **compute tax** is a very simple data transformation, it has many of the characteristics of the most complex transformations. Input data items are transformed by using an algorithm contained within the data transformation, and output data items are produced.

A *control transformation* is an operation that accepts either data or control items and applies an algorithm to produce control items that indicate the occurrence of an event or initiate some action. In essence, a control transformation may be viewed as the action that occurs when a "switch is thrown." That is, a single event will precipitate some action that is initiated by the control transformation. Examples of control transformations are: an operation that receives the **volume mute** control from a TV remote control unit and sends a **sound off** signal to the television's digital circuitry, an operation that monitors a **floor indicator** for a hotel elevator and then rings a chime when the selected floor is reached, and an operation that rings an alarm when an **entry indicator** is sensed for a home security system. Each of these control transformations accepts a control item as input and produces a control item as output.

To illustrate the use of control transformations, assume that CLSS must have a panic abort switch that can be used by an operator to shut down the conveyor line immediately. However, rather than simply cutting the power, CLSS software monitors the status of the switch and inititates a shutdown procedure if the switch is thrown. An operation called **monitor switch status** is a control transformation that receives a control item (**switch thrown**) as input and initiates a shutdown procedure that results in a control item (**turn-off-power**) as output.

Data and control transformations become one or more software modules (separately named components of the software) that must be designed and implemented in a programming language. Although our work during analysis is unlikely to identify every module that will be required, it gives us a good indication of the size and complexity of the software that must be built. In addition, the identification of operations (data and control transformations) will facilitate the development of a *flow model* for software—a topic to be discussed later in this chapter.

Table 3.2 lists CLSS operations and identifies whether each has data or control attributes. It should be noted that each operation could be translated into one or more modules that must be designed and implemented to accomplish CLSS software objectives.

Recognize and apply three fundamental analysis principles.

By identifying objects and operations, we have laid the groundwork for developing a model of the software that can be translated into a design. Before continuing with the steps required to complete the software model, we'll take a brief detour to consider fundamental analysis principles that are applicable to all problem solving. If you apply these principles, it is far more likely that the software model that you do develop will be a good one.

Chances for misinterpretation or misinformation abound throughout the analysis of software for a computer-based system. The dilemma that confronts a software engineer may best be understood by repeating the statement of an anonymous (infamous?) customer: "*I know you believe you understood what you think I said, but I am not sure you realize that what you heard is not what I meant . . .*"

Over the past decade, a number of software analysis and specification methods have been developed. Although each analysis method
has a unique notation and point of view, all analysis methods are related by a set of fundamental principles:

1. The *information domain*, as well as the functional domain, of a
problem must be represented and understood.
2. The problem must be *partitioned* in a manner that uncovers detail in
a layered (or hierarchical) fashion.
3. The system is first modeled by representing *essential* information
and then refined to specify *implementation detail.*

By applying these principles, the analyst approaches a problem systematically. The steps that follow discuss each principle and indicate
how it can be applied in a systematic fashion.

Analysis Principle 1: Evaluate each component of the information domain.

All software applications can be collectively called *data processing.*[*]
Interestingly, this term contains the key to our understanding of software requirements. Software is built to process *data*, to transform data
from one form to another; that is, to accept input, manipulate it in
some way, and produce output. This fundamental statement of objective is true whether we build batch software for a payroll system or
real-time embedded software to control fuel flow to an aircraft engine.

The information domain contains three different components of
the data that are processed by computer programs: (1) *data flow*, (2)
data content, and (3) *data structure.* To fully understand the information domain, each of these components must be analyzed.

Data flow represents the manner in which data or control change
as they move through a system. As illustrated in Figure 3.3, input is
transformed to intermediate data, which are further transformed to output. Along this transformation path (or paths), additional data may be
introduced from existing data stores (e.g., a disk file or memory buf-

---

[*] The term *data processing* is more commonly used to refer to business information system applications such as retailing, banking, payroll, and inventory
control. Until recently, these applications have been dominated by software developed in the COBOL programming language. In the context of our discussion, the
term *data* may be interpreted to mean numeric, alphanumeric, graphical, musical,
or any other information.

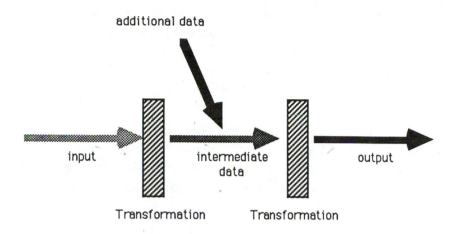

additional data

input

intermediate
data

output

Transformation   Transformation

Figure 3.3   A Data Flow Model

fer). The transformations that are applied to the data are the operations
that a program must perform. Information that moves between two
transformations (operations) may be either data or control items.

Data content represents the individual data items that comprise
some larger composite item of information. For example, **payroll
record** is a *composite data item* that comprises an **employee number,
pay rate, year-to-date wages, year-to-date taxes,** and so forth. The
content of **payroll record** is defined by the items that are contained
within it. To understand the processing that is to be applied to **payroll
record**, we must first understand its information content.

Data structure represents the logical organization of various data
items. Are data to be organized as a collection of individual data items,
as a two-dimensional array of numbers, or as a hierarchical record
structure that contains both numeric and alphanumeric information?
Within the context of the structure, what data items are related to other
data items? Is all information contained within a single information
structure, or are distinct structures to be used? How does information
in one structure relate to information in another structure? These questions and others are answered by an assessment of data structure.
Normally, a detailed consideration of data structure is postponed until
we begin software design (Chapter 4).

The application of the first analysis principle was initiated by creating object and operation tables (Tables 3.1 and 3.2). Later in this chapter, we will see that the information contained in these tables enables further analysis of the information domain.

Analysis Principle 2: Partition objects and operations to obtain a hierarchical view of the problem.

Problems are often too large and complex to be understood as a whole. For this reason, we tend to partition (divide) them into parts that can be easily understood. We then establish interfaces between the parts so that overall function can be accomplished. During requirements analysis, both objects and operations can be partitioned.

In essence, *partitioning* decomposes a problem into its constituent parts. Conceptually, we establish a hierarchical representation of function or information and then partition the uppermost element by (1) exposing increasing detail by moving vertically in the hierarchy or (2) decomposing the problem by moving horizontally in the hierarchy. To illustrate these partitioning approaches, let us reconsider the Conveyor Line Sorting System (CLSS) introduced in Chapter 2 and reconsidered earlier in this chapter.

A review of the statement of software scope and the object-oriented analysis applied to scope indicates that requirements for CLSS software may be analyzed by partitioning both objects and operations. Information contained in Tables 3.1 and 3.2 provides useful guidance for partitioning.

Figure 3.4 illustrates a simple *horizontal decomposition* of CLSS objects. Each object in the bottom row is actually a class from which lower-level objects may be derived. The problem is partitioned by representing constituent CLSS software objects, moving horizontally in the object hierarchy. Four object classes, each reducible to lower-level objects, are noted on the first level of the hierarchy.

Figure 3.5 shows a *vertical decomposition* of the object class **input objects**. The object **bar code data** is decomposed into **box identification format** and **customer destination**. Interestingly, **customer identification** does not appear in Table 3.1 or in the statement of scope. However, partitioning has uncovered this data item (and lower-level objects shown in the figure). Each object class shown in Figure 3.5 could be expanded in a similar manner.

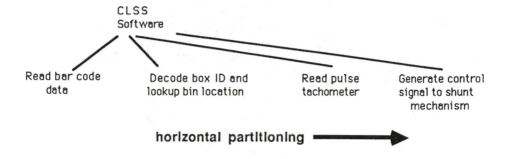

Figure 3.4 Horizontal Decomposition of Objects

CLSS operations can be partitioned in an analogous fashion. Examining the statement of scope and Table 3.2, a horizontal decomposition can be used to derive a set of generic operation categories—**input operations, data processing operations, control operations** and **output operations**. Each of these is then decomposed vertically using the statement of scope as a guide. A vertical partitioning for **data processing operations** is shown in Figure 3.6.

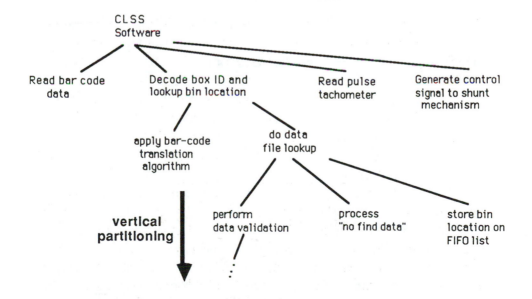

Figure 3.5 Vertical Decomposition of Objects

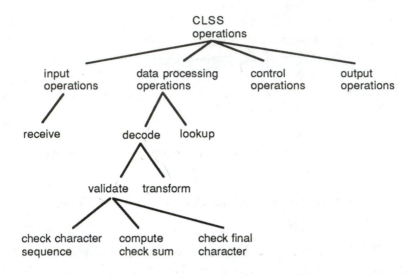

Figure 3.6   Vertical Partitioning for Input Operations

Analysis Principle 3: Create an essential model
of the system, and lay the foundation
for an implementation model.

The *essential model* of a program presents the objects and operations required to achieve system function without regard to implementation details. For example, the essential view of the CLSS operation **receive** (bar code data) does not concern itself with the physical form of the data or the type of bar code reader used. Similarly, an essential *data model* such as the object **data base** is represented without regard to the underlying data structures used to implement the data base. An essential representation of software requirements provides an important foundation for design.

The *implementation model* of software presents the real-world manifestation of processing functions and data structures. In some cases, an implementation model is developed as the first step in software design. However, most computer-based systems are specified in a manner that dictates certain implementation constraints. It is important to note that the modeling process often loops between essential and implementation considerations. The bottom line, however, is the implementation model. After all, the CLSS input device is a bar code reader, not a keyboard, a switch, or a TV camera! Therefore, we must recognize the constraints imposed by predefined system elements.

Software requirements analysis should focus on *what* the software is to accomplish, rather than on *how* processing will be implemented. However, the implementation model should not necessarily be interpreted as a representation of *how*. Rather, the implementation model represents the current mode of operation, that is, the existing or proposed allocation for all system elements. The essential model (of function or data) is generic in the sense that software realization of function or data is not explicitly indicated.

When things are uncertain, develop a prototype to help clarify requirements.

Problem analysis for software is often complicated by two factors. First, the customer may have a good overall understanding of objectives but may be unsure of specifics. Second, the customer may understand the processing that is required but may be unsure whether it will be accurate or fast enough.

For example, the customer may recognize the need for a highly interactive human interface but may be unsure of the form and style the interaction should take. Should the human use a mouse to select program functions represented as icons on a display screen, or should a command-oriented system be developed? Prototyping can help the customer to assess each approach and select the one that best meets the objectives of the system. Certain program functions may require the application of sophisticated computational algorithms. The software engineer may be unsure that an algorithm will function and perform properly, yet must specify many other features of the software on the assumption that the algorithm will perform correctly. Again, prototyping can help.

In some cases it is possible to apply fundamental analysis principles and derive a paper specification of software from which a design can be developed. In other situations, *requirements gathering* is conducted, the analysis principles are applied, and a model of the software to be built, called a *prototype,* is constructed for assessment by the customer and developer. In some circumstances, a working prototype is constructed at the beginning of analysis, since the prototype is the only means through which requirements can be effectively derived. The prototype then evolves into production software.

*Evaluate the software scope, and determine
whether the software to be developed
is a good candidate for prototyping.*

Not all software is amenable to prototyping. The application area, problem complexity, sophistication of the customer, and project time schedule have an important impact on our approach. In some cases, only one function, such as an interactive user interface, is a candidate for prototyping, while other functions must be specified using conventional approaches.

In general, any application that creates dynamic visual displays, interacts heavily with a human user, or demands algorithms or combinatorial processing that must be developed in an evolutionary fashion is a candidate for prototyping. However, these application areas must be weighed against application complexity. If a candidate application (one with the characteristics noted above) will require the development of tens of thousands of lines of code before any demonstrable function can be performed, it is likely to be too complex for prototyping. If, however, the complexity can be partitioned, it may still be possible to prototype portions of the software.

Because the customer must interact with the prototype in later steps, it is essential that the customer be (1) familiar with the prototyping process, (2) willing to spend the time to properly evaluate a prototype, and (3) capable of making requirements decisions in a timely fashion.

*Develop an abbreviated representation of requirements
using an object-oriented approach.*

Before construction of a prototype can begin, we must understand what objects and operations exist for a software solution and develop a reasonable approach to partitioning. Using the steps for identifying objects and operations presented earlier in this chapter, a basic model of the system is created. This model serves as a point of departure for the creation of a prototype.

To illustrate, reconsider the vertical partitioning of CLSS illustrated in Figures 3.5 and 3.6. The job of the software engineer is to select areas of uncertainty and focus attention there. For example, the customer may be unsure of the type of bar code reader and the resultant bar code input format. The software engineer decides that a software prototype of this function will be worthwhile, enabling the customer (and the software engineer) to better understand the pros and cons of different bar code formats. To develop this prototype, "mock-ups" of the objects **bar code reader** and **bar code data** are created. That is, a program that simulates the function of the **bar code reader** is written, producing an output data item that corresponds to the object **bar code data**. In addition, mock-ups of the operations **receive** and **decode** are implemented. Note that other objects and operations associated with CLSS are not to be implemented as part of this prototype but are specified and modeled using conventional methods.

Create a paper prototype.

A prototype need not be an executable model of the program. In many cases that involve human-machine interaction, it is possible to create a paper model. For example, consider a situation in which a customer wants a personal computer-based system that will assist in the design, layout, and representation of kitchen cabinets. The customer, a building supply firm, knows little about software interface design or computer graphics but does know what is required to design kitchens. After several conversations, the software engineer develops a statement of software scope, isolates important objects and operations, and then creates a paper prototype that contains pictures (in color, if appropriate) of each interactive "frame" (the image currently visible on the display device) with a description of what is happening between computer and user. Each frame is a screen image and shows icons, commands, menus, and graphics that result from human-machine interaction. The software engineer and the customer then walk through the paper prototype as if it were an operating program.

In most cases the paper prototype will suffice as a means of communicating interface requirements. However, it may still be necessary to build an operating model so that the user can get a dynamic feeling for the modes of interaction. In such cases, we apply the prototyping steps that follow.

Create an abbreviated design for the prototype.

Design must occur before prototyping can commence, but the depth and formality of design for the prototype will be different than design applied to production software. In many cases, the prototype is a "shell" of the production software. That is, the human interface or input/output functions may be implemented, but the computational or data processing internals are omitted. For this reason, the prototype design focuses only on the data structures and architectural and procedural components necessary to implement the shell. As we have already noted, horizontal and vertical partitioning that results in a description of objects and operations provides an important first step in the creation of a software prototype.

Create, test, and refine the prototype software.

A working prototype can be implemented using a conventional programming language (e.g., Pascal, C, or FORTRAN), an object-oriented language (e.g., Smalltalk, C++), a specialized language (e.g., Lisp or Prolog), a nonprocedural language that is used in conjunction with an existing data base system (e.g., NOMAD, FOCUS, INTELLECT), a code generator (e.g., TELON, SAGE), or a variety of specialized prototyping tools. Regardless of the implementation approach, the object is the same—to create a working model as rapidly as possible.

To illustrate how a simple prototype can be developed to help a customer better refine requirements for a sophisticated system, consider the development of a library information system described below:

The library information software will access a data base of all books currently held in a university library collection. Bibliographic information about each book will be maintained, as well as an extensive keyword index to assist in locating books by topic rather than by author. The user will interact with the data base through an interface ...

Tables of objects and operations are created using the steps described earlier in this chapter. It becomes apparent that the customer (the university librarian) has little knowledge of human-machine interface design and is unsure of how the user interaction should proceed. To assist the customer, the software engineer creates a mock-up of the library information system software using a data base system and query language (such as dBASE III) implemented on a personal computer. It should be noted that the personal computer prototype will be woefully inadequate for the production system but will serve nicely for prototyping.

A small data base of books is created, appropriate menus and interaction sequences are implemented, and a working prototype of the Librarian Information System software is created.

Present the prototype to the customer, who "test drives" the application and suggests modifications.

This step is the kernel of the prototyping approach. It is here that the customer (remember: in many cases you may be your own customer!) examines an implemented representation of software requirements, suggesting modifications that will enable the software to better meet actual needs.

Continuing with the Library Information System example, the librarian is asked to "test drive" the resultant prototype. Changes are requested and iteration occurs, but the result is a much more specific indication of the user interface for the Library Information System. For example, using the prototype, the software engineer finds that the librarian really wants two different interaction modes—one for students and faculty and another for the staff librarians themselves. This fact was not apparent in the problem statement.

Repeat prototyping steps iteratively until all requirements are formalized or until the prototype has evolved into a production system.

The prototyping paradigm can be conducted with one of two objectives in mind: (1) the purpose of prototyping is to establish a set of formal requirements that may then be translated into production software through the use of software engineering methods and techniques or (2) the purpose of prototyping is to act as the first step in a continuum that results in the evolutionary development of production software. Regardless of the objective that is chosen, prototyping provides an effective mechanism for solidifying software requirements and validating solutions that have technological risk.

Develop a flow model for the software.

Information is transformed as it flows through a computer-based system. The system accepts input in a variety of forms and applies hardware, software, data base, and human elements to transform input and produce output in a variety of forms. Input may be a control signal transmitted by a transducer, a series of numbers typed by a human operator, a packet of information transmitted on a network link, or a voluminous data file retrieved from disk storage. The transform(s) may comprise a single logical comparison, a complex numerical algorithm, or the rule-inference approach of an expert system. Output may light a single LED or produce a 200-page report. In effect, a *data flow model* can be applied to any computer-based system, regardless of size and complexity.

One method* for representing information flow through a computer-based system is illustrated in Figure 3.7. The overall function of the system is represented as a single information transform, noted as a *bubble* in the figure. One or more inputs, shown as labeled arrows, drive the transform to produce output information. It should be noted that the model may be applied to the entire system or to the software element only. The key is to represent the information fed into and produced by the transform.

Use data flow diagrams to indicate how data move through the software.

As information (objects that can be categorized as data and control items) moves through software, it is modified by a series of transformations. These transformations are analogous to the processing *operations* discussed earlier in this chapter. A *data flow diagram* (DFD) (also called a data flow graph or bubble chart) is a graphical technique that depicts data flow and the transforms that are applied as data move

---

*   It is important to note that there are many different methods that may be used to represent software requirements. The method presented in this book is derived from an approach called *Structured Analysis*. Other methods, such as *Data Structured Systems Development* (DSSD), *System Analysis and Design Technique* (SADT), and *Jackson System Development* (JSD) are used by software engineers. For additional references, see the Further Readings section at the end of this chapter.

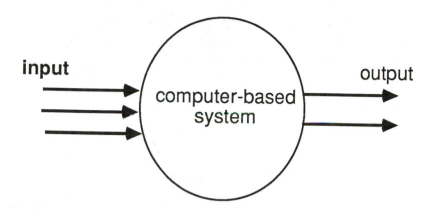

Figure 3.7 Representing Information Flow

from input to output. The basic form of a data flow diagram is illustrated in Figure 3.8.

Data or control items (**data$_1$**) are produced by an object (**originator$_1$**) that is an information source. **Data$_1$** flows into the system and is operated upon by **transform$_1$**, which produces another data item, **data$_2$**. Additional data objects are created through the application of other transforms or by retrieval from a data store. Ultimately, output, in the form **data$_6$**, is sent to an information sink, **receiver$_1$**.

The data flow diagram (DFD) may be used to represent a system or software at any level of abstraction. In fact, DFDs may be partitioned into levels that represent increasing information flow and functional detail. A level 01 DFD, also called a *fundamental system model*, represents the entire software element as a single bubble with input and output data indicated by incoming and outgoing arrows, respectively. Additional transforms and information flow paths are represented as the level 01 DFD is partitioned to reveal more detail.

DFD notation is illustrated in Figure 3.9. A rectangle is used to represent an *external object,* that is, a system element (e.g., hardware, a person) or another system that produces information for transformation by the software or receives information produced by the software. A circle or oval represents a *process* or *transform* that is applied to data and changes it in some way. An arrow represents one or more

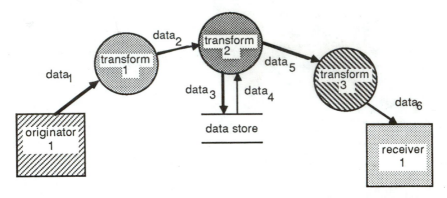

Figure 3.8 Data Flow Diagram

data items. All arrows on a data flow diagram should be labeled. The double line represents a *data store* —stored information that is used by the software. DFD symbology is exceptionally simple and is one reason that data flow-oriented analysis techniques are the most widely used.

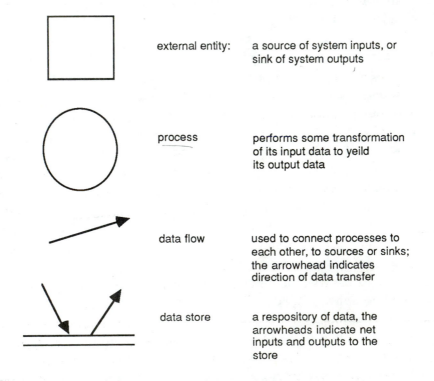

Figure 3.9 Data Flow Diagram Notation

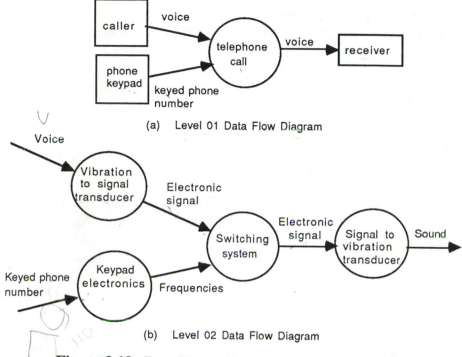

(a)   Level 01 Data Flow Diagram

(b)   Level 02 Data Flow Diagram

Figure 3.10 Data Flow Diagram for a Telephone Call

It is interesting to note that the objects determined as part of earlier steps correspond to boxes (information sources and sinks), arrows (data items), and double lines (data stores) on a DFD. Operations correspond to circles (transforms). Therefore, *the object and operation tables provide the basic information required to derive data flow diagrams.*

As a simple example of a data flow diagram, consider information flow for a typical telephone call (Figure 3.10). The level 01 DFD for a telephone call indicates that output is the sound of the caller's voice received by the listener. Input to the telephone call is the caller's voice and a keyed phone number. Figure 3.10b illustrates a level 02 refinement of the level 01 DFD. As shown in the figure, more information about both data flow and process function (transforms) is provided. The caller's action of depressing the key pad is transformed by associated electronics into a series of audible frequencies (tones). The frequencies flow to a switching system that performs requisite routing and establishes a link from sender to receiver. The sound of a human voice is transformed by a vibration transducer that produces a signal as output. The switching system moves the voice signal to a receiver that transforms the signal back to sound. It is important to note that the data flow diagrams for this example represent an entire system, not just software. In general, we use DFDs to represent only the software element of a system.

Although the above example is a gross oversimplification, the flow of information, represented by the data flow diagram, is easy to discern. Each transform in the diagram could be refined still further to provide greater detail about key pad processing, transducers, or the switching system. That is, the diagram may be *layered* to show any desired level of detail.

It is important to note that no explicit indication of the sequence of events (e.g., is phone number keyed before or after voice input?) is supplied by the diagram. Procedure or sequence may be implicit in the diagram, but explicit procedural representation is generally delayed until software design.

As we noted earlier, each of the bubbles may be refined or layered to depict more detail. Figure 3.11 illustrates this concept. A fundamental model for system F indicates that primary input is A and final output is B. We refine the F model into transforms f_1 to f_7. Note that *information flow continuity* must be maintained, that is, input and output to each level of refinement must remain the same. Further refinement of f_4 depicts detail in the form of transforms f_{41} to f_{45}. Again, the input (X,Y) and output (Z) remain unchanged.

The data flow diagram is a graphical tool that can be very valuable during software requirements analysis, establishing a foundation for subsequent software design. However, the diagram can cause confusion if a software engineer attempts to *design* a program using data flow notation. Software design requires a specification of program architecture, followed by a representation of the procedural details of program components (see Chapter 4 for an extended discussion of design). Because the data flow diagram notation cannot be applied to the representation of program architecture or processing details (e.g., loops, conditions), a DFD is inadequate as a design tool.

A few simple guidelines can aid immeasurably during derivation of data flow diagrams: (1) the level 01 data flow diagram should depict the software/system as a single bubble; (2) primary input/output/ files should be carefully noted; (3) all arrows and bubbles should be labeled with meaningful names; (4) information flow continuity must

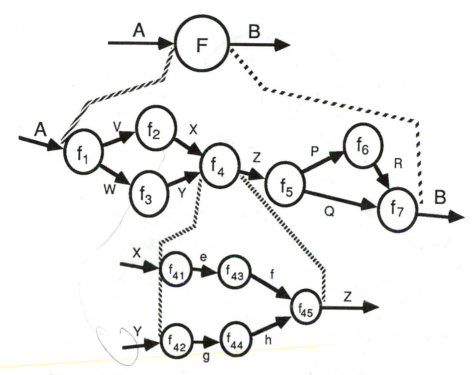

Figure 3.11   Hierarchical Layering for Data Flow Diagrams

be maintained; (5) <mark>one bubble at a time should be refined.</mark> There is a natural tendency to overcomplicate the data flow diagram. This occurs when we attempt to show too much detail too early or represent procedural aspects of the software in lieu of information flow.

> *Use control flow diagrams to indicate how control influences the software.*

The notation that we have developed for the data flow diagram does not explicitly represent control items and the transformations (operations) that process them. In many situations, information that indicates the occurrence of an event or initiates some action (a control item) and transformations that process control items are important to software function. Therefore, we need additional notation to accommodate control flow.

The convention established for data flow diagrams represents data items as a solid arrow. Control flow, however, is represented using

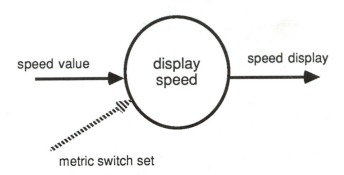

Figure 3.12   Representing Control Flow

a dashed or shaded arrow. Similarly, control transformation (an operation that produces control items) is represented by a dashed circle.

In Figure 3.12, a transform (operation) named **display speed** accepts a discrete data value, **speed value**, and produces another discrete output, **speed display**. **Display speed** also receives control information in the form of an *event flow*, **metric switch set**, that controls whether an English or metric conversion algorithm is used within the data transform. An event flow always represents a control item. In the example shown in the figure, the event flow "value" would indicate which measurement system is to be used.

Figure 3.13 illustrates a top-level view of a control process for a manufacturing cell.* As components are placed on fixtures, a status bit is set within a **parts status buffer** that indicates the presence or absence of each component. Event flows are used to set each bit, and the entire bit string is stored in a *control store*. Event information contained within the **parts status buffer** is passed to a *control process*, **signal robot arm**, that also receives other event flows as shown in the figure. The output of the control process is a control signal that invokes a robot controller.

The control flow represented in Figure 3.13 is expanded in Figure 3.14 to illustrate combined event and data flow. As shown in

---

* A manufacturing cell is a collection of machines, robots, tooling, and fixtures that are used in conjunction with one another to produce a specific manufactured component (e.g., a drive shaft, a circuit board). The equipment contained within the cell is monitored and controlled by one or more computers that communicate with a central computer for scheduling and reporting information.

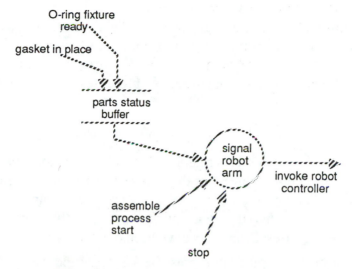

Figure 3.13 A Control Process for a Manufacturing Cell

Figure 3.14, the output of the control process described in the preceding paragraph is used to trigger a robot control system illustrated with a level 01 data flow diagram. From the DFD for the robot control system, we can see that **positioning commands** and **manipulation commands** are read from a **command file**. **Position coordinates** and **robot**

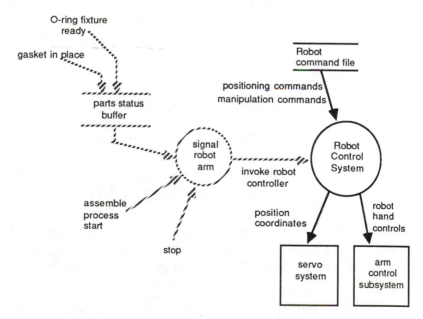

Figure 3.14 Combining Control and Data Flow

hand controls are produced by the system.

It is important to note that expansion of the robot control system portion of the flow diagram shown in Figure 3.14 may result in the representation of additional event flows and control processes. These may be combined with data transformation processes and conventional data flows.

Apply flow model assessment rules.

A flow model for software is a graphical notation that enables the software engineer to depict objects as they move through the system and the operations that act upon them. Like any graphical notation, flow models are most effective if they are applied consistently. For this reason, a number of assessment rules have been developed:

1. The flow model should be represented at a number of different levels of abstraction. That is, each new level should elaborate upon the preceding level, depicting more detail.
2. Data or control flow shown at one level must be maintained at lower levels. This data/control flow continuity is essential for creating a consistent model of the software.
3. The first level of a flow model should contain a single bubble that depicts the function of the entire software element.
4. A rule of thumb for expansion between levels is that one bubble at level *n* should expand to approximately three to five bubbles at level *n*+1.

Develop a data dictionary to represent object content.

Although the flow model is an important analysis representation, more information is required to create a complete analysis model. Each arrow of a flow diagram represents one or more data items. Therefore, some method for representing the content of each arrow (data item) should be available.

A *data dictionary* is a quasi-formal notation for describing the content of information as it flows through a system. The content of each object (data or control item) is represented using the notation shown in Figure 3.15. *Composite information* (either data or control) is represented in one of the three fundamental ways in which it can be constructed: (1) as a sequence of data or control items, (2) as a selection from among a set of data or control items, or (3) as a repeated

Data Construct	Notation	Meaning
Sequence	$=$	is composed of
	$+$	and
Selection	$[\ |\ ]$	either - or
Repetition	$\{\ \}^{n}$	n repetitions of
	$(\ )$	optional data
	$*\quad*$	comments

Figure 3.15 Data Dictionary Notation

grouping of data or control items. Each information item entry that is represented as part of a sequence, selection, or repetition may itself be another composite item that needs further refinement within the dictionary.

To illustrate the use of the data dictionary, let us return to the DFD for a telephone call, shown in Figure 3.10. In this figure, the data item **keyed phone number** is specified as input. But what exactly is a keyed phone number? It could be a seven-digit local number, a four digit extension, or a 25-digit long distance company sequence. The data dictionary provides us with a precise definition of **keyed phone number** for the DFD in question:

keyed phone number = [local extension|outside number| 0]

The above data dictionary statement may be read: **keyed phone number** is composed of either a **local extension** or an **outside number** or 0 (for operator). **Local extension** and **outside number** represent composite data items and are refined further in other data dictionary statements. The numeral 0 is *elementary data* and needs no further refinement.

Continuing the data dictionary entries for keyed phone number:

keyed phone number = [local extension|outside number| 0]
local extension= [2001|2002|...|2999|conference set]
outside number= 9 + [local number | long distance no.]
local number= prefix + access number
long distance no.= (0) + area code + local number
conference set = 2{# + local extension + #(#)}6

The data dictionary is expanded until all composite data items have been represented as elementary items or until all composite items are represented in terms that would be well known and unambiguous to all readers (e.g., **area code** is generally understood to mean a three-digit number with a 0 or 1 as the second digit).

The data dictionary defines information items unambiguously. Although we might assume that the phone call represented by the DFD in Figure 3.10 could accommodate a 25-digit long distance carrier access number, the data dictionary for the DFD tells us that such numbers are not part of the data that may be input. In addition, the data dictionary can provide information about function that may not be immediately obvious from an examination of the DFDs. For example, conference calling capability is implied by the entry for **conference set**, where between two and six extensions may be keyed (delimited by #) until two # signs are entered in a row. Each of these extensions, we infer, would be part of a conference call. It is important to note, however, that further information (external to the data dictionary) would have to be provided about conference calling capability.

A data dictionary can be used to describe any object or set of objects that can be processed by software. As another example, consider an object called **book** that contains all necessary information for a desk-top publishing system. The content of **book** can be represented using data dictionary notation:

book = front matter + {chapter}^{n} + end matter

where **front matter** is all the information that appears before chapters begin, multiple occurrences of **chapter** (note that the superscript n implies that there are n chapters), and **end matter** is all the information that appears after the last chapter. Refining each of the composite data items:

front matter = title page + table of contents + (dedication) + (acknowledgment) + (preface)
chapter = first page + {page}^{m} + (references) + (problems for solution)
end matter = (epilogue) + ({appendix}^{r}) + ([index |glossary])

It should be noted that each of the composite data items is itself composed of other composite items. Some of these items are optional (denoted by parentheses) while others represent multiple occurrences (e.g., m occurrences of **page** and r occurrences of **appendix**). Further refinement of **book** is left as an exercise to the reader.

Because the data dictionary focuses on the content of the information domain, it provides a software engineer with a "new look" at the requirements for a program. The small amount of time spent examining data content (rather than rushing into programming) will pay important dividends when design and implementation commence.

For large computer-based systems, the data dictionary grows rapidly in size and complexity. In fact, it is extremely difficult to maintain a data dictionary manually. For this reason, a number of automated data dictionary tools are available. In addition, new computer-aided software engineering (CASE) workstations support automated generation of DFDs and direct coupling and management of associated data dictionaries.

Write processing narratives for both data and control transforms.

Once a flow model has been created (using flow diagrams and the data dictionary), each transform (operation) should be described using natural language or some other stylized notation. The description is called a *processing narrative*.

One notation for processing narratives is called *program design language* (PDL). PDL incorporates basic procedural constructs—sequence, selection, and repetition—with English language phrases so that concise procedural descriptions can be developed for transforms represented within a flow diagram. In most cases, a simple English language description of a DFD bubble is sufficient for analysis purposes—the use of PDL is delayed until software design (Chapter 4). However, when an operation can be described only by specifying a complex set of logical conditions and actions, PDL is a useful alternative.

To illustrate the derivation of a processing narrative, we consider the data flow diagram shown in Figure 3.16. This DFD depicts the flow of information that occurs when a processing narrative is generated for a DFD bubble. The function of the bubble may be specified using an English language processing narrative:

A DFD bubble is selected and the software engineer determines whether it needs further refinement. If it does, the bubble is decomposed into two or more bubbles (with appropriate data flows). When no further refinement is required, a bubble is selected for description using program design language. The program design

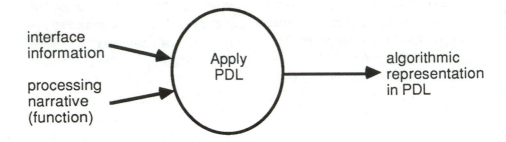

Figure 3.16 DFD for Applying Program Design Language

language description begins with a **procedure** statement that carries the name of the bubble. All processing tasks within the bubble are described using logical constructs that include sequence, if-then-else, and repetition. These are refined until the software engineer determines that sufficient detail has been specified.

Although the English language paragraph adequately describes the function of the bubble, there is no indication of processing logic. In most cases, this is acceptable for the software model that is created during problem analysis. However, for situations in which more precision is required, a program design language processing narrative may be used. A PDL version of the processing narrative of the DFD bubble follows:

```
procedure: Apply PDL;
select DFD bubble, call it target bubble;
do while target bubble needs further refinement
    if target bubble is multifunctional
        then decompose as required;
            select new target bubble;
        else no further refined needed;
    endif
enddo
use procedure statement to name target bubble;
describe sequence of process tasks;
repeat until all process tasks have been described
    case of process task logic
        case: process task includes a sequence;
            select: state sequence of steps;
```

```
      case: process task is a condition;
         select: use if-then-else to define condition;
      case: process task includes repetition;
         select: use do while or repeat until;
      case: process task includes a number of cases;
         select: use case of;
   endcase
endrep
review PDL  that has been generated;
modify as required using procedure Apply PDL;
end procedure
```

Program design language can often be combined with natural language descriptions to provide a complete description of either data or control transformations. During software design, the description is refined to provide additional procedural detail.

Begin thinking about software validation.

The analysis work that has been done has broadened our understanding and created a useful description of the software. Design and implementation steps will translate a *Software Specification* into a working program. But how can we assure ourselves that the program meets customer needs? The answer lies in a combination of *formal technical reviews* (see Appendix B) and testing.

Although it is too early to begin the design of test cases, the overall strategy for program validation (testing) and the classes of tests to be conducted later in the software engineering process can be defined at this time (subject to later modification). In essence, we ask the following question: *"How would I recognize a program that meets all customer objectives if it were dropped on my desk tomorrow?"*

At this stage, a description of testing strategy focuses on the order in which major software functions will be tested, the requirements for special testing resources (e.g., additional people, special hardware, simulation software), and the manner in which the program will be constructed. In addition, general classes of tests are described. For example, classes of tests for CLSS software (discussed earlier in this chapter) might be:

Class 1: Tests to validate proper decoding of bar code reader input
Class 2: Tests to ensure that identification codes contained in the data base are properly found and processed

Class 3: Tests to ensure that the proper shunt mechanism code is produced

Class 4: Tests to ensure that the control signal for the shunt mechanism is properly synchronized to box position

Class 5: Tests to validate proper error processing, i.e., situations in which the bar code is unreadable, the box ID does not exist in the data base, or hardware malfunctions

Each of the above classes of tests will result in many test cases that are developed using test case design techniques discussed in Chapter 6.

Put it all together
to form a *Software Specification.*

The *Software Specification* is produced as the culmination of the analysis step. The function and performance allocated to software are refined by establishing a complete information description, a detailed functional description, an indication of performance requirements and design constraints, appropriate validation criteria, and other data pertinent to requirements. The following simplified outline may be used as a framework for the specification:

Software Specification
1. Introduction
    1.1 system reference
    1.2 business objectives
    1.3 software project constraints
2. Software Description
    2.1 objects and operations
    2.2 flow model
    2.3 data dictionary
    2.4 system interface description
3. Processing Narratives
    3.n transform (operation) n description
        3.n.1 processing narrative
        3.n.2 restrictions/limitations
        3.n.3 performance requirements
        3.n.4 design constraints
        3.n.5 supporting diagrams
4. Validation Criteria
    4.1 testing strategy
    4.2 classes of tests

The *Introduction* states the goals and objectives of the software, describing it in the context of the computer-based system. Actually, the *Introduction* may be nothing more than a restatement of the software scope that was developed during the system engineering step.

The *Software Description* provides a detailed description of the problem that the software must solve. Objects and operations, a flow model, and the data dictionary are each presented. In addition, hardware, software, and human interfaces are described for external system elements and internal software functions.

A description of each operation required to solve the problem is provided in the *Processing Narratives* section. A processing narrative is provided for each function, design constraints are stated and justified, performance characteristics are stated, and one or more diagrams are included to graphically represent the overall structure of the software and the interplay among software functions and other system elements. This section forms the basis for software design. At this stage, however, we focus exclusively on *what* each operation must do, postponing a description of *how* it will be done until design begins.

The fourth section is probably the most important and, ironically, the most often neglected! The *Validation Criteria* section answers the following questions: How do we recognize a successful implementation? What classes of tests must be conducted to validate function, performance, and constraints? In the past we neglected this section because completing it demands a thorough understanding of software requirements—something that we often do not have. The *Validation Criteria* section acts as an implicit review of information and functional requirements. It is essential that time and attention be given to this section.

Finally, the *Software Specification* includes a *Bibliography* and *Appendix*. The *Bibliography* contains references to all documents that relate to the software. These include other planning phase documentation, technical references, vendor literature, and standards. The *Appendix* contains information that supplements the specification.

Tabular data, detailed description of algorithms, charts, graphs, and other material are presented as appendixes.

In many cases a *Software Specification* is accompanied by an executable prototype, a paper prototype, or a *Preliminary User's Manual*. The *Preliminary User's Manual* presents the software as a black box. That is, heavy emphasis is placed on user input and resultant output. The manual can serve as a valuable tool for uncovering problems at the human-machine interface.

Review the specification for correctness, consistency, and completeness.

A review of the *Software Specification* (and/or prototype) is conducted by both the software engineer and the customer. Because the specification forms the foundation of the development phase, extreme care should be taken in conducting this review. The format of the review may best be understood by considering some of the questions that must be answered:

- Do stated goals and objectives for software remain consistent with system goals and objectives?
- Have important interfaces to all system elements been described?
- Are information flow and structure adequately defined for the problem domain?
- Are diagrams clear? Can each stand alone without supplementary text?
- Do major functions remain within scope? Has each been adequately described?
- Are design constraints realistic?
- What is the technological risk of development?
- Have alternative software requirements been considered?
- Have validation criteria been stated in detail? Are they adequate to describe a successful system?
- Do inconsistencies, omissions, or redundancy exist?
- Is the customer contact complete?
- Has the user reviewed the *User's Manual* or prototype?
- How are the project estimates (for cost and schedule) affected by the results of analysis?

Once the review is complete, the *Software Specification* is "signed off" by both customer and software engineer. The specification becomes a "contract" for software development.   Changes in requirements will still be requested after the specification is finalized. But the customer will now be aware that each after-the-fact change is an extension of software scope and therefore can increase cost and/or protract the schedule.

Even with the best review procedures in place, a number of common specification problems persist. The specification is difficult to "test" in any meaningful way, and therefore inconsistency or omissions may pass unnoticed. During the review, changes to the specification may be recommended. It is extremely difficult to assess the global impact of a change, that is, how a change in one function affects requirements for other functions. Automated specification tools have been developed to help solve these problems, but to date they are used by only a small percentage of all software engineers.

Expect to iterate; avoid the temptation to rush into design or coding.

Problem analysis, regardless of which specific approach we apply, should be viewed as an iterative process. We examine the problem, gain greater insight into its intricacies, write down what we've learned, and review the results with the customer. Each review (in fact, each customer communication) is likely to uncover misunderstanding, omissions, or ambiguity that must be clarified.

Every software engineer has been tempted to "get on with it!" Time is passing, the delivery deadline is just over the horizon, we think we know enough, so why not start and fill in the details as we go? In fact, this is exactly what we will do. But before we can legitimately start, a solid description of the problem, the objectives to be addressed in solving it, and the requirements demanded of a solution must be identified and documented.

The steps that we have presented for problem analysis provide a good road map. The success of your journey through the remainder of the software engineering process is predicated on the quality of this road map. If it is incomplete, erroneous, or nonexistent, you'll make many false starts, wind up at too many dead ends, and likely get inextricably lost. You may finally stumble upon the solution, but not without much wasted time and substantial frustration. On the other hand, if the road map is complete, things will proceed smoothly as you progress toward your goal.

WHAT THIS MEANS TO YOU

If you've ever encountered a problem to be solved in software and not known where to begin, this chapter should help. No matter what the complexity of the problem, it can always be described in a brief English language paragraph. From this paragraph, you can derive the objects and operations that are relevant to problem solution. You can develop a flow model that depicts how information and control move through the software. You can refine the model to provide greater elaboration of detail. Each of these steps leads to the development of a specification or prototype for the software.

The steps described in this chapter take time, and it's reasonable to ask how this investment of time provides dividends. By analyzing the problem and creating a model of the software, you prove to yourself and your customer that you understand what needs to be done. You eliminate ambiguity, clarify intent, and uncover omissions. As important, you establish a foundation from which software design is derived and from which you can assess the quality of your work as you proceed toward implementation.

FURTHER READINGS

Atwood, J.W., *The Systems Analyst*, Hayden, 1977.
Boar, B., *Application Prototyping*, Wiley-Interscience, 1984.
DeMarco, T., *Structured Analysis and System Specification*, Prentice-Hall, 1979.

PROBLEMS AND POINTS TO PONDER

3.1 Early in this chapter we indicated that the statement of scope for software should be refined through a number of different levels of detail prior to the creation of object and operation tables. Three statements of scope are presented below. Acting as your own customer, refine each through two additional levels of detail.

a. Software for a grocery store scale acquires weight of the product to be sold (e.g., produce or meat) from scale hardware and the price per pound and product code from the grocery clerk. The software displays the overall price and weight on a digital display and prints a price label that is to be placed on the package.

b. Order entry software for a mail-order retailer accepts customer and product information as input and produces a packing slip and customer invoice as output. The software looks up unit price and availability, computes total price, applies any discounts, and computes sales tax and shipping charges for billing.

c. The software for an automatic teller machine (ATM) at a bank provides standard transactions that include funds transfer, cash withdrawal, bill paying and deposits. The software checks the user's security code, prompts for appropriate transaction type, and guides the customer through the transaction, requesting appropriate information as required.

3.2 Develop object and operation tables for each of the software applications described in problem 3.1. Use the refined statements of scope that you developed as part of problem 3.1.

3.3 As a software engineer, it's likely that you'll encounter more than one customer who has not taken the time to write a statement of scope for a new software application. Among the questions that you're likely to ask this customer are:

What does the system do?
What output does the software produce?
What is the input for the software?

In what order would you ask these questions? Does the order make a difference? If so, why?

3.4 In your own words, describe the difference between essential and implementation models for software.

3.5 Develop a paper prototype for a video game of your own creation.

3.6 List three software applications in which the benefits of prototyping would be open to question. Explain why.

3.7 Develop level 01 and 02 data flow diagrams for one or more (assigned by your instructor) of the software applications presented in problem 3.1.

3.8 Refine one data flow diagram developed in problem 3.7 to level 03.

3.9 Develop a data dictionary for one or more (assigned by your instructor) of the software applications presented in problem 3.1.

3.10 Develop a processing narrative for selected bubbles in the data flow diagrams for one or more (assigned by your instructor) of the software applications presented in problem 3.1.

3.11 Create a flow model of a software application that makes use of both data and control flow.

3.12 Complete the data dictionary for **book** that was started as part of this chapter.

3.13 Describe a series of validation tests for one or more (assigned by your instructor) of the software applications presented in problem 3.1.

CHAPTER 4
DESIGNING THE SOLUTION

Design lies at the kernel of all engineering disciplines. It provides us with a systematic method for deriving a solution to a problem and works best only when a problem has been thoroughly analyzed. Design enables us to represent the solution using a consistent notation and establish a foundation from which implementation proceeds. Most important, design provides us with a means for assessing the quality of the solution *before* it has been implemented, when changes are still relatively easy to make.

Software design is a natural outgrowth of the analysis steps that were described in the preceding chapter. The objects and operations, flow model, data dictionary, and process description are transformed into a data design, an architectural design, and a procedural design for the software. Each of these design representations is derived using the steps presented in this chapter.

Refine the *Software Specification* in preparation for design.

The *Software Specification* (described in Chapter 3) contains a relatively detailed description of software requirements. Problem analysis encompasses a series of steps that describe what is required of the software. Software design describes how the software solution will achieve requirements.

If the *Software Specification* has been developed with care, very little refinement will be required as a precursor to design. However, in many situations (more than we'd like), the information contained in the *Software Specification* must be further refined before design steps can commence. For example, the flow model contained in the specification may be adequate for problem analysis but require further expansion prior to architectural design (discussed later in this chapter).

Recognize and apply fundamental design concepts.

A set of fundamental software design concepts have evolved over the past three decades. Although the degree of interest in each concept has varied over the years, each has stood the test of time. Each provides the software engineer with a foundation from which more sophisticated design methods can be applied. Each helps the software engineer to answer the following questions:

- What criteria can be used to partition software into individual components?
- How is function or data structure detail separated from a conceptual representation of software?
- Are there uniform criteria that define the technical quality of a software design?

M.A. Jackson once said: "The beginning of wisdom for a computer programmer [software engineer] is to recognize the difference between getting a program to work, and getting it right." Fundamental software design concepts provide the necessary framework for "getting it right."

Design Concept 1: Derive representations for data, program structure, and procedural detail.

Software design is actually a three-step process. Initially, the content and structure of the data that are processed by a program are described. Next, the overall modular structure of a program is represented. Finally, the procedural detail that implements function within a given program module is depicted. Each of these steps, called *data design, architectural design,* and *procedural design,* respectively, is one part of the activity that we call software design. To produce high quality computer programs, we must perform all three design activities.

Design Concept 2: Understand the structural elements that comprise software architecture.

Software architecture refers to the hierarchical structure of procedural components, given the generic term *modules*. The term *module* is used to refer to a separately compilable program component. In FORTRAN a program component is called a *subroutine*. In the programming languages C and Pascal a program component is called a *procedure*. In the language Modula-2 a component is called a *module,* and in Ada a component is called a *package*. Software architecture is derived through a partitioning process that relates elements of a software solution to parts of a real-world problem implicitly defined during problem analysis.

Program structure represents the organization (often hierarchical) of program components (modules) and implies a hierarchy of control. It does not represent procedural aspects of software such as sequence of processes, occurrence/order of decisions, or repetition of operations.

Many different notations are used to represent program structure. The most common is the treelike diagram shown in Figure 4.1. The

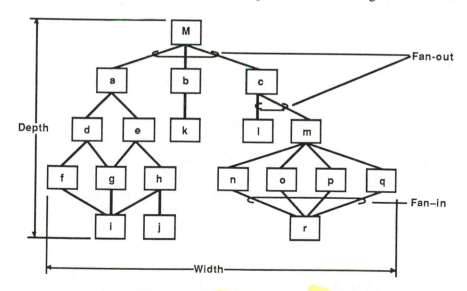

Figure 4.1 Program Structure Notation

diagram implies that a module M invokes (calls) modules a, b, and c. That is, logic within procedure M will cause procedures a, b, and c to be executed. Data and/or control items (information objects) may be passed between M and a, b, and c. Similarly, module a invokes modules d and e and so on.

In order to facilitate later discussions of structure, we define a few simple terms. As shown in Figure 4.1, *depth* and *width* provide an indication of the number of levels of control and overall span of control, respectively. *Fan-out* is a measure of the number of modules that are directly controlled by another module. *Fan-in* indicates how many modules directly control a given module.

The control relationship among modules is expressed in the following way: a module that controls another module is said to be *superordinate* to it, and conversely, a module controlled by another is said to be *subordinate* to the controller. For example, in Figure 4.1, module M is superordinate to modules a, b, and c. Module h is subordinate to module e.

Design Concept 3: Understand data structures and their impact on software design.

Data structure is a representation of the logical relationship among individual data items. Because the structure of information will invariably affect the final architectural and procedural design, data structure is as important as program structure to the representation of software design.

Data structure dictates the organization, methods of access, degree of associativity, and processing alternatives for information. Entire texts have been dedicated to these topics, and a complete discussion is beyond the scope of this book. However, it is important to understand the classic methods available for organizing information and the concepts that underlie information hierarchies.

The organization and complexity of a data structure are limited only by the ingenuity of the designer. There are, however, a limited number of classic data structures that form the building blocks for more sophisticated structures. These classic data structures are illustrated in Figure 4.2.

A *scalar item* is the simplest of all data structures. As its name implies, a scalar item represents a single element of information that

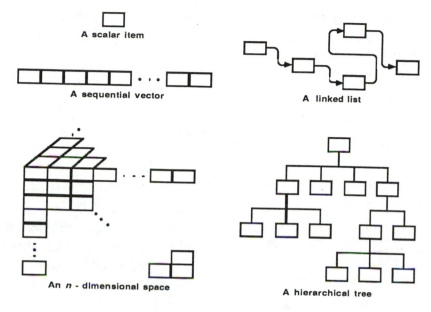

Figure 4.2 Classic Data Structures

may be addressed by an identifier; that is, access may be achieved by specifying a single address in memory. The size and format of a scalar item may vary within bounds that are dictated by a programming language. For example, a scalar item may be a logical entity one bit long, an integer or floating point number that is 8 to 64 bits long, or a character string that is hundreds or thousands of bytes long. In programming languages such as Pascal, scalar items are declared to identify their type. As an example, consider the scalar items required for a small Pascal program that computes sales tax:

```
var PurchasePrice, SalesTax, TotalPrice: real;
```

Three scalar items (Pascal variables) are defined as shown above.

The scalar item is the building block for all other data structures. For example, when scalar items are organized in a contiguous group, a *sequential vector* is formed. Vectors are the most common of all data structures and open the door to variable indexing of information. To illustrate we consider a simple Pascal example in which the grades for 20 students are averaged:

```
program TestAverage (input, output);
const n = 20;
var grade: array[1..n] of integer;
```

```
    sum, studentno, average: integer;
begin  (*main*)
    sum  := 0;
    for studentno := 1 to n do
    begin
        read (grade[studentno]);
        sum := sum + grade[studentno];
    end;
    average := sum div n;
    writeln ('  class average is  ', average);
end.  (*main*)
```

A sequential vector of 20 scalar integer items, **grade**, is defined. Access to each element of **grade** is indexed via the variable **studentno** so that elements of the data structure are referenced in a defined order.

When the sequential vector is extended to two, three, and ultimately an arbitrary number of dimensions, an *n-dimensional space* is created. The most common *n*-dimensional space is the two-dimensional matrix. In most programming languages, an *n*-dimensional space is called an *array*.

Items, vectors, and spaces may be organized in a variety of formats. A *linked list* is a data structure that organizes non-contiguous scalar items, vectors, or spaces in a manner that enables them to be processed as a list. A list is composed of *nodes* that contain a data structure and *pointers* referencing other (e.g., preceding and following) nodes. Nodes may be added at any location in the list by redefining pointers to accommodate the new list entry. For this reason, the linked list is an excellent design alternative when a set of items will be updated regularly.

Other data structures incorporate or are constructed using the fundamental data structures described above. For example, a hierarchical data structure, sometimes called a *record* structure, is constructed from different scalar items, vectors, and lists that are organized hierarchically. An additional layer of structure can be created by organizing records into *file structures*. To illustrate, consider a record structure that holds pertinent information about an individual (in Pascal):

```
type
    individual = record
        name:  string;
```

```
      address:    string;
      age:    integer;
   end;
```

The record structure **individual** is a data abstraction in the sense that a designer can use it to describe the characteristics of other objects in a program. That is,

```
var student: individual;
```

implies that the variable **student** is structured in the same manner as the record type **individual**. To create a collection of records representing all students, we use a file structure:

```
type studentbody = file of individual;
```

The concept of data design, however, goes beyond the simple definition of data structures in the programming language of choice. The designer must select data structures that are amenable to the requirements of the information domain, that will properly accommodate the data items described with a data dictionary (Chapter 3), and that will enable program architecture and procedural detail to be implemented effectively. These concepts are discussed later in this chapter.

Program and data structure are the foundation for good software design, and both are derived from work that we have already done during problem analysis. Program structure can be derived from the flow model of software (the data flow and control flow diagrams). Data structure is driven by specified functional requirements and the information content as described by the data dictionary.

Design Concept 4: Learn the difference between architectural and procedural representations of software.

Program structure defines control hierarchy without regard to the sequence of processing and decisions. Module procedure (Figure 4.3) focuses on the processing details of each module individually. Procedure must provide a precise specification of processing, including sequence of events, exact decision points, repetitive operations, and even data organization/structure. The flow chart shown in the figure depicts these important procedural constructs.

The flow chart is one of many graphical methods for representing procedural design information. Boxes represent sequential processing steps; diamonds represent decisions; arrows represent flow of control.

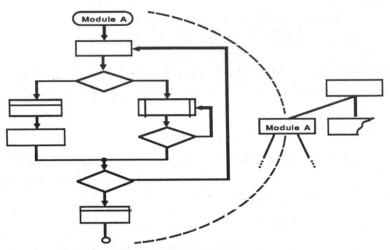

Figure 4.3 Architecture and Procedure

Other design representations, such as box diagrams or program analysis diagrams, accomplish the same objective using different notation. It should be noted, however, that many software engineers prefer program design language (PDL), a text-oriented design notation that was introduced in Chapter 2 and is presented in detail later in this chapter.

Structure and procedure are, of course, related. Processing indi-

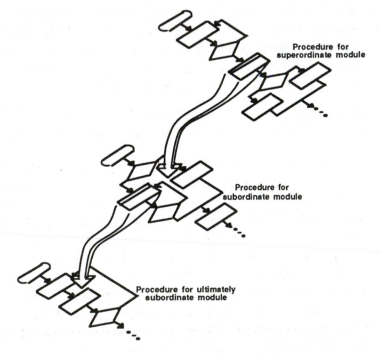

Figure 4.4 Conceptual Layering of Procedure

cated for each module must include a reference to all modules subordinate to the module being described. That is, a procedural representation of software is layered as illustrated in Figure 4.4.

Design Concept 5: Recognize the importance of refinement in the derivation of a design.

Stepwise refinement is a design strategy in which the design of a program is developed by successively refining levels of procedural detail. A hierarchy is developed by decomposing a macroscopic statement of function in a stepwise fashion until programming language statements are reached. An overview of the concept is provided by Niklaus Wirth:* "In each step (of the refinement), one or several instructions of the given program are decomposed into more detailed instructions. This successive decomposition or refinement of specifications terminates when all instructions are expressed in terms of any underlying computer or programming language ... As tasks are refined, so the data may have to be refined, decomposed, or structured..."

The process of program refinement proposed by Wirth is analogous to the process of refinement and partitioning that is used during problem analysis. The difference is in the level of detail that is considered, not the approach.

Refinement is actually a process of *elaboration*. We begin with a statement of function (or description of information) that is defined at a high *level of abstraction*. That is, the statement describes function or information conceptually but provides no information about the internal workings of the function or the internal structure of the information. Refinement causes the designer to elaborate on the original statement, providing more and more detail as each successive refinement (elaboration) occurs.

Stepwise refinement can be used to develop successive representation of any procedural operation. For example, the simple command

```
open the door;
```

is actually a procedural abstraction that can be refined through a number of successive levels of detail. The first refinement might be:

```
walk to the door;
determine whether it opens by pushing or pulling;
```

---

* Wirth, N., "Program Development by Stepwise Refinement," *CACM*, vol. 14, no. 4, 1971, pp. 221-227.

```
grasp the handle or door knob;
push or pull the door until it opens.
```

The first refinement provides basic procedural information, but much of the detail is missing. Each of the statements can be further elaborated as noted in the following refinement:

```
locate the door on the wall;
move to the door by walking;
examine the door to determine whether it is
locked;
if the door is locked,
     obtain a key and unlock the door;
examine the door to determine the direction for
opening;
if the door opens toward you,
     grasp the handle,
     pull, being sure to step out of the way;
if the door opens away from you,
     grasp the handle,
     push, being sure to move forward as the door
opens;
```

Needless to say, stepwise refinement of the procedural abstraction **open the door** is overkill. But it does illustrate a point. Any operation defined during software analysis can be refined in much the same way that we refined **open the door**. Using stepwise refinement to develop a procedural design, we are less likely to omit important details and more likely to move toward an accurate solution in a minimum amount of time.

Design Concept 6: Understand the importance of modularity for effective design.

The concept of modularity in computer software has been espoused for over three decades. Architecture embodies modularity; that is, software is divided into separately named and addressable elements, called *modules,* that are integrated to satisfy problem requirements.

Glenford Myers has stated that "modularity is the single attribute of software that allows a program to be intellectually manageable." Monolithic software (i.e., a large program made up of a single module) cannot be easily grasped by a reader. The number of control paths, span of reference, number of variables, and overall complexity would make understanding close to impossible. By dividing the

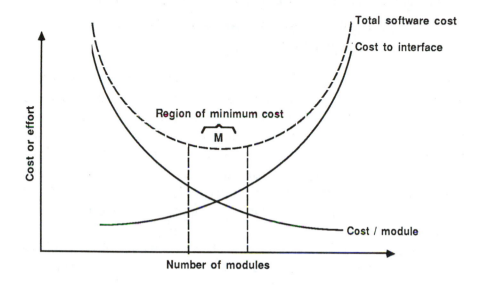

Figure 4.5 Modularity and Development Cost

program into modules, we make it easier to understand and less costly to develop.

It is possible to conclude that if we subdivide software indefinitely, the effort required to develop it will become negligibly small! After all, as each module becomes smaller it takes less time to design and implement it. Unfortunately, other forces come into play, causing this conclusion to be (sadly) invalid.

Figure 4.5 indicates that the effort to develop an individual software module decreases as the total number of modules increases. Given the same set of requirements, more modules means smaller individual size. However, as the number of modules grows, the effort associated with interfacing the modules also grows. These characteristics lead to a "total software cost" curve shown in the figure. There is a number, M, of modules that would result in minimum development cost, but we do not have the necessary sophistication to predict M with assurance.

The curves shown in Figure 4.5 do provide useful guidance when modularity is considered. We should modularize, but we should also take care to stay in the vicinity of M. Undermodularity or overmodularity should be avoided. But how do we know "the vicinity of

M"? How modular should we make software? We will soon see that the size of a module is dictated by its function and application.

Design Concept 7: Design software that exhibits information hiding.

The interrelated concepts of refinement and modularity lead every software designer to a fundamental question: "How do we decompose a software solution to obtain the best set of modules?" The principle of *information hiding* suggests that data structures and modules should be represented in a manner that precludes the need to understand their internal workings. In other words, modules should be specified and designed so that information (procedure and data) contained within a module is inaccessible to other modules that have no need for such information.

Hiding implies that effective modularity can be achieved by defining a set of independent modules that communicate with one another only that information that is necessary to achieve software function. Abstraction helps to define the procedural (or informational) entities that comprise the software. Hiding defines and enforces access constraints to both procedural detail within a module and any local data structure used by the module.

The use of information hiding as a design criterion for modular systems provides greatest benefits when modifications are required during testing, and also later during software maintenance. Because most data and procedure are hidden from other parts of the software, inadvertent errors introduced during modification are less likely to propagate to other locations within the software.

Design Concept 8: Define program components that exhibit effective modularity and functional independence.

Functional independence is a design concept that leads to guidelines for defining the proper "size" of a module. Functional independence is achieved by developing modules with "single-minded" function and an "aversion" to excessive interaction with other modules. Stated another way, we want to design software so that each module addresses a specific subfunction of requirements and has a simple interface when viewed from other parts of the program structure.

It is fair to ask why independence is important. Software with effective modularity, i.e., independent modules, is easier to develop because function can be compartmentalized and interfaces are simplified (consider the ramifications when development is conducted by a team of people). Independent modules are easier to maintain (and test) because: (1) secondary effects caused by design/code modification are limited, (2) error propagation is reduced, and (3) reusable modules are possible. To summarize, functional independence is a key to good design, and design is the key to software quality.

Independence is measured using two qualitative criteria: cohesion and coupling. *Cohesion* is a measure of the relative functional strength of a module. *Coupling* is a measure of the relative interdependence among modules.

A cohesive module performs a single task within a software procedure, requiring little interaction with procedures being performed in other parts of a program. Stated simply, a cohesive module should (ideally) do just one thing. As an example of low cohesion, consider a module that performs error processing for an engineering analysis package. The module is called when computed data exceed prespecified bounds. It performs the following tasks: (1) computes supplementary data based on original computed data, (2) produces an error report (with graphical content) on the user terminal, (3) performs follow-up calculations requested by the user, (4) updates a data base, and (5) enables menu selection for subsequent processing. Although these tasks are loosely related, each is an independent functional entity that might best be performed as a separate module. Combining the functions into a single module can only serve to increase the likelihood of error propagation (side effects) when a modification is made to one of the processing tasks.

Coupling is a measure of interconnection among modules in a software structure. Coupling depends on the interface complexity between modules, the point at which entry or reference is made to a module, and the data that pass across the interface.

In software design, we strive for lowest possible coupling. Simple connectivity among modules results in software that is easier to understand and less prone to a "ripple effect" that occurs when errors at one location cause problems to propagate throughout a system.

Relatively high levels of coupling (an undesirable characteristic) occur when modules are tied to an environment external to software. For example, I/O couples a module to specific devices, formats, and

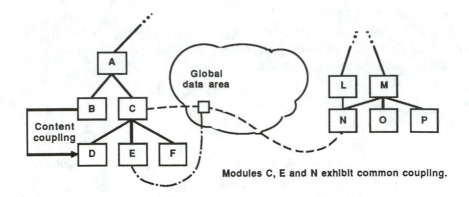

Modules C, E and N exhibit common coupling.

Figure 4.6 Common Coupling

communication protocols. External coupling is essential, but it should be limited to a small number of modules within a program structure.

High coupling also occurs when a number of modules reference a global data area. Common coupling, as this mode is called, is shown in Figure 4.6. Modules C, E, and N each access a data item in a global data area (e.g., a disk file, FORTRAN COMMON, a Pascal identifier defined in an outer procedural block and used in inner blocks that define other procedures, external data types in the C programming language). Module C reads the item, invoking E, which recomputes and updates the item. Let's assume that an error occurs and E updates the item incorrectly. Much later in processing, module N reads the item, attempts to process it, and fails, causing the software to abort. The apparent cause of abort is module N; the actual cause, module E. Diagnosing problems in structures with considerable common coupling is time consuming and difficult. However, this does not mean that the use of global data is necessarily "bad." It does mean that a software engineer must be aware of potential consequences of common coupling and take special care to guard against them.

Design Concept 9: Use abstraction as a means of refining software and creating effective design representations.

When we consider a modular solution to any problem, many levels of abstraction can be posed. At the highest level of abstraction, a solution is stated in broad terms using the language of the problem environment. At lower levels of abstraction, a more procedural orientation is taken. Problem-oriented terminology is coupled with implementation-oriented terminology in an effort to state a solution. Finally, at the lowest level of abstraction, the solution is stated in a manner that can be directly implemented.

Each step in the software engineering process is a refinement in the level of abstraction of the software solution. During system engineering, software is allocated as an element of a computer-based system. During software analysis, the requirements of the software solution are stated explicitly. As we move through design, the level of abstraction is reduced. Finally, the lowest level of abstraction is reached when source code is generated. Therefore, abstraction is not only a design concept but also applies during system engineering, problem analysis, design, and coding.

Different levels of abstraction are derived by refining (using the stepwise refinement approach) the initial statement of scope for software derived during problem analysis (Chapter 3). The initial statement of scope contains both procedural and data abstractions that we have called operations and objects, respectively.

To illustrate how different levels of abstraction can be derived from an initial statement of scope, consider the following excerpt from software scope derived during problem analysis for a text processing application:

Abstraction 0. *...the user can count the number of words contained in a document ...*

The above sentence fragment contains both procedural and data abstractions. **Count** is a procedural abstraction. **Words** and **document** are data abstractions. Because each represents a real-world operation or object (recall that initial levels of abstraction focus on the real world), we have no trouble understanding the *meaning* of the sentence fragment. However, the scope must be refined so that the meaning is translated into a form that can be implemented in software. Therefore, we respecify the problem at a slightly lower level of abstraction:

Abstraction 1. *... by selecting the **count-words** button with his mouse, the user initiates a counting function that accepts a document maintained as a text file as input and produces a word count as output to the screen.*

This abstraction moves us slightly closer to the machine. We learn how counting will be initiated, where the document is kept, and in what form the output count will be presented. But additional questions still remain. Most notably, how do we define a "word"? This leads us to the next level of abstraction:

Abstraction 2. ... *the counting function reads the text file on a character-by-character basis, searching for a transition from no-word to word and maintaining a count of these transitions. A word is defined as any sequence of alphanumeric characters except blanks, tabs, and newlines.* ...

The top-level procedural description of the abstraction **count** is specified (although important design details are still lacking) and a more detailed description of the data abstraction **word** is provided.

Abstractions 0, 1, and 2 would have been derived during problem analysis. However, subsequent abstractions will require a transition into design. Focusing our attention solely on the **count** operation,* we continue our refinement using program design language:

Abstraction 3.
```
Count-words function:
    get a text file;
    search for blank, newline, or tab characters;
    count transitions from no-word to word;
    produce output of word count to screen;
end.
```

At this level of abstraction, each of the major software operations associated with the **count-words** function is noted. Terms have moved away from the problem environment but are still not implementation specific. Narrowing our focus still more, we examine the search and count operations.

Abstraction 4.
```
procedure count-words;
 define all variable and files;
 do while characters remain to be analyzed
    if a character is a transition character
        then set a transition flag;
        else if transition flag is set
                then count a word;
                else skip;    *inside word, no count*
                endif
    endif
 enddo
end
```

* During design, all objects and operations associated with the text processing system would have to be refined.

Procedural logic appears for the first time at this level of abstraction. We have moved away from the real-world problem domain and toward a programming language-like representation. Design details still remain to be specified. The last refinement presents a program design language (PDL) representation of the search and count tasks for the *count-words* function.

Abstraction 5.

```
procedure count-words;
  define all variables and files;
  word count := 0;
  transition char := true;
  do while getcharacter(c) <> end-of-file
    if c = blank or c = newline or c = tab
      then transition char := true;
      else if (transition char = true)
        then increment word by 1;
        transition char := false;
        endif
    endif
  enddo
end
```

The design represented in abstraction 5 is reasonably detailed. Terminology is now software-oriented (e.g., the use of constructs such as *do while*), and an implication of modularity begins to surface.

It is interesting to note that the designer has used another procedural abstraction, **getcharacter**, to represent a character input operation. The **getcharacter** module is one of many building blocks that would be necessary to design and implement a text processing system.

The concepts of stepwise refinement and modularity are closely allied with abstraction. As the software design evolves, each level of modules in program structure represents a refinement in the level of abstraction of the software.

Data abstraction, like procedural abstraction, enables a designer to represent an object in various levels of detail and, more important, specify an object in the context of those operations (procedures) that can be applied to it. To illustrate, we consider an important data object that is used in all computer-aided design (CAD) systems. The data object, called **drawing**, connotes certain information when it is considered in the context of a CAD system.

The information contained within the object **drawing** will vary depending on the CAD application area. CAD systems are specifically designed to address application areas that include mechanical design, architectural drafting, electronic design, printed circuit board layout, and integrated circuit design. The contents of **drawing** will reflect the specific needs of the CAD application area.

At the system level, the first appearance of the data abstraction that we call **drawing** might appear in the following manner:

Abstraction 0.   *The system will store all design information as a drawing that is identified by a drawing number. The drawing contains the component geometry, alphanumeric notes that are associated with the geometry, and a bill of materials (BOM) that defines all parts that comprise the component.*

From the description contained in abstraction 0, it can be seen that **drawing** is composed of four data abstractions: **drawing number, component geometry, notes,** and **bill of materials.** As we reduce the level of abstraction with which these objects are represented, more design detail will begin to appear.

As problem analysis continues, we use data dictionary notation (Chapter 3) to expand the description of each of the objects within the abstraction **drawing**:

Abstraction 1.

drawing = drawing number + geometry + (notes) + (bill of materials)
drawing number = project ID + sequence number + revision level
component geometry = {line}^{a} + {circle}^{b} + {point}^{c} + {macro}^{d} +
    {symbol}^{e}
notes = *any alphanumeric information *
bill of materials = {component description + part number + quantity}^{f}

Further refinement of composite data items in the data dictionary would lead to additional levels of abstraction. Once software design begins, the software engineer applies data design (described later in this chapter) techniques to specify a data abstraction for **drawing** that could be easily transformed into a programming language realization.

Using PDL as our design notation, the internal details of **drawing** are defined by creating a record type data structure:

Abstraction n.

```
type drawing is defined
    number: integer;
    geometry = record called geomtype;
    notes = record called notetype;
```

```
     BOM = record called bomtype;
END  drawing;
```

In the design language description above, **drawing** is defined in terms of its constituent parts and represented as a *type,* that is, a data abstraction that can be assigned to other objects in a program. For example, when the type **integer** is assigned to a designer-specified variable, the variable takes on all of the attributes of **integer**. Similarly, if the type **drawing** were assigned to another object, the object would take on all of the attributes of **drawing**.

Therefore, the type **drawing** (an abstract data type) can be used to describe other data objects, without the need to reference the internal details of drawing. For example, at another location in the data design, we might say:

```
blueprint: drawing
```
or
```
schematic: drawing
```

implying that **blueprint** and **schematic** take on all characteristics of **drawing** as defined above. This typing process is called *instantiation.*

Once a data abstraction is defined, a set of operations that may be applied to it is also defined. For example, we might identify operations such as **erase, save, catalog,** and **copy** for the abstract data type **drawing**. By definition (literally), each of these procedures can be specified without the need to define details of **drawing** every time the procedure is invoked.

A number of programming languages (e.g., Ada, C++, Smalltalk) provide mechanisms for creating abstract data types. For example, the Ada package is a programming language mechanism that provides support for both data and procedural abstraction. The original abstract data type is used as a template or generic data structure from which other data structures can be instantiated.

Begin data design by extending work done during problem analysis.

Many experienced software engineers believe that once the data design is complete, the rest is easy! But what is a data design?

Data design is a series of design steps that enable us to select the structural representations for data objects identified during problem analysis (Chapter 3). In some cases, data objects are simple items that require little additional design attention. In other cases, however, a data object may be a file or a sophisticated data base that must be designed with care.

It is important to note that data design begins during problem analysis (e.g., the data dictionary is a data design tool) and continues throughout the design process. What we attempt to do at this stage is to solidify the representation of important program data structures, files, and any data base arrangement that may be required.

To help illustrate data design steps, we consider the following statement of scope that describes order-processing software that has been requested for a mail order company, called the *Software Store,* that sells personal computer software:

Information from each mail order is entered into the order-processing system (OPS) via an interactive terminal. The OPS assigns an order number to each order. Information that is entered includes customer name, customer address, order date, software catalog number, quantity, and a credit card number. The software catalog number is used to reference a product data base that contains all software titles, author name, unit price, and other special inventory information. OPS produces a bill/packing list on a multipart form printer that includes all information pertinent to the order.

Recalling the object-oriented approach suggested in Chapter 3, we can create Table 4.1. Once important objects are identified, further analysis steps enable us to create a data dictionary as shown below:

```
order number = month + date + year + sequence
month = [01|02| ... |12]
date  = [01|02| ... |31]
sequence = *assigned by system, nnnnn*
order = order data + order list
order data = order number + order date + customer name +
customer address + credit card number
order list = {software number + software title + author + quantity +
unit price + total price} k
customer name = last name + , + first name
last name = *alpha string*
first name = *alpha string*
customer address = company + street + city + state + zip
company = *alpha string*
street = *number* + *alpha street name*
```

Table 4.1 OBJECT TABLE FOR SOFTWARE STORE

Object	Alias	Type
information	mail order	external
OPS		external
terminal		originator
order number		data item
customer name		data item
customer address		data item
order date		data item
software catalog number		data item
quantity		data item
credit card number		data item
product data base		data store
software title		data item
author name		data item
unit price		data item
special inventory information		data item
bill/packing list		data item
multipart form printer		receiver

city = *city name, up to 20 chars*
state = *std. postal abbreviation*
zip = *numeric sequence of the form nnnnn-nnnn*
order date = *assigned by system*
software catalog number = category + code
category = [B|E|H|M|G]
code = *numeric sequence of the form nnnnn*
quantity = *numeric*
credit card number = *nnnn-nnnn-nnnnn + exp*
exp = *expiration date of the form month/year*
product data base = *to be defined*
software title = *alphanumeric, up to 32 chars.*
author = *see customer name*
unit price = *$xxx.xx*
special inventory information = bin location + no. avail
bin location = row + bin number
row = *alpha*
bin number = *numeric*
no. avail = *numeric*
bill/packing list = *to be defined*

It is important to note that the data dictionary introduces a number of lower-level data items that are required to define the objects contained in Table 4.1. In addition, careful study of the data dictionary may uncover important questions about the manner in which data are stored and processed. For example, what happens if a given software title has two or more authors? What happens if the order is accompanied by a check or cash? What happens if two or more software titles are requested in one order? Interestingly, the data dictionary helps us to discover that these questions need to be asked.

Review the data dictionary,
and select candidate data structures.

Because the data dictionary contains descriptions of all important data and control objects, it is relatively easy to select those objects that must be implemented as a data structure. Most objects can be represented as simple scalar data items or simple combinations of data items and do not require formal data design. However, data stores and sophisticated output data are often good candidates for data design. In the data dictionary for the *Software Store,* two objects become immediate candidates for data design: **product data base** and **bill/packing list.** In the discussion that follows we consider the design of **product data base**.

If complex data structures are to be created,
simplify their organization.

In applications such as the *Software Store*, the organization of data structures can have a profound impact on the efficiency with which information can be accessed and the overall simplicity of a program design. It is often possible to simplify the organization of record and file structures, thereby facilitating the design of a data base. A data design technique called *normalization* is used to simplify the data structure.

The normalization process identifies redundant data that may exist in the data structure, determines unique keys that are needed to access data items, and helps to establish necessary relationships among data items. Three levels of normalization, called *normal forms,* can be achieved. To illustrate the normalization process, we revisit the *Software Store* example and consider the design of the record and file structures for **product data base**. The product data base contains much of the information described in the data dictionary for the Software Store OPS. To normalize these data, all *repeating groups* of data (in this case, the list of software ordered, order list) are separated so that no file has any repeating groups. This level of simplification is called *first normal form (1NF)*. We may represent this 1NF data structure in the following manner (using Pascal):

```
orderinfo = record
    orderno: integer;
    softwareno: string;
    title: string;
    author:  string;
    quantity: integer;
    unitprice:  real;
    totalprice:  real;
end;
customer = record
    orderno: integer;
    orderdate:  string;
    customername:  string;
    address:  string;
    creditcardno:  string;
end;
orderlist = file of orderinfo;
orderdata = file of customer;
```

Further normalization can be accomplished by identifying key and non-key data items. A *key data item* is used to identify one or more other non-key items. For example, **softwareno**, a key data item, uniquely identifies **title, author, unit-price**. In this example, **softwareno** and **orderno** are key data items. For the data structures above, **quantity** is termed *fully functionally dependent* because it can be obtained only if both key data items (**orderno** and **softwareno**) are known. The non-key item **title** is not fully functionally dependent because we need know only one key, **softwareno**, to access it.

To achieve *second normal form (2NF)*, data structures are reorganized so that all non-key data items are fully functionally dependent. Examples of 2NF relations follow:

```
orderinfo = record
    orderno: integer;
    softwareno: string;
    quantity: integer;
```

```
      totalprice:  real;
end;
customer = record
      orderno:  integer;
      orderdate:   string;
      customername:   string;
      address:   string;
      creditcardno:   string;
end;
software = record
      softwareno: string;
      title:  string;
      author:   string;
      unitprice:   real;
      inventoryinfo:   string;
end;
orderlist = file of orderinfo;
orderdata = file of customer;
softwareinfo = file of software;
```

Third normal form (3NF) simplification can be achieved if all conditions for 2NF are met and no non-key data item can be derived from a combination of other non-key data items in any of the relations. For example, total-price can be computed as the sum of the products of unit-price and quantity. Therefore, it need not be maintained in the data structure. The normalization process simplifies data structures and removes redundancy and unnecessary data items from a data base.

Select appropriate internal data structures.

An internal data structure may be used to communicate data between programs, tasks, or modules (e.g., a buffer or queue) or to serve as a temporary storage place for data to be processed (e.g., vectors, tables, lists). The selection of an internal data structure can occur only after the program structure has been defined and the function of each module identified.

In most cases, the procedural design of an algorithm is intimately connected to the data structures that the algorithm must manipulate. If data are to be stored in an array, it is likely that the resultant algorithm would be considerably different from one to be used for data stored in a linked list. Therefore, data structures must be chosen with care.

A detailed discussion of data structures and the algorithms that process them is beyond the scope of this book. Interested readers should refer to the Further Readings section for addition information and references.

If a data base management system
is appropriate, acquire one!

Today, hundreds of off-the-shelf data base management systems (DBMS) are available for computing environments that range from mainframes to personal computers. Such DBMS often contain support software that enables relatively easy interface with custom-designed applications, a query language that can sometimes obviate the need to design a custom application, and a file structure that has been proved in practice. For these and many other reasons, it is foolhardy to try to build your own.

Derive the architectural design.

Data design is the first step toward a complete derivation of software architecture. The second step is the design of program structure—the hierarchy of modules that are the procedural components of the software.

Program structure (as shown in Figure 4.1) depicts the control relationship between software modules. But how is the program structure derived? It would seem that there are a large number of possibilities and many methods for deriving program structure, and in fact there are.* In the steps that follow, however, we explore one method for the design of program structure—a method that is tied to the flow model that was created during problem analysis.

Refine the flow model in preparation for design.

The flow model (data flow and/or control flow diagrams) created during problem analysis serves as the basis for architectural design. To be effective in this role, the flow model must exhibit sufficient detail.

* Although there are a number of excellent software design methods available (see Further Readings section for additional information), not all focus attention on program structure. For example, *structured programming*—a widely applied design approach—provides guidance for deriving good procedural designs. *Object-oriented design*—a relatively new software development approach—defines *objects* as the primary program component and does not stress modular hierarchy.

That is, transforms shown in the flow model must have a direct correspondence to modules in the program structure.

In an earlier discussion of modularity in this chapter, the concept of functional independence (cohesion and coupling) was presented. Each module in the program structure should exhibit high cohesion (perform a single, bounded function) and low coupling (have a limited interface to the outside world). The flow model is reviewed to assess the functional independence of each transform (bubble). If low cohesion exists (the transform does too many different things), it is further refined. If high coupling is evident, the overall flow through the system is examined to determine if a more loosely coupled approach may be possible.

As an example of flow model refinement, we consider software for the digital dashboard of an automobile. Software scope is described in the following manner:

Digital dashboard software (DDS) is designed to monitor drive wheel rotation and fuel flow rate and display instantaneous speed and fuel consumption on a digital dashboard display. A rotation signal is converted from analog to digital form and translated to mph using physical parameters such as wheel size. Fuel flow rate is monitored and converted into gallons per hour value. Speed and fuel consumption are then combined, and an instantaneous value for miles per gallon is displayed.

DDS software also supports an overspeed indicator that monitors current speed and rings a chime synchronized to the difference between the current speed (if greater than 55 mph) and 55 mph.

As an exercise, each reader should develop an object and operation table for DDS. Once procedural and data abstractions are defined, each should be elaborated to provide greater detail. For the purposes of this example, we move directly to the flow model representation.

A level 01 data flow diagram (DFD) for DDS is shown in Figure 4.7. The level 01 DFD illustrates primary input and output, along with an important data store. The data dictionary corresponding to the level 01 model is shown below:

transducer signals = rotation signal + fuel flow signal
rotation signal = *pulses counted over a 500 msec interval*
fuel flow signal = *pulse (corresponding to 1 ml) counted over a 1 second
    interval*
dashboard output = mph display + mpg display + odometer + chime
    ... further definitions would follow

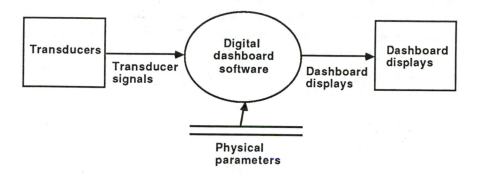

Figure 4.7 Level 01 DFD for Digital Dashboard Software

The next flow model produced during problem analysis represents the "macro operations" shown in Figure 4.8. An analysis of the functional independence of these transforms indicates that further refinement is in order. For example, the transform **compute dashboard data** actually implies a number of rather different calculations (i.e., fuel consumption, speed) that would be better separated to achieve high cohesion.

We refine the level 02 DFD produced during problem analysis

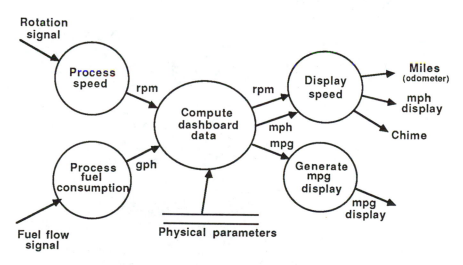

Digital dashboard software—level 02

Figure 4.8 Level 02 DFD for Digital Dashboard Software

and develop the level 03 DFD shown in Figure 4.9. Each bubble (transform) in Figure 4.9 exhibits high cohesion and reasonably low coupling—desirable attributes for effective modularity.

Incoming data flow at the upper left is a converted rotation signal that is read and converted into signals per second. Time average and change in signal [measured in signals per second (sps)] are used to drive speedometer functions.

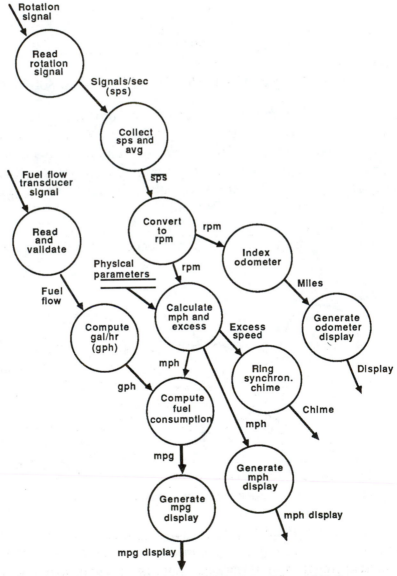

Figure 4.9 Level 03 DFD for Digital Dashboard Software

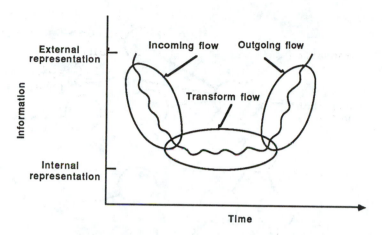

Figure 4.10   Time History of Data Flow

Once average sps is converted to rpm, speed (in mph) is developed and used to ring a synchronous chime (if speeding!), to generate mph display, and as one data item required to compute fuel consumption in miles per gallon (mpg). The odometer function also uses rpm as incoming data. All of these functions lead to displays on the dashboard.

A second incoming path collects fuel flow data and combines them with speed data. Both are then converted to gallons per hour for fuel efficiency calculation and display.

Determine whether the flow model has transform or transaction characteristics.

Information must enter and exit software in an "external world" form. For example, data typed on a terminal keyboard, tones on a telephone line, and pictures on a computer graphics display are all forms of external world information. Such externalized data must be converted into an internal form for processing. For the digital dashboard system, external world data are manifested by analog rotation and fuel flow rates that must be converted to digital form and then scaled and processed to provide meaningful data for the driver (i.e., it would do little good to display speed in revolutions per second for the drive wheels!).

An illustration of the time history of data as they flow through a system is shown in Figure 4.10. Information enters the system along paths that transform external data into an internal form and will be

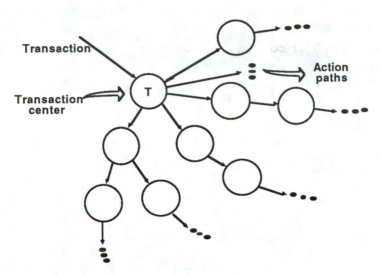

Figure 4.11 Transaction Flow

identified as *incoming flow*. At the kernel of the software, a transition occurs. Incoming data are passed through a *transform center* and begin to move along paths that now lead "out" of the software. Data moving along these paths are called *outgoing flow*. When a segment of a data flow diagram exhibits these characteristics, *transform flow* is present.

Because all level 01 flow models exhibit the characteristics described above, it is possible to characterize all data flow as transform flow. However, it is useful to examine data flow at lower levels and to characterize the flow somewhat differently when a single data item, called a *transaction,* triggers other data flows along one of many paths. When a DFD takes the form shown in Figure 4.11, *transaction flow* is present.

Transaction flow is characterized by data moving along an incoming path that converts external world information into a *transaction*. The transaction is evaluated, and depending on its value, flow is initiated along one of many *action paths*. The hub of information flow from which many action paths emanate is called a *transaction center* (labeled as "T" in the figure). Such flows are common in many software application areas. For example, whenever a user selects one of many functions from a menu presented on a display device, it is likely that transaction flow will follow.

It should be noted that within a DFD for a large system, both transform and transaction flow may be present. For example, in a transaction-oriented flow, data flow along any one action path may have transform flow characteristics.

To illustrate, consider a software application called "Grade Book." Grade Book allows a professor to enter student grades, compute weighted averages, perform simple statistical analysis, and provide hardcopy output for the registrar. The menu for Grade Book displayed on a personal computer screen might be:

```
Please select one of the following program options:
   1   enter grades
   2   compute student averages
   3   determine standard deviation
   4   print out grade report
   5   quit program
```

When the professor selects a value between 1 and 5, a transaction has been specified. The transaction (e.g., enter grades) causes data to flow along a path that will request the student name (input), prompt for all grades and their weights for the student (input), store the data in a data base (processing), and echo the data (output) for verification. The input-processing-output characteristic along the "enter grades" path indicates transform flow that has been triggered by an initial transaction (the menu selection). It is likely that the DFD for the Grade Book application would take on the characteristics of a transaction flow.

Derive program structure using transform mapping when transform flow is present.

In general, information flow within a system can always be represented as transform flow. However, when an obvious transaction characteristic (Figure 4.11) is encountered, a different design mapping is recommended and is considered in later steps. For this step, it is assumed that the designer has selected transform flow as a global (software-wide) flow characteristic based on the prevailing nature of the DFD. To illustrate transform mapping, we revisit the digital dashboard software example.

Evaluating the dashboard DFD (Figure 4.9), we see data entering the software along two incoming paths and exiting along five outgoing paths. No distinct transaction center is implied (although the transform

calc mph and **excess** could be perceived as such). Therefore, an overall transform characteristic will be assumed for data flow.

Isolate the transform center by specifying incoming and outgoing flow boundaries.

We have described incoming flow as a path in which information is converted from external to internal form; outgoing flow converts from internal to external form. The first step in transform mapping is to represent incoming and outgoing flow boundaries. That is, the point in flow at which incoming data stop and another point at which outgoing data begin. It is sometimes possible to define flow boundaries by focusing on those transforms (bubbles) that reside with them. Transforms with names beginning with compute, look-up, modify, calculate and other processing-oriented operations are likely to reside within the boundaries.

Nevertheless, incoming and outgoing flow boundaries are open to interpretation. That is, different designers may select slightly different points in the flow as boundary locations. In fact, alternative design solutions can be derived by varying the placement of flow boundaries. Although care should be taken when boundaries are selected, a variance of one bubble along a flow path will generally have little impact on the final program structure.

Flow boundaries for the digital dashboard example are illustrated in Figure 4.12. The transforms (bubbles) that comprise the transform center lie within the two boundaries that run from top to bottom in the figure. An argument can be made to readjust a boundary [e.g., an incoming flow boundary separating **read and validate** and **compute gal/ hr (gph)** could be proposed]. In this design step, there should be an emphasis on selecting reasonable boundaries rather than lengthy argument on placement of divisions.

Perform "first-level factoring."

Program structure represents a top-down distribution of control. *Factoring* results in a program structure in which top-level modules perform decision making and low-level modules (that is, modules that are located at the lowest levels of the hierarchical tree structure) perform most input, computational, and output work. Middle-level modules perform some control and do moderate amounts of work.

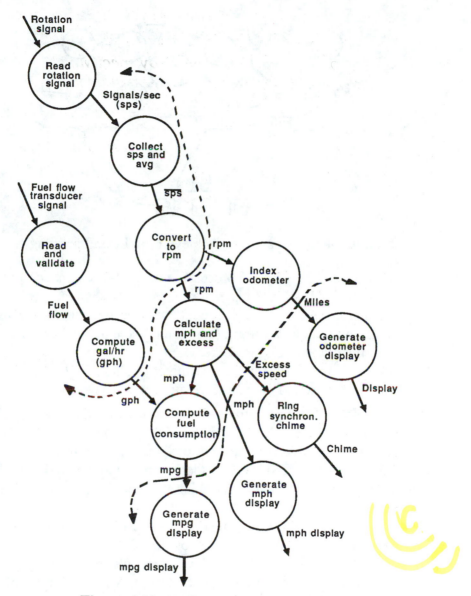

Figure 4.12 Defining Flow Boundaries

When transform flow is encountered, a DFD is mapped to a specific structure that provides control for incoming, transform, and outgoing information processing. This *first-level factoring* is illustrated in Figure 4.13. A control module, C_m, resides at the top of the program structure and serves to coordinate the following subordinate control functions:

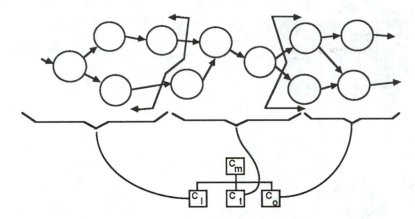

Figure 4.13 Mapping to Achieve First-Level Factoring

- An incoming information processing controller, C_i, that coordinates receipt of all incoming data
- A transform center controller, C_t, that supervises all operations on data in internalized form (e.g., a module that invokes various "number crunching" procedures)
- An outgoing information processing controller, C_o, that coordinates production of output information

Although a three-pronged structure is implied by Figure 4.13, complex flows in large systems may dictate two or more control modules for each of the generic control functions described above. The number of modules at the first level should be limited to the minimum that can accomplish control functions and still maintain good coupling and cohesion characteristics.

To illustrate first-level factoring, we present two examples that continue our discussion of Grade Book and Digital Dashboard Software. Level 01 and 02 DFDs for the Grade Book are shown in Figure 4.14a and b. To illustrate first-level factoring, we consider the transform flow represented by the **enter grades** transform (Figure 4.15a) as if it were a simple program separated from the remainder of the application. We produce a program structure for **enter grades** (Figure 4.15b) that is similar to the template shown in Figure 4.13. For this simple example, it is unlikely that further expansion of the structure is necessary. However, more complex application will often require additional factoring.

To illustrate further levels of factoring, we again consider the

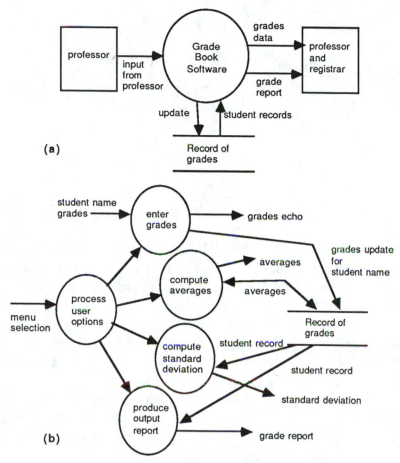

Figure 4.14 Level 01 and 02 DFD for Grade Book

digital dashboard example, using first-level factoring to develop program control modules as shown in Figure 4.16. Each control module is given a name that implies the function of the subordinate modules it controls.

Perform second-level factoring to derive a preliminary program structure.

Second-level factoring is accomplished by mapping individual transforms (bubbles) of a DFD into appropriate modules within the program structure. Beginning at the transform center boundary and moving outward along incoming and then outgoing paths, transforms are mapped into subordinate levels of the program structure. The general approach to second-level factoring is illustrated in Figure 4.17.

Expanding **enter grades** transform:

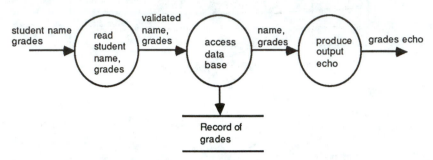

Figure 4.15a   DFD for **Enter Grades**

Although Figure 4.17 illustrates a one-to-one mapping between DFD transforms and modules, different mappings frequently occur. Two or even three bubbles can be combined and represented as one module (recalling potential problems with cohesion), or a single bubble may be expanded to two or more modules. Practical considerations and design quality dictate the outcome of second-level factoring.

Program structure derived from the incoming flow paths of the dashboard software DFD (Figure 4.12) is shown in Figure 4.18. A simple one-to-one mapping of bubbles to modules can be observed by following flow backward from the transform center boundary. Review and refinement may lead to changes in this structure, but the mechanical mapping can serve as a "first-cut" design.

Performing first level factoring:

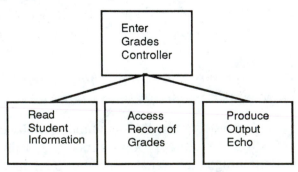

Figure 4.15b   First-Level Factoring for **Enter Grades**

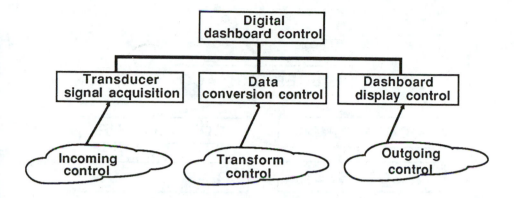

Figure 4.16 First-Level Factoring for DDS

Second-level factoring for the transform center of Digital Dashboard Software is shown in Figure 4.19. Each of the data conversion or calculation transforms of the DFD is mapped into a module subordinate to the transform controller. Finally, outgoing flow is mapped into program structure as illustrated in Figure 4.20. Factoring is

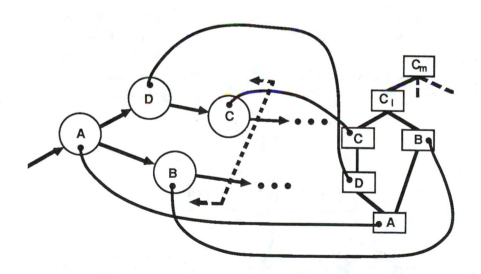

Figure 4.17 Second-Level Mapping

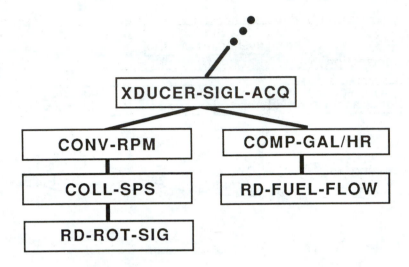

Figure 4.18 Unrefined Incoming Structure for DDS

again accomplished by moving outward from the transform center boundary.

Refine processing narratives for each module in the program structure.

Each of the modules shown in Figures 4.18, 4.19, and 4.20 represents an initial design of program structure. Because of the one-to-one mapping between data flow bubbles and program modules, the processing narrative developed for each transform should apply to its corresponding module. The narrative should be reviewed for accuracy

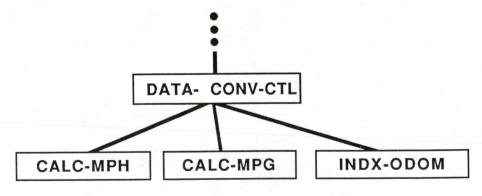

Figure 4.19 Unrefined Transform Structure for DDS

and becomes part of the design description. At this stage, the narrative describes:

- Information that passes into and out of the module (an interface description)
- Information that is retained by a module (e.g., data stored in a local data structure)
- A procedural narrative that indicates major decisions points and tasks
- A brief discussion of restrictions and special features (e.g, file input/output, hardware-dependent characteristics, special timing requirements).

The collection of narratives and the representation of program structure serve as a rudimentary *Design Document*. However, further refinement and additions occur regularly during this period of design.

*Refine the "first-cut" program structure
using fundamental design concepts.*

A first-cut program structure can always be refined by applying concepts of module independence. A module can be *exploded* (broken into two or more modules), or modules can be *imploded* (two or more modules can be combined to form a single module) to produce sensible factoring, good cohesion, minimal coupling, and, most important, a structure that can be implemented without difficulty, tested without confusion, and maintained without grief.

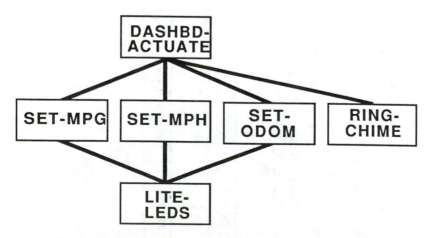

Figure 4.20 Unrefined Outgoing Structure for DDS

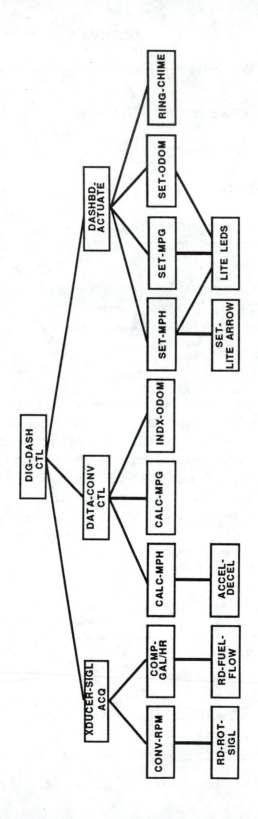

Figure 4.21 Refined Program Structure

134

Refinements are dictated by practical considerations and common sense. There are times, for example, when the controller for incoming data flow is totally unnecessary, when some input processing is required in a module that is subordinate to the transform controller, when high coupling due to global data cannot be avoided, or when optimal structural characteristics cannot be achieved. Software requirements coupled with human judgment are the final arbiter.

Modifications can be made to the first-cut structure developed for the digital dashboard example. Among many possibilities: modules CONV-RPM and COLL-SPS in the incoming structure branch can be imploded. Collection of transducer signals and conversion to an RPM measure are sequentially related and make sense in this context.

The refined program structure for the digital dashboard is shown in Figure 4.21. Design constraints (e.g., memory limitations or run-time performance) may dictate further revisions. For example, RD-ROT-SIGNAL and CONV-RPM could be imploded (at the expense of relatively low cohesion), or DATA-CONV-CTL could be removed and control functions performed by DIG-DASH-CTL.

The objective of the preceding steps is to develop a global representation of software. That is, once structure is defined, we can evaluate and refine software architecture by viewing it as a whole. Modifications made at this time require little additional work, yet they can have a profound impact on software quality and maintainability.

You should pause for a moment and consider the difference between the design approach just described and the process of "writing programs." If code is the only representation of software, the developer will have great difficulty evaluating or refining at a global or holistic level and will, in fact, have difficulty "seeing the forest for the trees."

Derive program structure using transaction mapping when transaction flow is present.

In many software applications, a single data item triggers one or a number of data flows that effect an operation implied by the triggering data item. The data item, called a transaction, and its corresponding flow characteristics have been illustrated in Figure 4.11.

An extension of the digital dashboard software presented earlier in this chapter is used to illustrate the design approach for transaction

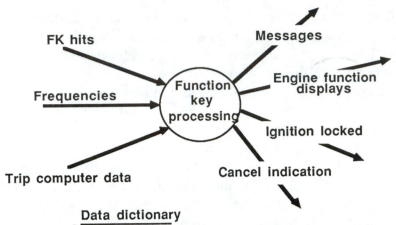

Data dictionary

FK hits = [menu select | ignition code | keyed data]
menu select = [1 | 2 | 3 | 4 | 5 | 6]
and so on ...

Figure 4.22a   Level 01 DFD for Extended DDS

flow. The basic dashboard system has optional features that include an "electronic key" and a "function selection/display" facility. An ignition start-up sequence of numbers is keyed via a key pad and replaces the ignition key. The array is also used to initiate the following functions:

Button	Function Selected
1	Initiate ignition start-up sequence
2	Activate radar detector (only available where legal!)
3	Activate display of various engine functions including oil pressure, temperature, etc.
4	Display trip computer data
5	Enter trip computer data
6	Cancel previous key (clear)

Applying the data flow notation described in Chapter 3, level 01 and 02 data flow diagrams and corresponding data dictionary are developed (Figure 4.22a and b). Further refinement results in the level 03 DFD shown in Figure 4.22c.

As shown in Figure 4.22c, the array button or "function key" hit is a primary input that drives subsequent flow. After the key is validated, flow moves along one of a number of paths depending on what button was pressed. In the figures, paths for buttons 1 and 2 are shown in detail, while other paths are indicated with single shaded transforms to simplify the drawing. To develop a complete design, these shaded bubbles would have to be refined.

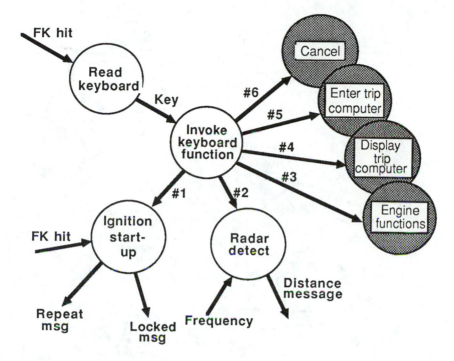

Figure 4.22b   Level 02 DFD for Extended DDS

It should be noted that information flow along both paths 1 and 2 incorporates additional incoming data. Each path also produces displays, messages and/or alarms.

> *Identify the transaction center and the*
> *flow characteristics of each action path.*

Design steps for transaction analysis are similar and in some cases identical to steps for transform analysis. A major difference lies in the mapping of DFD to program structure.

The location of the transaction center can be immediately discerned from the DFD. The transaction center lies at the origin of a number of information paths that flow radially from it. For dashboard flow shown in Figure 4.22c, the **function key actions** bubble is the transaction center.

The incoming path (i.e., the flow path along which a transaction is received) and all action paths must also be isolated. Boundaries that define a reception path and action paths are shown in Figure 4.23. Each action path must be evaluated for its individual flow

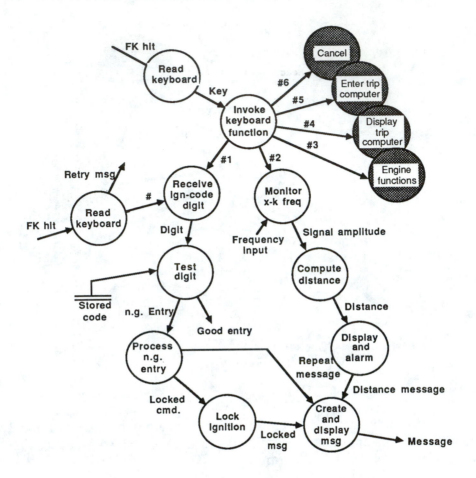

Figure 4.22c Level 03 DFD for Extended DDS

characteristics. For example, the radar detection path (shown enclosed by a shaded area in Figure 4.23) has transform characteristics. Incoming, transform, and outgoing flow are indicated with dashed boundaries.

*Map the DFD into a program structure
amenable to transaction processing.*

Transaction flow is mapped into a program structure that contains an incoming branch and a dispatch branch. Structure for the incoming branch is developed in much the same way as transform analysis. Starting at the transaction center, bubbles along the incoming path are mapped into modules. The structure of the dispatch branch contains a

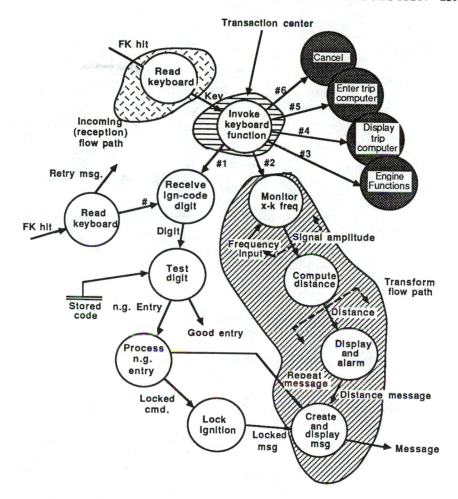

Figure 4.23   Level 03 DFD Showing Transform Region

dispatcher module that controls all subordinate action modules. Each action flow path of the DFD is mapped to a structure that corresponds to its specific flow characteristics. This process is illustrated in Figure 4.24.

The digital dashboard data flow represented in Figure 4.23 leads to first-level factoring as shown in Figure 4.25. Module READ-KEYBD performs reception (input) operations passing the transaction (a function key hit) via the transaction controller, FUNC-KEY-CTL, to the dispatcher module, INVOKE-KEYBD-FUNCTIONS. Subordinate to the dispatcher, modules IGN-CODE-EVALUATION, RADAR-DETECT, and others act as control modules for each action.

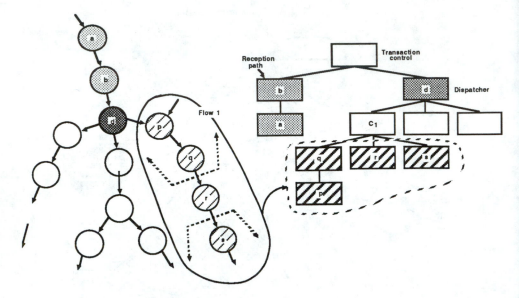

Figure 4.24 Transaction Mapping

*Factor and refine the transaction structure
and the structure of each action path.*

Each action path of the data flow diagram has its own information
flow characteristics. We have already noted that transform or transaction flow may be encountered. A *substructure* related to each action

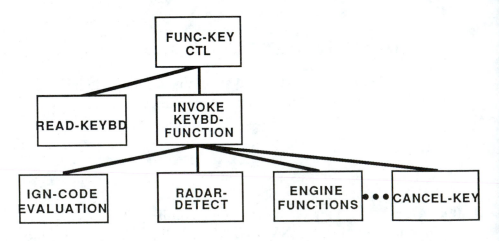

Figure 4.25 First-Level Factoring

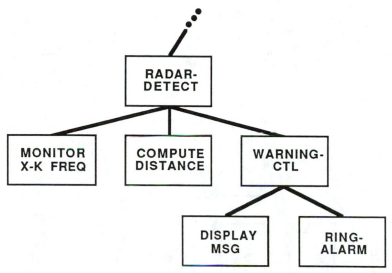

Figure 4.26 Program Substructure for RADAR-DETECT

path is developed using the design steps discussed in this and the preceding section.

As an example, consider the radar detector information flow shown (inside shaded area) in Figure 4.23. The flow exhibits classic transform characteristics. Frequencies are monitored (incoming flow), producing input to a transform center when a signal is received. An alarm and warning message (outgoing flow) are then produced. The structure for the resultant action path is shown in Figure 4.26.

A RADAR-DETECT module serves as the main controller. The incoming flow is mapped into a MONITOR-X-K-FREQ module. Module COMPUTE-DISTANCE performs transform functions, and WARNING-CTL acts as the outgoing branch controller. To maintain high cohesion, two modules, DISPLAY-MSG and RING-ALARM, perform reporting functions as subordinates to the outgoing controller. The DFD transform **create and display message** is mapped into a utility module (i.e., a module called by two or more modules) that is used by two action flow structures.

The overall program structure is illustrated in Figure 4.27. Ignition code and radar detection functions are factored to illustrate development of action branches. It should be noted that within each transform substructure input is acquired and output is produced. The DISPLAY-MSG module is subordinate to two action paths, exhibiting *fan-in*, a common feature of transaction structures.

Again, we refine the "first-cut" program structure using funda-

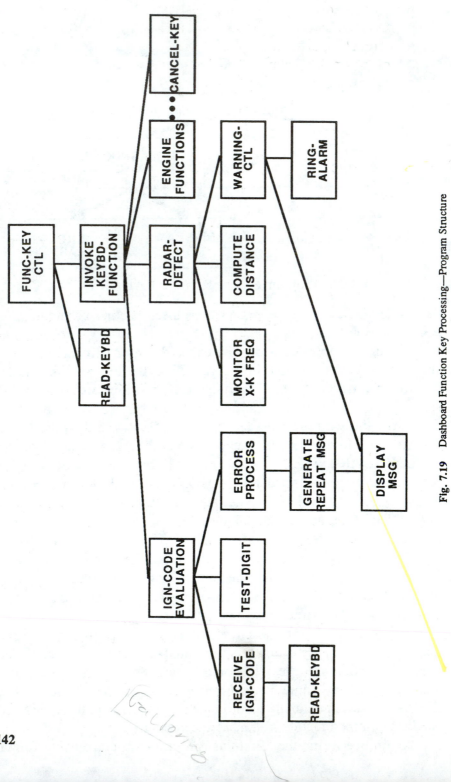

Fig. 7.19 Dashboard Function Key Processing—Program Structure

142

mental design concepts as a guide. This step for transaction analysis is identical to the corresponding step for transform analysis. In both design approaches, criteria such as module independence, practicality (efficacy of implementation and test), and maintainability must be carefully considered as structural modifications are proposed.

Derive a procedural design for each module depicted in the program structure.

The procedural design, also called the *detail design,* presents a description of each module. The description finalizes the design of all data structures internal to a module and provides a representation of program logic at a fairly low level of abstraction. That is, the procedural design is "close" to the level of detail required for a programming language implementation of a module.

The procedural design, when successfully completed, accomplishes three objectives: (1) the design is a product for review, enabling us to uncover logic errors prior to programming; (2) the design serves as a template for coding, and (3) the design provides important input for the derivation of test cases (Chapter 6).

Apply the structured programming philosophy when deriving the procedural design.

In the late 1960s, Dijkstra and others proposed the use of a set of simple logical constructs from which any program could be formed. The constructs emphasized "maintenance of functional domain." That is, each construct had a predictable logical structure, was entered at the top, and exited at the bottom, enabling a reader to follow procedural flow more easily.

The constructs are *sequence, condition,* and *repetition.* Sequence implements processing steps that are essential in the specification of any algorithm. Condition provides the facility for selected processing based on some logical occurrence, and repetition provides for looping. These three constructs are fundamental to *structured programming.*

The structured constructs were proposed to limit the procedural design of software to a small number of predictable logical operations. The use of the structured constructs reduces program complexity and thereby enhances readability, testability, and maintainability. The use of a limited number of logical constructs also contributes to a human understanding process that psychologists call *chunking.* To under-

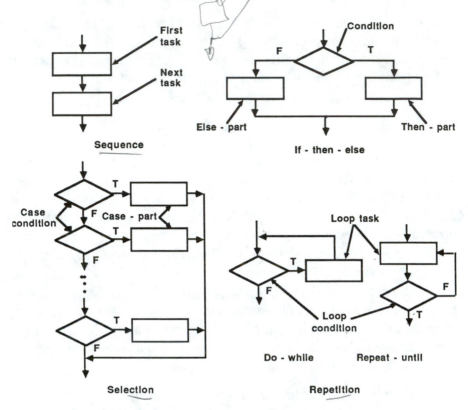

Figure 4.28 The Structured Constructs

stand this process, consider the way in which you are reading this page. You do not read individual letters; you recognize patterns or chunks of letters that form words or phrases. The structured constructs are logical chunks that allow a reader to recognize procedural elements of a module, rather than reading the design or code line by line. Understanding is enhanced when readily recognizable logical forms are encountered.

Any program, regardless of application area or technical complexity, can be designed and implemented using only the three structured constructs. Figure 4.28 illustrates the three structured constructs using flow chart notation. Sequence is represented as two processing boxes connected by a line (arrow) of control. Condition, also called *if-then-else,* is depicted as a decision diamond which if true causes *then-part* processing to occur and if false invokes *else-part* processing. Repetition is represented using two slightly different forms. The *do-while* tests a condition and executes a *loop task* repetitively as long as the condition holds true. A *repeat-until* executes the loop task first, then

do (while rep
if then else
sequence
TRUE

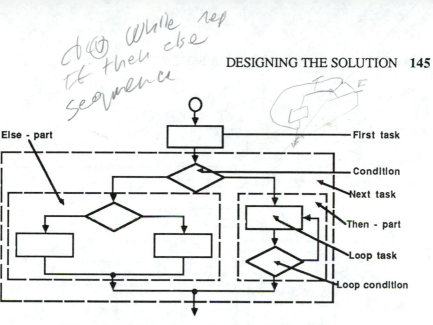

Else - part

First task

Condition

Next task

Then - part

Loop task

Loop condition

Figure 4.29 Nesting Structured Constructs

tests a condition and repeats the task until the condition fails. The *se-lection* (or *case*) construct shown in the figure is actually an extension of the if-then-else. A parameter is tested by successive decisions until a true condition occurs and a case-part processing path is executed.

The structured constructs can be nested within one another as shown in Figure 4.29. In the figure, a *repeat-until* forms the *then-part* of an *if-then-else* (shown enclosed by the outer dashed boundary). Another if-then-else forms the *else-part* of the larger condition. Final-ly, the condition itself becomes a second block in a sequence. By nest-ing constructs in this manner, a complex logical schema may be devel-oped. It should be noted that any one of the blocks in Figure 4.29 could reference another module, thereby accomplishing procedural layering implied by program structure.

A more detailed structured flow chart is shown in Figure 4.30. As an exercise, the reader should attempt to identify each construct. Upon completion of the exercise, two things will be apparent. The entire procedure is constructed using the constructs shown in Figure 4.28, and as the constructs are "boxed," boundaries of the boxes never cross. That is, all constructs have a single entry and single exit.

The use of only structured constructs can at times introduce com-plications in logical flow. For example, assume that as part of process **i** (Figure 4.30) a condition **z** may arise that requires an immediate branch to process **j**. A direct branch violates the logical constructs by escaping from the functional domain of the repeat-until of which pro-cess **i** is a part. To implement the above branch without violation,

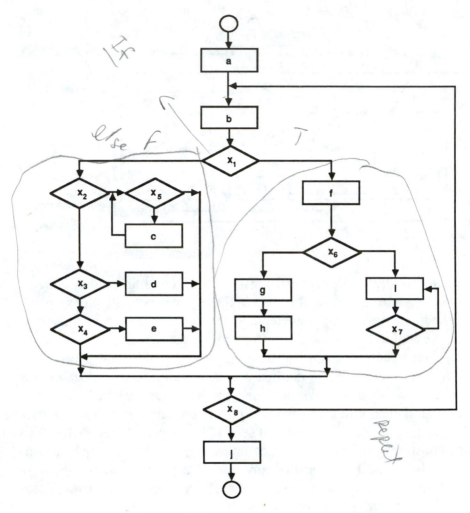

Figure 4.30 A Structured Flowchart

tests for condition z must be added to x_7 and x_8. These tests will occur repeatedly, even if the occurrence of z is rare. We have introduced additional complication and potential execution inefficiency.

The use of only structured constructs can introduce problems when an escape from a set of nested loops or nested conditions is required. More important, additional complication of all logical tests along the path of escape can cloud software control flow, increase the possibility of error, and have a negative impact on readability and maintainability. What can we do?

The designer is left with two options: (1) the procedural representation is redesigned so that the "escape branch" is not required at a nested location in the flow of control; or (2) the structured constructs are "violated" in a controlled manner—that is, a constrained branch out of the nested flow is designed. Option 1 is obviously the ideal approach, and in most cases the algorithm can be redesigned so that the required branch does not have to occur from within nested program logic. In situations where redesign is not possible, option 2 can be accommodated without violating the spirit of structured programming.

Refine the processing narratives for each module.

We have already noted that design is a process of refinement. The processing narratives originally developed for each flow model transformation are refined to become processing narratives for each module in the program structure. Likewise, each module processing narrative is refined to become a detailed procedural design representation. At each step along the way, we reduce the level of abstraction with which the software is represented.

Use program design language (PDL) to represent data structures and procedural logic.

Program design language (PDL), also called *structured English* or *pseudocode,* is a programming language-like notation that combines a formal syntax for data design and procedural design with the free syntax of a natural language such as English. At first glance PDL looks like Pascal or any other high-level programming language. The difference between PDL and a real high-level programming language lies in the use of narrative text (e.g., English) embedded directly within PDL statements. Given the combined use of narrative text embedded directly into a syntactic structure, PDL cannot be compiled (at least not yet!). However, PDL "processors" exist to translate PDL into a graphical representation (e.g., a flow chart) of design and produce nesting maps, a design operation index, cross reference tables, and a variety of other information.

A program design language may be a simple transposition of a language such as Pascal or may be a product purchased specifically for procedural design. Regardless of origin, a design language should have the following characteristics:

- A fixed syntax of *keywords* that provide for all structured constructs, data declaration, and modularity characteristics
- A free syntax of natural language that describes processing features
- Data declaration facilities that should include both simple (scalar, array) and complex (linked list or tree) data structures
- Subprogram definition and calling techniques that support various modes of interface description

Today, a high-order programming language is often used as the basis for a PDL. For example, Ada-PDL is widely used in the Ada community as a design definition tool. Ada language constructs and format are "mixed" with English narrative to form the design language. For our purposes, we consider a PDL that is modeled after the structure of the Pascal programming language. In essence, Pascal language constructs are mixed with English language phrases to describe the inner workings of a module at a level of abstraction that is higher than code itself.

Our basic PDL syntax will include Pascal-like constructs for: data declaration, subprogram definition, interface description, condition constructs, repetition constructs, and I/O constructs. The format and semantics of the example PDL are presented in the following paragraphs.

During earlier discussions of design, we emphasized the importance of data structure on both a local (per module) and global (programwide) scale. Our PDL contains data declaration capabilities that correspond directly to Pascal constructs used for that purpose. For example,

```
TYPE label = packed array [1..n] of char;
or
TYPE colors = (red, green, blue, yellow, orange);
```

are legitimate Pascal statements and are equally legitimate PDL statements. However, the following statement is also legitimate PDL:

```
type UserInfo = name, address, and account number;
```

but would generate compiler errors in Pascal. In the above PDL statement, we have used the form of Pascal but incorporated the English language phrase "name, address, and account number." Using **record**, **file**, and **listnode** and other Pascal keywords, we can describe complex data structures as part of our design activities.

Referring back to the CAD system example presented earlier in this chapter, we can use PDL to define a drawing. A drawing is composed of different data types in a specific hierarchy and is therefore characterized as a *heterogeneous structure*. Recalling the earlier PDL definition:

```
type drawing is defined
   number: integer;
   geometry = record called geomtype;
   notes = record called notetype;
   BOM = record called bomtype;
END drawing;
```

The above PDL (which is *not* valid Pascal) implies that **drawing** is composed of a drawing number, a geometry, notes, and a bill of materials (BOM). The details of each type implied by the PDL can also be defined. For example:

```
Type geomtype = record;
   lines: (x,y) start;  (x,y) end;  linetype;
   circle: (x,y) center,  radius,  arcangle;
   point: (x,y);
   macro = record called componentmacro;
   symbol: symbolset;
end;
```

The correct Pascal implementation of the PDL for drawing will be postponed until coding. However, the above PDL provides important information about the design—information that can be reviewed for correctness.

It is important to reemphasize that the above description of **drawing** is not a programming language description. The designer should follow the overall syntax of the PDL but can define the constituent parts of **drawing** in whatever manner is appropriate (and informative). Obviously, the translation of PDL into programming language source code must follow a precise syntax.

The PDL description for **drawing** can be expanded using stepwise refinement so that each of the constituent parts of **geometry**, **notes**, and **BOM** is described in some detail. **Geometry**, the most complex component of the drawing data structure, is composed of many different data and user-defined types.

The procedural elements of PDL are *block structured*. That is, pseudocode may be defined in blocks that are executed as a single entity. A block is delimited in the following manner:

```
Begin <block-name>
    <pseudocode statements>;
end;
```

where `<blockname>` may be used (but is not required) to provide a mode for subsequent reference to a block and `<pseudocode state-ments>` are a combination of all other PDL constructs. For example:

```
Begin <draw-line-on-graphics-terminal>
    get end-points from display list;
    scale physical end-points to screen coordinates;
    DRAW a line using screen coordinates;
end;
```

The above block makes use of pseudocode statements that describe appropriate processing. The use of a specialized keyword, DRAW, illustrates the use of a previously defined procedural abstraction and the manner in which a PDL may be customized to address a specific application.

The condition construct in PDL takes a classic *if-then-else* form (varying slightly from Pascal):

```
If <condition-description>
then <block or pseudocode statement>;
else <block or pseudo-code statement>;
endif
```

where `<condition-description>` indicates the logical decision that must be made to invoke either *then-part* or *else-part* processing. For example, the following PDL segment describes a decision sequence for a payroll system:

```
If yeartodateFICA < maximum
    then begin
    FICAdeduction := 0.0715*gross wage;
        If (yeartodateFICA + FICAdeduction) > maximum
        then FICAdeduction := maximum - yeartodateFICA;
        else skip;
    endif
    end;
    else set FICAdeduction := 0;
endif
```

Two nested IFs are shown in the PDL segment above. The *then-part* of the outer IF contains a block that combines the inner IF with pseudocode statements. The `else skip` indicates that else-part processing is skipped. The `endif` is used to indicate unambiguous termination of the construct and is particularly useful when nested IFs are represented. The `end` following the first `endif` terminates the block that processes FICA information.

The selection (case) construct, actually a degenerate set of nested IFs, is represented:

```
case of <case-variable-name>:
    when<case-condition-1>select<block or pseudocode
    statement>;
    when<case-condition-2>select<block or pseudocode
    statement>;
        . . .
    when<last-case-condition>select<block or pseudocode
    statement>;
    default: <default or error case: block or pseudo-
    code statement>;
endcase
```

In general, this construct tests a specific parameter, the *case-variable,* against a set of conditions. Upon satisfaction of a condition, a block or individual pseudocode statement is invoked.

The case construct is almost always encountered in transaction flows. As an example of the CASE construct in PDL, we consider a segment of a word processing system that is invoked when file processing occurs:

```
case of fileprocessingcommand:
    when "new" select CreateNewFile;
    when "open" select begin
       get file name;
       open file;
       read file into page buffer;
       end;
    when "close" select begin
       determine if changes have been made since last
       "save";
       if changes have been made, request a resave;
       close file;
       end;
    when "save" select begin
```

```
        if file is untitled, then request file name;
        write file to disk;
    end;
    default: display "invalid command";
endcase
```

PDL repetition constructs include pretest and posttest loops as well as an indexing loop:

```
do while <condition-description>
    <block or pseudocode statement>;
enddo
```

```
repeat until <condition-description>
    <block or pseudocode statement>;
endrep
```

```
do for <index> = <index list, expression or sequence>
    <block or pseudocode statement>;
endfor
```

As an example of PDL repetition constructs, consider the following analysis loop, which tests for convergence of two calculated values:

```
epsilon := 1.0;
numbertries := 0;
do while (epsilon > 0.001 and numbertries < 100)
    calculate value1 := f(x,y,z);
    calculate value2 := g(x,y,z);
    epsilon := ABSVAL (value1 - value2);
    increment numbertries by 1;
enddo
```

It should be noted that the loop condition must be defined so that escape from the loop is guaranteed. The `numbertries` counter is established for this purpose.

Subprograms and corresponding interfaces and input/output operations are defined using PDL constructs that correspond directly to the target programming language (in this case, Pascal). I/O specification is frequently expanded to include operations that support specialized input/output such as audio output or graphical display.

It should be noted that PDL can be extended to include keywords for multitasking and/or concurrent processing, interrupt handling, interprocess synchronization, and many other features. The software designs for which PDL is to be used should dictate the final form for the design language.

To illustrate the use of PDL, we present a more detailed example of a procedural design for monitoring software for a Home Security System. The Home Security System monitors alarms for fire, smoke, burglar, water, and temperature (e.g., furnace breaks while home owner is away during winter); produces an alarm bell, and calls a monitoring service, generating a synthesized voice message. In the PDL that follows, we illustrate some of the important constructs that have been discussed. Recall that PDL is not a programming language. The designer can adapt as required without worry of syntax errors. The designer can also provide additional detail for those portions of the design that require further elaboration. To determine the quality of the design, a review of the PDL is conducted (see Appendix B for details), and the design is further refined before code is written.

```
procedure SecurityMonitor (input, output);
type
    signal = record
        name: char;
        address: integer;
        boundvalue: integer;
        message: char;
    end;
var systemstatus; boolean;
    smokealarm: signal;
    firealarm: signal;
    wateralarm: signal;
    tempalarm: signal;
    burglaralarm: signal;
    phoneno defined as area code + 7-digit number;
    . . .
initialize all system ports and reset all hardware;
case of controlpanelswitches (cps):
    when cps = "test" select
      set alarmbell to "on" for testtime in seconds;
    when cps = "alarm-off" select DeactiviateAlarm;
    when cps = "new bound temp" select KeypadInput;
    when cps = "burglar alarm off" select Deactivate-
    Signal [burglaralarm];
      . . .
    default:   none;
endcase
```

```
repeat until activateswitch is turned off
   reset all signalvalues and switches;
   do for alarmtype = smoke,fire,water,temp,burglar;
      read address[alarmtype] signalvalue;
      if signalvalue > bound [alarmtype]
         then  phonemessage = message[alarmtype];
         set alarmbell to "on" for alarmtime seconds;
         MakePhoneCall(message[alarmtype], phoneno)
         else skip
      endif
   endfor
endrep
end SecurityMonitor
```

Note that the designer for the SecurityMonitor procedure has made reference to a number of other procedures (e.g., DeactivateAlarm, KeypadInput) that would be defined elsewhere in the procedural design.

Develop a preliminary test strategy to accommodate the data and program structure.

A test strategy (described in Chapter 6) provides guidance for the construction and testing of the program. Our first concern with testing occurred during problem analysis, when overall software validation criteria were established. Now we can be more specific about our approach to ensuring that these criteria have been met. A detailed discussion of test strategies is presented in Chapter 6.

Put it all together to create a *Design Document*.

We have created three complementary representations: data design, architectural design, and procedural design. These must be documented in a manner that will (1) enable us to conduct reviews to assess the technical correctness of the design, (2) serve as a guide for implementation, and (3) provide information to others who will maintain the software. The *Design Document* provides a template for satisfying each of these objectives. Each section of the *Design Document* is composed of numbered paragraphs that address different aspects of the design representation.

Software Design Document

1.0 Scope
    1.1 system objectives
    1.2 hardware, software, and human interfaces
    1.3 major software functions
    1.4 externally defined data base
    1.5 major design constraints, limitations
2.0 Reference Documents
    2.1 existing software documentation
    2.2 system documentation
    2.3 vendor (hardware or software) documents
    2.4 technical reference
3.0 Design Description
    3.1 data description
        3.1.1 review of data flow
        3.1.2 review of data structure
    3.2 derived program structure
    3.3 interfaces within structure
4.0 Modules
For each module:
    4.1 processing narrative
    4.2 interface description
    4.3 design language (or other) description
    4.4 modules used
    4.5 data organization
    4.6 comments
5.0 File Structure and Global Data
    5.1 external file structure
        5.1.1 logical structure
        5.1.2 logical record description
        5.1.3 access method
    5.2 global data
    5.3 file and data cross reference
6.0 Requirements Cross Reference
7.0 Test Provisions
    7.1 test guidelines
    7.2 integration strategy
    7.3 special considerations

8.0 Special Notes

9.0 Appendixes

The documentation outline presents a complete design description of software. The numbered sections of the *Design Document* are completed as the designer refines his or her representation of the software.

The overall scope of the design effort is described in section 1.0. Much of the information contained in this section is derived from the *Software Specification* (described in Chapter 3). Specific references to supporting documentation are made in section 2.0.

Section 3.0, the design description, is completed as part of architectural design. We have noted that design is information-driven—that is, flow and/or structure of data will dictate the architecture of software. In this section, data flow diagrams or other data representations, developed during problem analysis, are refined and used to derive data and program structures. Because data flow diagrams are available, interface descriptions may be developed for software modules.

Sections 4.0 and 5.0 evolve as preliminary design moves into detail design. Modules—separately addressable components of software such as subroutines, functions, or procedures—are initially described with an English language processing narrative. The processing narrative explains the function of a module. Later, PDL is used to translate the narrative into a structured procedural description.

A description of data organization is contained in section 5.0. File structures maintained on secondary storage media are described during preliminary design; global data are assigned (when no alternative to their use exists), and a cross reference that associates individual modules to files or global data is established.

Section 6.0 of the *Design Document* contains a requirements cross reference matrix. Two objectives of this cross reference matrix are: (1) to establish that all requirements described in the *Software Specification* are satisfied by the software design and (2) to indicate which modules are critical to the implementation of specific requirements.

The first stage in the development of test documentation is contained in section 7.0 of the *Design Document*. Once software architecture and interfaces have been established, we can develop guidelines for testing of individual modules and integration of the entire package.

 In some cases, a detailed specification of test procedure occurs in parallel with design. In such cases, this section may be deleted from the *Design Document* and included with test documentation.

Sections 8.0, 9.0, and 10.0 of the *Design Document* contain supplementary data. Algorithm descriptions, alternative procedures, tabular data, excerpts from other documents, and other relevant information are presented as a special note or as a separate appendix. It may be advisable to develop a *Preliminary Operations/Installation Manual* and include it as an appendix to the *Design Document*.

Review the *Design Document* for conformance to software requirements and technical quality.

Reviews for software design focus on data structure, program structure, and procedure. In general, two types of design reviews are conducted. The *preliminary design review* assesses the translation of requirements to design and focuses on software architecture. The second review, often called a *design walkthrough*, concentrates on the procedural correctness of algorithms as they are implemented within program modules. The following checklists are useful for each review:

Preliminary Design Review

1. Are software requirements reflected in the software architecture?
2. Has effective modularity been achieved? Are modules functionally independent?
3. Is the program architecture factored?
4. Are interfaces defined for modules, and are external system elements accurate and consistent?
5. Are data structures consistent with the information domain?
6. Are data structures consistent with software requirements?
7. Has maintainability been considered?

Design Walkthrough

1. Does the algorithm implemented for a given module accomplish the module's desired function?
2. Is the algorithm logically correct?
3. Is the module interface consistent with architectural design?
4. Is the module's logical complexity reasonable?
5. Have error handling and "anti-bugging" been specified?

6. Has the local data structure been properly defined?
7. Are structured programming constructs used throughout?
8. Is the design detail amenable to the programming language to be used for implementation?
9. Are there operating system or language dependent features?
10. Has compound or inverse logic been used to an excessive degree?
11. Has maintainability been considered?

Design is the cornerstone to successful software engineering, and design reviews are essential for successful design. A more detailed discussion of software reviews is contained in Appendix B.

WHAT THIS MEANS TO YOU

Would you attempt to build a house without blueprints? Would you travel over a bridge that was built without regard to accepted quality criteria? Would you purchase an automobile that was assembled "on the fly" without regard to some master production plan? Of course not! Yet many people attempt to build computer programs "without blueprints," without regard to quality criteria, without a production plan—without *design*.

In this chapter you have seen that designing a program is very much like designing a house. First, the requirements (how many bedrooms, baths, etc.?) must be defined. Next, an architectural model must be created. Finally, detailed design drawings are developed. Your approach to software should be the same. First, understand and refine requirements. Next, create an architectural model (for data and the program). Finally, develop a detailed procedural design.

Software design is the technical kernel of software engineering. Without it, you'll have difficulty translating a customer's requirements into operational software; you'll be unsure of the quality of the program that you've built, and you'll struggle to make it all come together. With design, you'll create high quality software that has been engineered to meet the needs of your customer.

FURTHER READINGS

Freeman, P. and A. Wasserman, *Software Design Techniques,* fourth edition, IEEE Computer Society, 1985.
Kruse, R.L., *Data Structures and Program Design,* Prentice-Hall, 1984.

Martin, J. and C. McClure, *Diagramming Techniques for Analysts and Programmers,* Prentice-Hall, 1985.

Mills, H., R. Linger, and B. Witt, *Structured Programming,* Addison-Wesley, 1979.

Peters, L., *Software Design: Methods and Techniques,* Yourdon Press, 1981.

Pressman, R.S., *Software Engineering: A Practitioner's Approach,* McGraw-Hill, second edition, 1987.

Yourdon, E. and L. Constantine, *Structured Design,* Yourdon Press, 1979.

PROBLEMS AND POINTS TO PONDER

4.1 Data, architectural, and procedural design are fundamental to software engineering. Are there analogies to these design activities in the hardware world? If so, what are they?

4.2 The program structure notation shown in Figure 4.1 provides no information to answer the questions: In what order does module M invoke modules a, b, and c? Under what conditions are a, b, and c invoked? How many times are a, b, and c invoked? Where would we find answers to these questions?

4.3 You've been asked to develop a "checkbook" program for a personal computer. Develop a statement of software scope, identify objects and operations, define DFDs, and recommend data structures that would be useful for this application.

4.4 For the checkbook program introduced in problem 4.3, develop an architectural design.

4.5 For the checkbook program introduced in problem 4.3, use stepwise refinement techniques to develop a procedural design. The first refinement (abstraction 0) might be: Maintain all checkbook information and perform all checkbook operations.

4.6 Describe information hiding in your own words, and discuss how it is related to functional independence.

4.7 Continuing the refinement of the applications introduced in problem 3.1 (Chapter 3), develop a data design, an architectural design, and a procedural design for one of the systems.

4.8 Using the normalization technique described in this chapter, develop a set of simplified data structures for an order-entry system for a lumberyard:

> The order entry software produces an invoice that includes customer information and products ordered information. The customer information includes an account number, name, billing address, ship-to address, order number, project name, total dollar amount ordered, customer discount, current balance, and past due amounts. Products ordered information includes item number, quantity, description, item discount, unit price, quantity price, taxes, total due, and total past due.

4.9 Orders for the lumberyard application are entered at interactive terminals. Derive your own set of requirements, develop a flow model and derive a program structure using the mappings described in this chapter.

4.10 Using a transaction mapping, derive the program structure that corresponds to the DFD shown below. Note that this DFD contains a number of subflows, labeled regions 1, 2, and 3, that have other transform and transaction flows. Your mapping should result in a one-to-one correspondence between bubbles in the DFD and modules in the program structure. Note: You will have to add additional control modules. These should be labeled X_i.

4.11 Why do we strive to design factored software architectures? What are the benefits of this approach?

4.12 Represent the structured programming constructs in whatever programming languages you are using for this course. If you know other languages, represent the constructs in them as well.

4.13 How close to code should PDL be? Is it necessary to qualify your answer?

4.14 Using the PDL described in this book, develop a procedural design for one or more of the following applications:

a. A module that performs simple numerical integration for a function $f(x)$ for values $a \leq x \leq b$.

b. A module that counts the number of occurrences of a given word in a paragraph of text.

c. A module that isolates individual words in a text file and compares each word against an existing list of keywords, keeping track of all "hits" on the list.

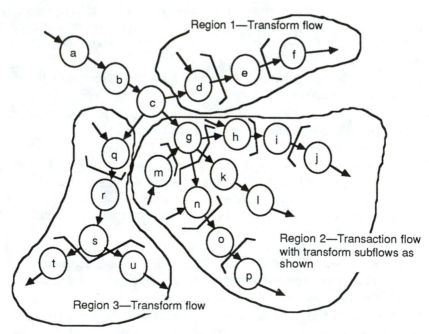

Figure for Problem 4.10

CHAPTER 5
CODING THE PROGRAM

Just as we cannot drive the mechanical drawings that represent an automobile or live in the blueprint that depicts the design of a house, we cannot "execute" the *Design Document* that represents software. A car or a house is manufactured using raw materials, larger prefabricated components, and a wide variety of specialized tools. People are involved, but over the years, the level of human involvement in the manufacturing process has been dramatically reduced. Fewer discrete parts are necessary, some having been replaced by components or modules that are prefabricated elsewhere. The result is a "building process" that takes less time and often produces higher quality.

The "manufacture" of a computer program is considerably different. Although small pockets of automation have surfaced and a few reusable components have been developed, *coding* remains an essentially human activity. People provide the human creativity involved in the derivation of a design. The raw materials used to create a program include the programming language that is used to translate the design into an executable program. The tools that we use encompass programming language compilers to effect the translation and a variety of editors, debuggers, and other code-oriented tools.

From a software engineering perspective, coding may be viewed as a natural outgrowth of software design. During design we represent each of the important aspects of a computer program—data structure, program structure, and procedural detail. Coding implements these design characteristics in the programming language at hand. In fact, it can be argued that coding is a rather mechanistic outgrowth of design and involves relatively little creativity. The creative process occurs during analysis, design, and (surprising as it seems) testing.

In this chapter we examine the steps required to implement a program. We assume that a design has been created and reviewed for correctness. Coding without a design is analogous to building a house without blueprints. It's likely that all the pieces will ultimately be constructed, but the degree to which they fit, their overall utility, and the satisfaction of the end user are all suspect.

Use the *Design Document* as a guide.

Each of the three elements of design—data design, architectural design, and procedural design—comes into play during the coding process. For this reason, the design document is an invaluable guide throughout the implementation of a program. Because coding focuses on module-level detail, the primary source of information is the procedural design description of each module. However, a description of internal data structures (as well as global data structures) and files is essential for implementation. In addition, the program architecture is used to establish proper interfaces between modules and to validate the control linkages throughout the modular hierarchy.

Use the program structure to determine the order in which modules will be coded.

The order in which modules are coded will affect the manner in which the program is constructed (integrated) and the speed with which operating program functions can be demonstrated. In general, we begin coding using a strategy that implements one *vertical branch* of the program structure. A vertical branch of a program structure includes the main control program, a module directly subordinate to it, and all modules that are subordinate to the directly subordinate module. Modules M, A, E, and G (Figure 5.1) form one vertical branch of a program structure. It should be noted that all PDL and/or code segments implied by the program structure in Figure 5.1 reference procedures

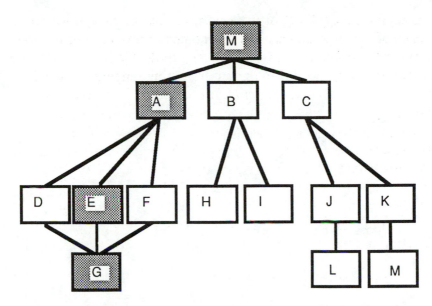

Figure 5.1 Branch Strategy for Coding

such as *procX*, where X is the corresponding module name shown in the figure. Therefore, G would be referenced as *procG*.

During design (Chapter 4), we attempted to develop a *factored* structure in which control modules exist at high levels in the program structure and "worker" modules comprise the lower levels. A branch strategy for implementation enables us to code and then test a major program function relatively early. This gives the software engineer confidence and enables the customer to see at least one part of an operating program.

But where do we begin coding? Should we start by coding the main control module or by coding the low-level modules associated with I/O or computations? Before coding starts in earnest, it is often worthwhile to create an "outline" of the program that reflects the program structure. For example, an "outline" for the program shown in Figure 5.1 might be:

```
program procM;
{declare global variables and data structures}
    procedure procA;
```

```
{declare data for procA}
begin
    procD;
    procE;
    procF;
end;
procedure procB;
{declare data for procB}
begin
    procH;
    procI;
end;
procedure procC;
{declare data for procC}
begin
    procJ;
    procK;
end;
{similar outline definition is created for modules
D, E, F, G, H, I, J, K, L, M}
begin {progM}
    procA;
    procB;
    procC;
end.  {progM}
```

The outline can be "fleshed out" by adding programming language statements that implement all major logical operations, computation, output, and input that have been specified as part of software design.

> *Begin coding modules that reside at
> low levels in the program structure.*

The creation of the programming language "outline" described above satisfies a natural tendency to begin coding at the top of the program structure (i.e., we code the main control program first). However, once the outline has been created, it is often better to complete the coding of low-level modules first. Low-level modules perform basic I/O operations or implement the computational kernel of the program. These low-level modules (recall factoring) perform processing work and are much easier to test in stand-alone mode (see module testing in Chapter 6).

In the context of the program structure and branch implementation strategy depicted in Figure 5.1, the first module to be coded might be G. It is likely that G is an input module (it resides on the input branch of a transform structure). Beginning with a module outline of the form

```
procedure procG;
    {declare data for procG}
    begin
        {processing statements}
    end;
```

all local initialization and input statements would be implemented, along with any logical tests and/or loops required to implement the input function specified for *procG*. Using a program design language (PDL) description of G as a guide, the module outline is "fleshed out."

To illustrate this process, assume that one of the following PDL descriptions has been developed for *procG:*

Version 1. *procG* is described with PDL at a fairly high level of abstraction. A representation at this level would be appropriate when (1) the module logic is reasonably straightforward and (2) the designer will also code the module.

```
procedure   procG;
  {declare data for procG}
  begin
    define an array that holds up to 10 parameter
    values;
    ask user for units system and number of parameters
    to be input;
    do appropriate error checking on these inputs;
    read parameter values until the number of inputs
    has been met;
  end;
```

Version 2. *procG* is described with PDL at a lower level of abstraction. A representation at this level would be appropriate when (1) the module logic is more complex or (2) the code will be written by someone other than the designer. PDL for *procG* follows:

```
procedure procG (unittype, numinput, parametervalue);
type  numinput, inputcounter, unittype: integer;
```

```
type parametervalue: real array [1..10];
   ASK "what type of units are you using" 1=english,
   2=metric";
   ANSWER unittype=1, 2;
   check ANSWER to ensure proper response, provide ap-
   propriate error message;
   ASK "how many parameters will you enter?";
   ANSWER placed in numinput, 0<numinput<10;
   check ANSWER to ensure proper response, provide
   appropriate error message;
   inputcounter = 0;
   do while (numinput > inputcounter)
       increment inputcounter;
   ASK "enter parameter"; ANSWER parametervalue
   [inputcounter];
   enddo
end procG;
```

Code is derived from the procedural design. Obviously, the lower the level of abstraction at which PDL is represented, the more mechanical the coding process becomes. A rendition of *procG* using Pascal follows:

```
procedure procG (var unittype, numinput: integer;
        var parametervalue: array{1..10] of real);
   {a module prologue (to be discussed later in this
   chapter) goes here}
var inputcounter: integer; errorflag: boolean;
begin
errorflag:=true;
writeln ('What type of units are you using for
     parameter input?');
while errorflag do begin
   writeln ('Type 1 for English or 2 for metric.');
   readln (unittype);
   if unittype < 1 or unittype > 2      {error test}
      then begin
         errorflag:=true;
         writeln ('ERROR --You must type either 1 or 2
         to indicate the units you'll use.');
         writeln ('Please try again');
      end
      else errorflag:= false;
end;
```

```
      errorflag:=true;
      writeln ('How many values will you input
      for parameters?");
      while errorflag do begin
         writeln ('Type an integer number between 1 and
         10');
         readln (numinput);
         if numinput < 1 or numinput > 10   {error test}
         then begin
            errorflag:=true;
            writeln ('ERROR--You must type an integer
            number between 1 and 10 for parameters');
            writeln ('Please try again');
         end
         else errorflag:= false;
      end;
      inputcounter := 0;
      while numinput >= inputcounter do begin
         inputcounter := inputcounter + 1;
         writeln ('Enter parameter value (a floating
         point number)');
         readln (parametervalue[inputcounter]);
      end;
end.
```

The Pascal procedure *procG* is a mechanical transformation of the procedural design described above. Although the design didn't indicate an error processing module, it becomes apparent that such a module (we'll call it *inputcheck*) could be put to good use in the service of *procG*. It is not at all uncommon for such discoveries to occur during coding. After a review to ensure that *inputcheck* will not create unforeseen side effects, design documentation (the program structure chart and description) is modified to reflect the change and the module *procG* is recoded to reflect the new error processing module.

Develop code for global data structures.

Although the use of global data structures should be avoided (they tend to increase the amount of coupling within a program), there are some instances when global data are the only effective means for communicating information to different modules. When global data are used, code for their implementation should be developed early. In this way, the implementation of each program module (hopefully, a limited number!) that accesses the global data will have a defined template for the data. This is likely to reduce interfacing errors that commonly occur.

To begin the coding of global data we revisit the original program "outline" (described earlier) and add code that declares all global data structures. For the purposes of this discussion, let us assume that *progM* (presented earlier in this chapter) is a computer-aided design (CAD) application that implements the data structure **drawing** described in Chapter 4. We assume further that drawing must be globally available to all modules in program M. Using the PDL description presented in Chapter 4 as a guide, we implement Pascal code for global data. Returning to the outline for *progM:*

```
program procM;
    {program prologue}
type
    LineChoices = (narrow, bold, dashed, dotted,
    double, invisible);
    PartCodes = (ma, mb, mc, md, ca, cb, cc, cd, xx,
    yy, zz);
    BOMnodePointer = ^integer;
    number: integer;
    line = record
        xCoordstart: real;
        yCoordstart: real;
        xCoordend: real;
        yCoordend: real;
        linetype: LineChoices;
    end;
    { ... other geometry components follow ... }
    BOMnode = record
        nodeNo: integer;
        description: char;
        partno1: PartCodes
        partno2: integer;
        NextnodePointer = ^integer;
    end;
procedure procA;
    {declare data for procA}
    begin
        procD;
        procE;
```

```
{ ... the outline for procM continues ... }
end.  {progM}
```

Recall that the use of global data tends to reduce functional independence by coupling all modules in a system through a data structure. For this reason, the use of global data, regardless of the programming language, should be restricted to those situations in which no other choice is available.

If a block-structured programming language (e.g., Pascal) is used, the scope of a data structure can be limited by organizing modules within appropriate blocks. In older programming languages such as FORTRAN, the scope of global data can be limited by using labeled COMMON.

It is often useful to develop a global data cross reference matrix that lists all global data structures and the corresponding modules that require access to them. In actuality, the cross reference matrix should be developed as part of the data design step. However, it can also be created during coding.

> *Examine internal data structures, and determine*
> *how they can be implemented using*
> *programming language constructs.*

Each programming language has its own set of constructs for describing data structures. Some languages (such as Pascal) have a rich set of constructs that enables a wide variety of data structures (e.g., enumerated types, linked lists, arrays, records) to be implemented directly. Other programming languages (such as FORTRAN) have more limited data declaration capabilities and therefore require more inventiveness (and often, more frustration) on the part of the programmer when "unsupported" data structures are specified as part of a design.

Just as we began the design process by considering data design, we begin the coding process by focusing on the data structures that will be manipulated by the program. We have already noted that the internal data structures required for most modules will be quite simple (e.g., scalar variables and simple arrays). In other cases, however, both internal and global data structures may be relatively complex (e.g., heterogeneous data structures such as the Pascal record type, shown above for **drawing**) and may therefore offer some challenge in design to code translation.

The naming conventions for internal data are dictated by the programming language in use. By definition, an internal data structure is locally defined and has meaning only within the scope of a specific module. Therefore, most programming languages (e.g., Pascal, FORTRAN) allow local variables to take on the same identifying names as variables outside the scope of a module. Confusion can arise when the same identifier is used in two different modules, if it refers to entirely different data.

For example, in an engineering application in Pascal, the following declaration is made internal to the procedure *ComputeTemp:*

```
type vector = array [1..100] of real;
var TempData: vector;
```

where the identifier `TempData` might be used in a module that computes engine temperature given other transducer inputs. In another module, *ModifyTemp,* of the same program, `TempData` is declared:

```
type SmallVector = array [1..10] of real;
var TempData: SmallVector;
```

In this case, however, `TempData` is used to store intermediate calculations for subsequent temperature processing in the module. Although both versions of `TempData` are local to their respective modules, the use of the same identifier name could be psychologically ambiguous. Unless there is a compelling reason to do so, don't use the same identifier to represent different data.

Define all data files using
programming language conventions.

A data file is nothing more than an external data structure, and therefore all comments made about data apply equally to data files. In addition, the programmer must observe appropriate conventions for the definition of the files and the requirements for opening and closing the files that are specific to each programming language.

Generate programming language source code
using the procedural design as a guide.

We have developed a procedural design for each module using a program design language (PDL) described in Chapter 4. In some cases, the translation between PDL and the target programming language may be trivially simple. For example, a PDL statement such as

```
Increment order number sequence by 1;
```

can be translated into a programming language statement that takes the form

```
OrderNoSeq := OrderNoSeq + 1;
```

Other situations, however, are not so obvious. For example, the PDL statement:

```
Perform a search on a list of sorted items;
```

implies that a search algorithm must be implemented. A good software engineer will recognize that a number of different search algorithms are available and will select one that best meets the requirements of the system. Before coding can commence, the design must be elaborated (using stepwise refinement). After researching the subject, the designer selects a binary search algorithm and expands the PDL statement, obtaining:

```
procedure BinarySearch;
    select a value that approximates the "middle" of
    the list of items, thereby dividing the list into
    two  sublists;
    determine which sublist the item to be found lies
    within and progressively subdivide the sublist
    until the item is found or the sublist is length 1,
    i.e., the item is not found;
end;
```

Refining the procedural design further:

```
procedure BinarySearch;
    {NOTE: the list to be searched is assumed to have
    been sorted in ascending order elsewhere.}
    select the entire list as the sublist to be
    searched;
    do while the sublist length is greater than 0 and
    the item has not been found;
        find the middle position in the sublist by
        middle := (firstindex + lastindex)/2;
        compare the target item (being searched) for
        with the item at the middle position;
        if target item = middle item then begin
            target item is found {search succeeds};
```

```
            set found flag to true;
        end;
        if target item > middle then begin
            last half of list is new sublist;
            first := middle + 1;
        end;
        if target item < middle item then begin
            first half of list is new sublist;
            last := middle - 1;
        end;
    end;
    if found flag is true then target item searched for
    is at middle; otherwise it is not in the list;
end;
```

This PDL description can be expanded into a Pascal implementation that looks like:

```
procedure BinarySearch (var item: list;
    numitems: integer; targetitem: datatype;
    var found: boolean; var location: integer);
{
This procedure conducts a binary search for a
targetitem that may be contained in a list of items
that is numitems long. If targetitem is found, a flag
is set to true and the index of the targetitem in the
list is placed in location. NOTE: List is assumed to
have been sorted in ascending order.
}
var first, last, middle: integer;
begin
first := 1;
last := numitems;
found := false;
while (first <= last) and (not found) do begin
    middle := (first + last) div 2;
    if targetitem = item[middle] then begin
        found := true;
        location = middle
    end {if}
    else if targetitem > item[middle] then
        first := middle + 1
    else
        last := middle - 1
end {while}
end {BinarySearch};
```

Because the procedural design for the binary search algorithm was specified in detail in PDL, coding could have been accomplished with equal facility in any modern programming language.

In summary, the level of procedural abstraction with which PDL is represented will have a strong bearing on the ease with which programming language source code is generated. If the level of abstraction is high, more time and effort will be required to derive the appropriate source code to achieve the specified procedural abstraction (unless a module already exists to implement the abstraction). If, however, the level of abstraction is low, the relationship between PDL and the programming language source code may approach one-to-one and coding becomes a mechanistic outgrowth of design.

Learn the elements of good coding style, and apply them.

Even when a procedural design is represented in considerable detail, the programmer has some latitude in choosing the style with which a program is implemented. The choice of variable names, the manner in which data are declared, the use of comments, and many other features are style dependent. Good programming style can aid immeasurably in program testing, debugging, and maintenance. Poor style can detract significantly from an otherwise excellent design.

A number of textbooks have been written on the subject of programming style. The premier source of information is a book by Kernighan and Plauger (*The Elements of Programming Style,* second edition, McGraw-Hill, 1982).

The following coding rules summarize some of the more important points associated with programming style.

Coding Rule 1: Always strive for simplicity and clarity; never be purposely obtuse.

More than a few misguided programmers believe that the more complex and convoluted their code, the more sophisticated their skills. Nothing could be further from the truth! A truly elegant program is generally quite simple. The underlying meaning of the procedure represented in programming language source code should be obvious to the reader.

Coding Rule 2: Use meaningful variable names and consistent typing conventions.

Variable names such as `InputData` or `x001yz` are to be avoided at all cost. In general, variables and more complex data structures should be named in a manner that enables the reader to infer their meaning within the context of the procedure at hand and/or their correlation with some real-world object. In addition, variable naming conventions should be established in advance so that variable names are not misinterpreted by an uninitiated reader.

For example, a program that performs sophisticated heat transfer computations might establish a convention that defines all variable names with the prefix `Temp` to contain temperature-related data. It would be poor style to define an loop index somewhere in the program with the name `TempIndex` (in this case, meaning temporary counter). The potential for misinterpretation is obvious.

Compilers for programming languages with strong data typing will enforce the consistent use of data types. However, other programming language compilers allow the coder great flexibility in the use of data types (e.g., FORTRAN) and therefore do little to discourage poor programming style. If the compiler does not directly enforce the consistent use of data types, this important element of good programming style should be enforced by the programmers themselves.

Coding Rule 3: Use a prologue to describe each module.

A *prologue* (sometimes called a *header*) is a group of comment statements at the beginning of each module that describe the overall function of the module and provide a variety of other information. The format for such comments is:

1. A statement of purpose that indicates the function of the module
   a. English language processing description
   b. PDL excerpt
2. An interface description that includes:
   a. a sample "calling sequence"
   b. a description of all arguments
   c. a list of all modules called by this module

3. A discussion of pertinent data such as important variables and their use; restrictions and limitations; other important information
4. A development history that includes:
   a. module designer (author)
   b. reviewer (auditor) and date
   c. modification dates and description

As an example of a module prologue, we return to the binary search procedure discussed earlier in this chapter. The simple statement of purpose contained in the initial source code is expanded to become a complete module prologue:

```
procedure BinarySearch (var item: list;
    numitems: integer; targetitem: datatype;
    var found: boolean; var location: integer);
{MODULE PROLOGUE
Purpose:
    This procedure conducts a binary search for target-
    item that may be contained in list, a list of items
    containing numitems. If targetitem is found, the
    flag found is set to true and the location of the
    targetitem in the list is contained in location.
    NOTE: List is assumed to have been sorted in as-
    cending order.
Procedural Design Description:
do while the sublist length is greater than 0 and the
targetitem has not been found;
        find the middle position in the sublist by
        middle := (firstindex + lastindex)/2;
        compare the targetitem (being searched for) with
        the item at the middle position;
        if targetitem = middle item then begin
           targetitem has been found {search succeeds};
           set found flag to true;
        end;
        if targetitem > middle then begin
           last half of list is new sublist;
           first := middle + 1;
        end;
        if targetitem < middle item then begin
           first half of list is new sublist;
           last := middle - 1;
        end;
    end;
```

```
      if found flag is true then targetitem searched for
      is at middle; otherwise item is not in the list;
end;
Interface Description:
      Sample calling sequence:
          BinarySearch(list, numitems, targetitem, found,
          location);
List of Arguments:
      list = ordered input vector of datatype, items to
      be searched
      numitems = input integer, number of items in the
      list
      targetitem = input datatype, item to be found
      found = output boolean, true if search successful
      location = output integer, location of targetitem
      in list
List of modules called:   none
Programming notes: This algorithm will work only for an
ordered list.
Development history:
      Module designer (author):  P. Simon, 6-01-88
      Reviewer (auditor) and date:  A. Rivers, 6-06-88
Modification dates and description:   none
END PROLOGUE }

   { ... source code for the module follows ... }
```

Much of the information contained in the *BinarySearch* module prologue can be excised directly from the *Design Document*. It is included here to combine both code and design information, making it easier to read and understand the program and thereby simplifying software maintenance.

Coding Rule 4: Establish effective commenting conventions.

Source code comments can improve overall understanding of a complex algorithm or sophisticated data structure. However, when used improperly, comments can also make code more difficult to read and in some cases mislead the reader.

Descriptive comments are embedded within the body of source code and are used to describe processing functions. A primary guideline for such commenting is: "comments should provide something extra, not just paraphrase the code." In addition, descriptive comments should:

- Start with an effective module prologue
- Describe blocks of code, rather then commenting every line
- Use blank lines or indentation so that comments can be readily distinguished from code
- Answer the question "why?" as well as "what?"
- Be correct; an incorrect or misleading comment is worse than no comment at all

With proper identifier mnemonics and good commenting, adequate internal documentation is ensured.

When a detailed procedural design is represented using a program design language, design documentation can be embedded directly into the source listing as comment statements. This technique helps to ensure that both code and design will be maintained when changes are made to either.

The form of the source code as it appears within the listing is an important contributor to readability and serves as an indirect "comment" on procedural flow. Source code indentation indicates logical constructs and blocks of code by indenting from the left margin so that these attributes are set off visually. Like commenting, the best approach to indentation is open to debate. Ideally, source code is indented automatically using a software tool. Manual indentation can become complicated as code modification occurs, but many software engineers feel that indented code aids understanding.

Coding Rule 5: Use simple statement construction and program layout.

The description of a program's logical flow is established during design. The construction of individual statements, however, is part of the coding step. Statement construction should abide by one overriding rule: each statement should be simple and direct.

Many programming languages allow multiple statements per line. The space-saving aspects of this feature are hardly justified by poor readability that can result if it is used without consideration for style. Consider the following two code segments (presented without comment statements):

```
repeat   while Data[left]<StarterValue do
left := left + 1;   while StarterValue < Data[right] do
right := right + 1;
if left <= right then begin temp := Data [left];
```

```
Data[left] := Data[right]; Data[right] := temp; left :=
left + 1; right := right - 1;
end; until right <= left; if start < right
    then sort (start, right, Data);
if left < finish then sort (left, finish, Data);
```

The loop structure and conditional operation contained in the above segment are masked by multi-statement per line construction. Reorganizing the form of the code:

```
repeat
while Data[left]<StarterValue do
    left := left + 1;
while StarterValue < Data[right] do
    right := right + 1;
    if left <= right then begin
        temp := Data [left];
        Data[left] := Data[right];
        Data[right] := temp;
        left := left + 1;
        right := right - 1
    end;
until right <= left;
if start < right then sort (start, right, Data);
if left < finish then sort (left, finish, Data);
```

Here, simple statement construction and indentation illuminates the logical and functional characteristics of the segment. Individual source code statements can be simplified by:

- Avoiding the use of complicated conditional tests
- Eliminating tests on negative conditions
- Avoiding heavy nesting of loops or conditions
- Using parentheses to clarify logical or arithmetic expressions
- Using spacing and/or readability symbols to clarify statement content
- Using only ANSI standard features
- Thinking: "Could I understand this if I was not the person who coded it?"

Each of the above guidelines strives to "keep it simple."

It is important to note that in certain circumstances multiple programming language statements can be typed on a single line without negative affects. For example, the set of statements:

```
left := left + 1; right := right - 1;
```

from the above code segment can be combined on the same line without loss of clarity.

> ### *Coding Rule 6: Code all input and output to enhance ease of data transfer and improve error checking.*

The style of input and output is established during software requirements analysis and design, not during coding. However, the manner in which I/O is implemented can be the determining characteristic for system acceptance by users.

Input and output style will vary with the degree of human interaction. For batch-oriented I/O, logical input organization, meaningful input/output error-checking, good I/O error recovery, and rational output formats are desirable characteristics. For interactive I/O, a simple, guided input scheme, extensive error-checking and recovery, human-engineered I/O, and consistency of I/O format become primary concerns.

Regardless of the batch or interactive nature of software, a number of I/O style guidelines should be considered during design and coding:

- Validate all input data
- Check the plausibility of important combinations of input items;
- Keep input format simple
- Use end-of-data indicators, rather than requiring a user to specify "number-of-items"
- Label interactive input requests, specifying available choices or bounding values
- Keep input format uniform when a programming language has stringent formatting requirements
- Label all output and design all reports

The style of I/O is affected by many other characteristics such as I/O devices (e.g., terminal type, computer graphics device, mouse), user sophistication, and communication environment.

> ### *Coding Rule 7: Strive for efficient code, but not at the expense of readability or simplicity.*

In well-engineered systems, there is a natural tendency to use critical resources efficiently. Processor cycles and memory locations are often viewed as critical resources, and the coding step is seen as the last point where microseconds or bits can be squeezed out of the software. Although efficiency is a commendable goal, three maxims should be stated before we discuss the topic further. First, efficiency is a performance requirement and should therefore be established during problem analysis. Software should be as efficient as is required, not as efficient as is humanly possible! Second, efficiency is improved with good design. Design modifications can often provide macroscopic efficiency improvement, while coding modifications provide only microscopic improvement. Third, code efficiency and code simplicity go hand in hand. In general, don't sacrifice clarity, readability, or correctness for nonessential improvements in efficiency.

The efficiency of source code is directly tied to the efficiency of algorithms defined during procedural design. However, coding style can have an effect on execution speed and memory requirements. The following set of guidelines can always be applied when procedural design is translated into code:

- Simplify arithmetic and logical expressions before committing to code
- Carefully evaluate nested loops to determine if statements or expressions can be moved outside
- When possible, avoid the use of multi-dimensional arrays
- When possible, avoid the use of pointers and complex lists
- Use "fast" arithmetic operations
- Don't mix data types, even if the language allows it
- Use integer arithmetic and boolean expressions, whenever possible

Many modern programming language compilers have optimizing features that automatically generate efficient code by collapsing repetitive expressions, performing loop evaluation, using fast arithmetic, and applying other efficiency-related algorithms. For applications in which efficiency is paramount, such compilers are indispensable coding tools.

Review the resultant code for correctness and readability.

Programming language source code should be directly traceable to the procedural design description. A review of the source code for each module should consider the following questions:

- Does the source code properly reflect the design's intent?
- Are data structures implemented properly?
- Have operators been used correctly? That is, have we used a "+" sign where we meant to use a "*" sign?
- Are all loops and logical tests nested properly?
- Do we have a proper escape mechanism for all loops? That is, have we ensured against an infinite loop?
- Have all variables been assigned explicit data types? Are inconsistent data types combined in an inappropriate manner?
- Have meaningful variable names been chosen?
- Does a module prologue exist? Is it complete?
- Do comments add to the understanding of the source code rather than parroting the code?
- Is the layout (e.g., comments, indentation, white space) of the code conducive to good readability?

Each of these questions should be applied to the code for every module in a program.

WHAT THIS MEANS TO YOU

A master carpenter builds a house using a design created by an architect. In most cases, the carpenter follows the "outline" provided by the design. However, every craftsperson has the ability to interpret the design in a way that is most likely to achieve a high quality end result. The carpenter draws on experience to develop a style that yields high quality construction. A software engineer does very much the same thing. Like the carpenter, the software engineer builds programs by following an "outline" established during design. Like any craftsperson, a software engineer follows a set of style guidelines to ensure that the product to be built will exhibit high quality.

All of us, students and practitioners, hackers and software engineers, enjoy building software by coding in our favorite programming language. Coding enables us to realize what we've designed, to create a working program where nothing existed previously. Coding translates design into realization, but coding itself is not a particularly creative process. It only seems creative because many of us implicitly design as we code. During design we create, during coding we build.

In this chapter we've discussed the manner in which design-to-code translation occurs and a set of style guidelines for effecting the translation. Whether you code in Pascal, C, Ada, COBOL, or FOR-TRAN, the coding process is essentially the same. Software architecture, data structure, and procedural logic are implemented, and a working program results. But the growing importance of software demands more that a "working" program. Software must be readable, testable, reliable, maintainable—the list of attributes could fill three or four lines of text. Good coding can help you to achieve some of these attributes, and for this reason we develop guidelines for coding style. Use them.

FURTHER READINGS

Kernighan, B. and P. Plauger, *The Elements of Programming Style*, McGraw-Hill, second edition, 1978.
Ledgard, H. and M. Marcotty, *The Programming Language Landscape*, SRA, 1981.
Leffick, B.W., *The Software Developer's Sourcebook*, Addison-Wesley, 1985.
Pratt, T., *Programming Languages*, second edition, Prentice-Hall, 1984.
Weiland, R.J., *The Programmer's Craft*, Reston Publishing, 1983.

PROBLEMS AND POINTS TO PONDER

5.1 Using a programming language suggested by your instructor, implement one or more of the procedural designs that were developed as part of problem 4.15 (Chapter 4).

5.2 Using a programming language suggested by your instructor, implement the data structure that was developed for problem 4.8 (Chapter 4).

5.3 Some people argue that PDL is redundant and that source code should be the mechanism for representing procedural design. How do you respond?

5.4 When a factored program structure has been designed, we suggest beginning coding with modules that reside low in the structure. Do you agree with this suggestion? Why?

5.5 Analyze, design, and then code a software tool that will automatically indent programming language source code to better represent data and control structure. Ideally, the tool should be capable of working with a number of different programming languages.

5.6 In the example on page 166 we used the abstractions ASK and ANSWER for the PDL representation of a procedural design. Develop a list of other generic procedural abstractions that could be represented as PDL and then easily translated into source code.

5.7 Implement the Binary Search program presented on page 172 in a programming language other than Pascal. Does the PDL provide you with sufficient guidance?

5.8 Develop a series of programming language examples that illustrate the underlying rationale for each of the programming rules presented in this chapter.

5.9 Develop a complete module header for the program that you implemented in problem 5.1.

5.10 Suggest additional review questions similar to those presented at the end of this chapter. Examine a fellow student's program and conduct a review using these questions as a guide.

CHAPTER 6
TESTING THE RESULT

A major automobile manufacturer brags about the fact that a new car has undergone 3 million miles of road testing; an appliance manufacturer demonstrates the quality of its product by describing over 300 separate "quality checks" to ensure that it works properly; a computer manufacturer runs diagnostic tests day and night for three weeks to ensure that its hardware is functioning properly. In each of these cases, a hardware builder uses the thoroughness of testing as a sales tool to convince customers that a product has reliability and quality. How often have you heard a software builder use the same approach?

Although everyone who has developed a computer program (both large and small) recognizes the importance of testing, few software developers perform testing in an effective manner. In most cases, testing occurs late in a software project, when time is short, budgets are nearly exhausted, managers are nervous, and customers are anxious. As a result, testing often gets the short end of the stick.

Testing need not be conducted in an ad hoc fashion. Rather, the design characteristics of the software can be used as a foundation from which test cases are derived. Test case design methods enable us to improve the thoroughness with which software tests are conducted and increase the probability that testing will achieve its primary objective: *to find the largest number of errors in the least amount of time with a minimum allocation of resources*. In this chapter, we examine the steps that are required to conduct systematic testing for computer software.

Develop a test plan that describes both strategy and specifics.

The formality of a *Software Test Plan* is almost always proportional to the overall criticality of the software and its size. For small projects with average criticality, the test plan may be nothing more than a brief "paper" that describes the overall strategy for testing and delineates the test cases that will be used to demonstrate that the software works according to its specifications. In some cases, this information may be incorporated into a *Design Document*. For large, highly critical projects, the test plan may be a 200 - 300 page document that contains a detailed integration and validation strategy along with page after page of test cases and expected results. Obviously, the software engineer must use common sense to determine which approach to test planning is viable for the project at hand. In every case, however, test planning should occur.

In actuality, test planning begins during the problem analysis process. The validation requirements section of the *Software Specification* (Chapter 3) is a precursor to the test plan, delineating important classes of tests that will be used to demonstrate valid operation of software. The work performed as part of software analysis and specification is expanded during test planning.

The overall strategy for software testing can best be understood by considering it in the context of the entire software engineering process. Software engineering activities begin with system engineering and culminate with testing. Initially, system engineering defines the role of software and leads to software requirements analysis, where the information domain, function, performance, constraints, and validation criteria for software are established. Analysis establishes the foundation for design and design provides an outline for coding. To develop computer software, we spiral inward, passing through each of the major steps that we've already discussed in this book. With each loop around the spiral, the level of abstraction with which we represent software decreases.

A strategy for software testing may also be viewed in the context of a spiral. The first testing step, *module testing,* begins at the vortex of the spiral and concentrates on each software component that has been implemented in source code. Testing progresses by moving outward along the spiral to *integration testing,* where the focus is on the construction and verification of the program structure and associated data structures. Taking another turn outward on the spiral, we encounter *validation testing,* where requirements established as part of software requirements analysis are validated against the software that has been constructed. Finally, we arrive at *system testing,* where the software and other system elements are tested as a whole. To engineer software, we spiral inward toward code. To test software, we spiral outward, beginning with a focus on code and terminating with a system-level perspective. The scope of testing is broadened with each turn.

Define an approach for testing each module in the program structure.

Once each program module is coded, a series of tests are conducted to uncover errors in (1) the module interface, (2) the algorithm implemented by the module, (3) the internal data structures, (4) error handling, and (5) each independent path through the program.

To design a complete set of module tests, two complementary points of view are taken. In the first, the module is treated as a "black box." That is, the internal workings of the module are not considered when test cases are designed. Rather, we provide input to the module and then evaluate the output produced against expected results. The second view of module testing, sometimes called *white-box testing,* applies test case design methods that are driven by the procedural design (the internal workings) of the module. Both black-box and white-box testing techniques are described in more detail later in this chapter.

It is important to note that not all modules are amenable to module-level testing. In general, modules that reside at low levels of the program structure are relatively easy to test at the module level. These modules are the "workers" (see Chapter 4) and require relatively little information from modules subordinate to them. Modules higher in the program structure can be more difficult to test in stand-alone fashion because their operation requires data provided by subordinates.

Develop an integration strategy for constructing the program structure.

A newcomer to the software world might ask an innocent question once all modules have been tested in stand-alone fashion: "If they all work individually, why do you doubt that they'll work when we put them together?" The problem, of course, is "putting them together"— *integration*. Data can be lost across an interface; one module can have an unexpected adverse effect on another; subfunctions, when combined, may not produce the desired major function; individually acceptable imprecision may be magnified to unacceptable levels; global data structures can present problems. The list goes on and on.

Integration testing is a systematic technique for constructing the program structure while at the same time conducting tests to uncover errors associated with interfacing. The objective is to take tested modules and build a program structure that has been dictated by design.

There is often a tendency to attempt nonincremental integration; that is, to construct the program using a "big bang" approach. All modules are combined in advance. We cross our fingers and test the entire program as a whole. Chaos usually results! A set of errors are encountered. Correction is difficult because isolation of causes is complicated by the vast expanse of the entire program. Once these errors are corrected, new ones appear, and the process continues in a seemingly endless loop.

Incremental integration is the antithesis of the big bang approach. The program is constructed and tested in small segments, where errors are easier to isolate and correct; interfaces are more likely to be tested completely, and a systematic test approach may be applied. In the sections that follow, a number of different incremental integration strategies are discussed.

Integrate modules using both top-down and bottom-up testing.

Top-down integration is an incremental approach to construction of program structure. Modules are integrated by moving downward through the control hierarchy, beginning with the main control module (main program). Modules that are subordinate to the main control module are incorporated into the program structure in either a *depth-first* or *breadth-first* manner.

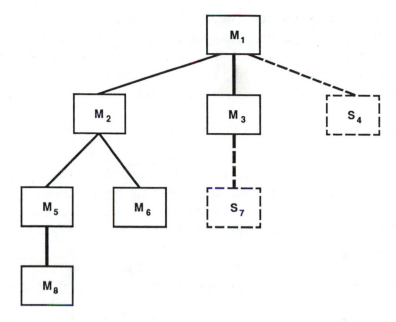

Figure 6.1 Depth-First Integration

As illustrated in Figure 6.1, *depth-first integration* (also called a branch integration strategy) integrates all modules on a major control path of the structure. Selection of a major path is somewhat arbitrary and depends on application-specific characteristics.* To illustrate we refer once more to Figure 6.1.

Selecting the left-hand path of the program structure, we integrate modules M_1, M_2, and M_5 first. Before tests can be executed for M_1 and M_2, a *stub* for M_5 is created. Stubs are dummy modules that replace an actual module until it is ready to be integrated. A stub for M_5 enables tests designed for M_2 to cause it to "call" M_5 without generating an error. Stubs can be designed to serve more sophisticated functions, but for the most part they merely act as place markers until the actual module is integrated.

Continuing with the left-hand branch of the program structure (Figure 6.1), M_8 or M_6 would be integrated. Then the central and

---

* In some cases, however, project schedule or customer desires may dictate the order in which paths are integrated. For example, a customer may be eager to "see progress" and "try out" an interactive system for design. The software engineer selects the input path for integration (delaying work on other paths) so that some human interaction can be demonstrated early.

right-hand control paths would be built.

Breadth-first integration incorporates all modules directly subordinate at each level, moving across the structure horizontally. The figure shows that modules M_2, M_3, and M_4 (a replacement for stub S_4) would be integrated first. The next control level, M_5, M_6, etc., follows.

The integration process is performed in a series of five substeps:

1. The main control module is used as a test driver (the module that acts as the main program to control testing), and stubs are substituted for all modules directly subordinate to the main control module.
2. Depending on the integration approach selected (i.e., depth- or breadth-first), subordinate stubs are replaced one at a time with actual modules.
3. Tests are conducted as each module is integrated.
4. On completion of each set of tests, another stub is replaced with the real module.
5. *Regression testing* (i.e., conducting all or some of the previous tests) may be conducted to ensure that new errors have not been introduced.

The process continues from step 2 until the entire program structure is built. Figure 6.1 illustrates the process. Assuming a depth-first approach and a partially completed structure, stub S_7 is next to be replaced with module M_7. M_7 may itself have stubs that will be replaced with corresponding modules. It is important to note that at each replacement, tests are conducted to verify the interface.

A *top-down integration* strategy verifies major control or decision points early in the test process. In a well-factored program structure, major decision making occurs at upper levels in the module hierarchy and is therefore encountered first. If major control problems do exist, early recognition is essential. If depth-first integration is selected, a complete function of the software may be implemented and demonstrated. For example, consider a classic transaction structure (Chapter 4) in which a complex series of interactive inputs are requested, acquired, and validated via an incoming path. The incoming path may be integrated in a top-down manner. All input processing (for subsequent transaction dispatching) may be demonstrated before other elements of the structure have been integrated. Early demonstration of functional capability is a confidence builder for both the software engineer and the customer.

Top-down strategy sounds relatively uncomplicated, but in practice, logistics problems can arise. The most common of these problems occurs when processing at low levels in the hierarchy is required to adequately test upper levels. Stubs replace low-level modules at the beginning of top-down testing; therefore, no significant data can flow upward in the program structure. The tester is left with three choices: (1) delay many tests until stubs are replaced with actual modules, (2) develop stubs that perform limited functions that simulate the actual module, or (3) integrate the software from the bottom of the hierarchy upward.

The first approach (delay tests until stubs are replaced by actual modules) causes us to lose some control over correspondence between specific tests and incorporation of specific modules. This can lead to difficulty in determining the cause of errors and tends to violate the highly constrained nature of the top-down approach. The second approach is workable but can lead to significant overhead, as stubs become more and more complex. The third approach, called *bottom-up testing,* sometimes offers an appealing alternative.

Bottom-up integration testing, as its name implies, begins construction and testing with "worker" modules (i.e., modules at the lowest levels in the program structure). Because modules are integrated from the bottom up, processing required for modules subordinate to a given level is always available and the need for stubs is eliminated.

A bottom-up integration strategy may be implemented with the following steps:

1. Low-level modules are combined into *clusters* (sometimes called *builds*) that perform a specific software subfunction.
2. A *driver* (a control program for testing) is written to coordinate test case input and output.
3. The cluster is tested.
4. Drivers are removed and clusters are combined, moving upward in the program structure.

Integration follows the pattern illustrated in Figure 6.2. Modules are combined to form clusters 1, 2, and 3. Each of the clusters is tested using a driver (shown as a dashed block). Modules in clusters 1 and 2 are subordinate to M_a. Drivers D_1 and D_2 are removed and the clusters are interfaced directly to M_a. Similarly, driver D_3 for cluster 3 is removed prior to integration with module M_b. Both M_a and M_b will ultimately be integrated with module M_c, and so forth.

As integration moves upward, the need for separate test drivers lessens. In fact, if the top two levels of program structure are integrated top down, the number of drivers can be reduced substantially and integration of clusters is greatly simplified.

There has been much discussion of the relative advantages and disadvantages of top-down versus bottom-up integration testing. The major disadvantage of the top-down approach is the need for stubs and the attendant testing difficulties that can be associated with them. Problems associated with stubs may be offset by the advantage of testing major control functions early. The major disadvantage of bottom-up integration is that top-level control modules are not tested until late in the testing process. This is tempered to some extent by easier test case design.

Selection of an integration strategy depends on software characteristics and sometimes on project schedule. In general, a combined approach (sometimes called *sandwich testing*) that uses the top-down approach for upper levels of the program structure coupled with a bottom-up approach for subordinate levels may be the best com—promise.

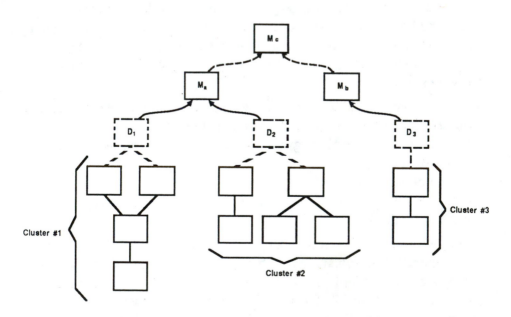

Figure 6.2   Bottom-Up Integration Strategy

Define a validation testing strategy to be
conducted prior to release.

Validation testing is a final series of tests that are designed to ensure
that software meets all requirements defined as part of the *Software
Specification.* In many cases, however, validation testing goes beyond an assessment of conformance to software requirements. Validation tests encompass procedures to verify that user manuals and other
user-oriented documentation properly reflect the correct operation of
the software and have been designed for ease of use. Also, the final
steps in validation testing may include a *configuration review* to ensure that all elements of the software have been properly documented
and archived.

Recognize and apply fundamental testing principles.

We have already noted that testing has been the weak link in the software development process. Most testing is done in an ad hoc fashion.
In fact, in many cases the people conducting tests are more interested
in "getting the product out the door" than in applying an effective quality assurance mechanism.

   If we understand the basic principles that underlie all software
testing and apply systematic test case design techniques, we can dramatically improve the effectiveness of software testing and at the same
time increase the reliability of software.

Testing Principle 1: Design test cases with the objective
of uncovering errors in the software.

The primary objective of software testing is to uncover defects that
have been inadvertently introduced into software during design and
implementation. It is often stated that software testing can show the
presence of bugs but can never show their absence. For this reason,
test cases should be designed to show the presence of bugs. As a by-
product, tests will provide us with an indication that software function
and performance have been adequately achieved and that overall software quality and reliability are adequate. However, we should not de-
lude ourselves into thinking that because a few test cases worked
properly, the software is error free. This unfortunate extrapolation has
caused many programs to be released to customers prematurely.

*Testing Principle 2: Design tests systematically;
don't rely solely on intuition.*

A number of excellent black-box and white-box test case design methods (to be discussed in this chapter) are available for the software engineer. These methods enable us to design test cases that are derived from program design characteristics.

*Testing Principle 3: Establish a testing strategy
that begins at the module level.*

All testing should first be conducted "in the small." That is, testing begins at a module level. Only after each module has been individually tested should we move on to integration testing—the process that enables us to construct the system while at the same testing the viability of the program structure.

*Testing Principle 4: Record all testing results, and save all
test cases for reapplication during software maintenance.*

The results of software testing are extremely useful during the software maintenance process, when changes to the software must be validated. A testing approach called *regression testing* is applied in the following manner:

1. A change to the software is made based on a specific attempt to correct an error, adapt the software to some change in its external environment, or provide a functional or performance enhancement.
2. Tests specific to the change are conducted to ensure that the modification associated with the change has been properly implemented.
3. Regression tests, using a subset of all test cases used prior to the release of the software, are conducted to ensure that the change has not propagated unforeseen side effects that may cause problems elsewhere in the program.

A record of the results of all tests should be maintained to assist in the evaluation of regression testing, and as part of the overall record of quality assurance for the software.

Design tests using white-box techniques.

White-box testing is a test case design method that uses the control structure of the procedural design to derive test cases. Using white-box testing methods, the software engineer can derive test cases that (1) guarantee that all statements within a module have been exercised at least once; (2) exercise all logical decisions on their true and false sides; (3) execute all loops at their boundaries and within their operational bounds; and (4) exercise internal data structures to ensure their validity.

A reasonable question might be posed at this juncture: "Why spend time and energy worrying about (and testing) logical minutiae when we might better expend effort assuring that program requirements have been met?" As Boris Beizer has stated: "Bugs lurk in corners and congregate at boundaries." White-box testing is likely to uncover them.

Derive test cases using the basis path technique.

Basis path testing is a white-box testing technique first proposed by Tom McCabe. The basis path method enables the test case designer to derive a logical complexity measure of a procedural design and use this measure as a guide for defining a *basis set* of execution paths. Test cases derived to exercise the basis set are guaranteed to execute every statement in the program at least one time during testing.

A basis set is a collection of program paths that, when taken together, will result in the execution of every program statement. To guarantee that we have defined a basis set, all paths in the set must be *independent paths,* that is, each path must introduce one new set of processing statements or one new condition that has not been introduced by other paths in the collection.

To illustrate the derivation of a basis set, consider the following PDL:

```
do while condition 1
  process 2;
  if condition 3
    then begin
      process 4;
      process 5;
    end;
    else if condition 6
      then process 6;
      then process 7;
    endif
  endif
enddo;
```

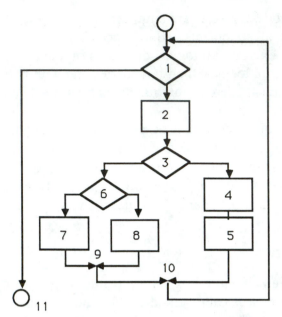

Figure 6.3 Flow Chart Corresponding to PDL

The PDL may be represented as a flow chart shown in Figure 6.3. Note that we have identified additional locations 9, 10, and 11 on the flow chart to help represent logical flow in the discussion that follows. Each decision diamond of the flow chart corresponds to a *simple logical test* (a logical test containing only one logical operator) represented by conditions 1, 3, and 6 in the PDL.

When stated in terms of a flow chart, an independent path must move along at least one arrow (control flow) that has not been traversed before the path is defined. For example, a set of independent paths for the flow chart illustrated in Figure 6.3 is:

Path 1: 1-11
Path 2: 1-2-3-4-5-10-1-11
Path 3: 1-2-3-6-8-9-10-1-11
Path 4: 1-2-3-6-7-9-10-1-11

Note that each new path introduces a new flow arrow. The path 1-2-3-4-5-10-1-2-3-6-8-9-10-1-11 is not considered to be an independent path because it is simply a combination of already specified paths and does not traverse any new arrows (program statements).

Paths 1, 2, 3, and 4 defined above comprise a basis set for the flow chart in Figure 6.3. That is, if tests can be designed to force execution of these paths (a basis set), every statement in the program will have been guaranteed to be executed at least one time. Stated differently, every condition will have been executed on its true and false side. It should be noted that the basis set is not unique. In fact any number of different basis sets can be derived for a given procedural design.

How do we know how many paths to look for? The computation of *cyclomatic complexity*—a formal measure for a module's logical complexity—provides the answer. When used in the context of the basis path testing method, the value computed for cyclomatic complexity defines the number of *independent paths* in the *basis set* of a program and provides us with an upper bound for the number of tests that must be conducted to ensure that all statements have been executed at least once.

If a flow chart is used to describe a procedural design, cyclomatic complexity can be computed easily if each decision diamond contains a simple condition—that is, a condition that contains only one logical comparision. For example, $(a < b)$ is a simple condition but $(a<b$ **or** $c<d)$ is a compound decision and must be reduced to two simple tests. If only simple conditions are represented, cyclomatic complexity for a procedure G, represented as $V(G)$, can be computed with one of three simple algorithms: (1) by counting the number of areas enclosed by control flow arrows of a flow chart and adding 1; (2) by using the relationship:

$$V(G) = P + 1$$

where P is the number of simple logical tests (decision diamonds) for the procedure G, or (3) for PDL design representations, by counting the number of simple conditions and adding 1.[*]

Referring once more to the PDL and corresponding flow chart in Figure 6.3, we see that the cyclomatic complexity can be computed using each of the algorithms noted above:

1. The flow chart encloses three areas, bounded by the loop from location 10 to condition 1, the condition 3 if-then-else, and the condition

___

[*] In actuality, it is not really necessary to draw flow charts to compute cyclomatic complexity. An assessment of PDL or programming language source code and the application of the third algorithm will do the trick. However, the flow chart provides us with a "picture" of the module's processing logic. Some people find this easier to use when test cases are being designed.

6 if-then-else. Hence, the cyclomatic complexity is 4.

2. $V(G) = 3$ decision diamonds + 1 = 4.

3. There are three simple logical tests (conditions 1, 3 and 6). Therefore, cyclomatic complexity is:

$$\text{(number of simple logical tests)} + 1 = 4.$$

The value for $V(G)$ provides us with an upper bound for the number of independent paths that comprise the basis set and, by implication, an upper bound on the number of tests that must be designed and executed to guarantee coverage of all program statements.

The basis path testing method can be applied to a detailed procedural design or to source code. To illustrate the steps of the basis path method, we use the procedure described in the PDL that follows:

```
PROCEDURE average (input: value, maximum, minimum;
           output: average, totalinput, totalvalid;)
{Purpose:
This procedure computes the average of 100 or fewer
numbers input as an array and terminated by eof (a
constant indicating end of file). Only those numbers
that lie within bounding values, minimum and maximum,
are considered in the computation of the average. The
procedure also determines the total number of input
values and the number of valid inputs, i.e., input
values that lie between minimum and maximum.
}
type value: real array [1:100];
type average, totalinput, totalvalid,
     maximum, minimum, sum: real;
type counter: integer;
counter := 1;
totalinput := totalvalid := sum := 0;
do while value[counter] <> eof and totalinput < 100
    increment totalinput by 1;
    if value[counter] ≥ minimum and
       value[counter] ≤ maximum
       then begin
          increment totalvalid by 1;
          sum := sum + value[counter];
          end;
       else skip
    endif
    increment counter by 1;
enddo;
```

```
totalinput := counter - 1;
if totalvalid > 0
     then   average := sum / totalvalid;
     else   average := "null";
endif
end average.
```

Note that **average**, although an extremely simple algorithm, contains compound conditions and loops.

Draw a flow chart, using the design or code as a guide.

Although the creation of a flow chart is not absolutely essential, it will assist us in computing the cyclomatic complexity, and more important, provide a graphical means for assessing each path to be tested. Referring to the PDL for **average**, a flow chart is created by first numbering those PDL statements that will be mapped into corresponding flow chart symbols. The numbering scheme (shown below) identifies conditional logic and processing statements within the PDL:

```
1: counter  := 1;
1:   totalinput := totalvalid := sum := 0;
2:   do while value[counter] <> eof and
3:               totalinput < 100
4:       increment totalinput by 1;
5:       if value[counter] ≥ minimum and
6:       value[counter] ≤ maximum
7:          then begin
7:              increment totalvalid by 1;
7:              sum := sum + value[counter];
7:              end;
8:          else skip
8:       endif
8:       increment counter by 1;
9:   enddo;
10:  totalinput := counter - 1;
10:  if totalvalid > 0
11:      then   average := sum / totalvalid;
12:      else   average := "null";
13:  endif
```

It is important to note that each simple logical condition is assigned its own number when compound logical statements are encountered. For example, number 2 refers to the condition

```
value[counter] <> eof
```

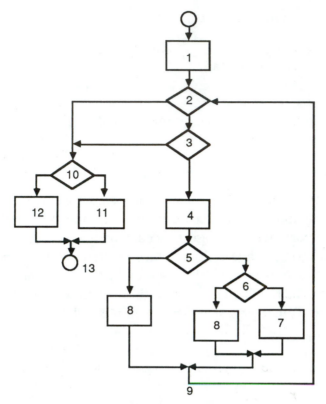

Figure 6.4 Flow Chart for **Average** Procedure

and number 3 refers to

$$totalinput < 100$$

The flow chart that corresponds to the PDL for **average** is shown in Figure 6.4.

Determine the cyclomatic complexity of the resultant flow chart.

The cyclomatic complexity, $V(G)$, is determined by applying the simple algorithms described earlier. It should be noted that $V(G)$ can be determined without developing a flow chart by counting all conditional statements in the PDL (for the procedure **average**, compound conditions count as 2).

From Figure 6.4:

$$V(G) = 5 \text{ enclosed areas} + 1 = 6$$

$$V(G) = 5 \text{ decisions} + 1 = 6$$

We shall see that the number derived for $V(G)$ provides an upper bound for the number of test cases that must be executed to ensure statement coverage.

Determine a basis set of linearly independent paths.

The value of $V(G)$ provides us with the number of linearly independent paths through the program control structure. In the case of procedure **average**, we expect to specify six paths:

    Path 1: 1-2-10-11-13
    Path 2: 1-2-10-12-13
    Path 3: 1-2-3-10-11-13
    Path 4: 1-2-3-4-5-8-9-2-...
    Path 5: 1-2-3-4-5-6-8-9-2-...
    Path 6: 1-2-3-4-5-6-7-8-9-2-...

The ellipsis (...) following paths 4, 5, and 6 indicates that any path through the remainder of the program logic is acceptable. It is often worthwhile to identify decision points as an aid in the derivation of test cases. In this case, 2, 3, 5, 6, and 10 are decision points.

Prepare test cases that will force execution
of each path in the basis set.

Data should be chosen so that conditions at the decision points are appropriately set as each path is tested. Test cases that satisfy the basis set described above are:

Path 1 Test Case:
    value(k) = valid input, where k = i − 1 for i defined below
    value(i) = eof where $2 \leq i < 100$
Expected results: correct average based on k values and proper totals
Note: cannot be tested stand-alone; must be tested as part of path 4, 5, and 6 tests.

Path 2 Test Case:
    value(1) = eof
Expected results: average = "null"; other totals at initial values

Path 3 Test Case:
    attempt to process 101 or more values
    first 100 values should be valid
Expected results: same as test case 1

Path 4 Test Case:
   value(i) = valid input where $2 \leq i < 100$
   value(k) < minimum where $k \leq i$
Expected results: correct average based on $i-1$ values and proper totals

Path 5 Test Case:
   value(i) = valid input where $2 \leq i < 100$
   value(k) > maximum where $k \leq i$
Expected results: correct average based on $i-1$ values and proper totals

Path 6 Test Case:
   value(i) = valid input where $i < 100$
Expected results: correct average based on i values and proper totals

Each test case is executed and compared to expected results. Once all test cases have been completed, the software engineer can be sure that all statements in the program have been executed at least once.

It is important to note that some independent paths (e.g., path 1 in our example) cannot be tested in stand-alone fashion. That is, the combination of data required to traverse the path cannot be achieved in the normal flow of the program. In such cases, these paths are tested as part of another path test.

Basis path methods work well for the design of test cases for small programs (less than 100 lines of source code) and for selective testing of specific program modules. However, it is often impractical to apply the basis path testing method to all modules in a large program. In most cases, we reserve the basis path approach for modules that have high values of cyclomatic complexity [in general, $V(G) > 7$]. In addition, the manual application of basis path methods can be tedious (and itself error prone) for large programs. A number of automated software tools have been developed to assist in deriving test cases using the basis path method.

Use loop testing techniques to uncover errors in loops.

Loops are the cornerstone for the vast majority of all algorithms implemented in software. And yet, we often pay them little heed while conducting software testing.

Loop testing is a white-box testing technique that focuses exclusively on the validity of loop constructs. Four classes of loops can be defined: *simple loops, concatenated loops, nested loops,* and *unstructured loops* (Figure 6.5).

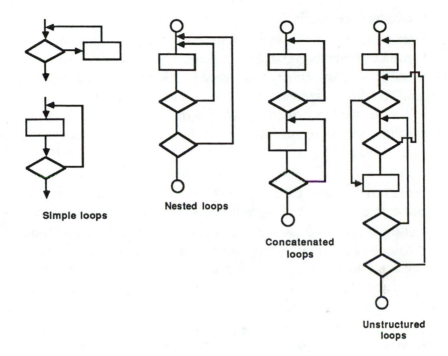

Figure 6.5 Types of Loops

Basis path analysis will isolate all independent paths within a loop. However, a special set of additional tests can be recommended for each loop type. These tests are intended to uncover initialization errors, indexing or incrementing errors, and bounding errors that occur at loop limits.

Simple Loops. The following set of tests should be applied to simple loops, where n is the maximum number of allowable passes through the loop.

1. Skip the loop entirely.
2. Only one pass through the loop.
3. Two passes through the loop.
4. m passes through the loop, where $m < n$.
5. $n-1$, n, $n+1$ passes through the loop.

Nested Loops. If we were to extend the test approach for simple loops to nested loops, the number of possible tests would grow geometrically as the level of nesting increases. This would result in an impractical number of tests. Beizer[*] suggests an approach that will

---

[*] Beizer, B., *Software Testing Techniques,* Van Nostrand-Reinhold, 1983.

help to reduce the number of tests:

1. Start at the innermost loop. Set all other loops to minimum values.

2. Conduct simple loop tests for the innermost loop while holding the outer loops at their minimum iteration parameter (e.g., loop counter) values. Add other tests for out-of-range or excluded values.

3. Work outward, conducting tests for the next loop but keeping all other outer loops at minimum values and other nested loops to "typical" values.

4. Continue until all loops have been tested.

Concatenated Loops. Concatenated loops can be tested using the approach defined above for simple loops, if each of the loops is independent of the other. Two loops are independent if processing of the first loop will have no direct affect on the processing of the second loop. If, however, the loops are not independent (e.g., the loop counter for loop 1 is used as the initial value for loop 2), the testing approach applied to nested loops is recommended.

Unstructured Loops. Whenever possible, this class of loops should be redesigned to reflect the use of the structured programming constructs (Chapter 4).

To illustrate the use of loop testing, we consider a procedure for performing a quicksort.*

```
procedure Quicksort (start, finish: integer; var Data:
TheArrayType));
{
This module recursively sorts an array named Data using
a Quicksort algorithm.The array is bounded by values
Start and Finish.
}
var  StarterValue; left, right, temp: integer;
begin {procedure Quicksort}
    left := start;
    right := finish;
    StarterValue := Data [(start+finish) div 2];
    repeat
    while Data[left]<StarterValue do
      left := left + 1;   {find a bigger value on the left}
    while StarterValue < Data[right] do
      right := right - 1;   {find a smaller value on the right}
```

---

* A *quicksort*, sometimes called a *partition exchange sort*, is one of the better algorithms for sorting items in a list.

```
   if left <= right then begin   {if we haven't gone too far}
      temp := Data [left];        {switch them }
      Data[left]  := Data[right];
      Data[right] := temp;
      left  := left + 1;
      right := right - 1;
   end;
  until right <= left;
  if start<right then Quicksort (start, right, Data);
  if left<finish then Quicksort (left, finish Data)
end;
```

The **Quicksort** procedure contains three loops. Two small *while-do* loops are nested within a larger *repeat-until* loop. Following the procedure for nested loops, we start with one of the innermost loops (in this case either of the *while-do* loops will suffice). Arbitrarily, the loop

```
while Data[left] < StarterValue do
   left := left + 1;
```

is chosen. For the first set of test cases, outer loop values should be set at minimum (or initial) values. Therefore, `start` and `finish` should be initial values (assuming a test array, `Data`, containing 10 values, `start` and `finish` will be 1 and 10, respectively. Then, applying the tests for simple loops:

Test Case 1. Skip the loop entirely.

   Data [1] $\geq$ StarterValue

Expected results: left = start upon loop exit

Test Case 2. One pass through the loop.

   Data [1] < StarterValue; Data [2] $\geq$ StarterValue

Expected results: left = Start +1 upon loop exit

Test Case 3. Two passes through the loop.

   Data [i] < StarterValue, where i $\leq$ 2

   Data [k] $\geq$ StarterValue, where k > 2

Expected results: left = start + k - 1 upon loop exit

Test Case 4. A general *m* passes test. For example:

   Data[1..10] = 2, 1, 3, 7, 5, 4, 3, 8, 9, 6 where StarterValue = 5

Expected results: left = start + 4

Test Cases 5, 6. Upper-bound tests.

   Data[p-1] $\geq$ StarterValue and Data[p] $\geq$ StarterValue,

   where p = number of array elements including StarterValue

Expected results:
    left = start + p-1; test case 5.
    left = start + p; test case 6.

The test data for each of the above test cases are controlled through the contents of the input array, Data. Data contains the numbers to be sorted. For testing purposes, an array size no larger than 10 is recommended. A similar set of tests would be conducted on the other *while-do* loop.

The next set of test cases to be designed would be for the outer repeat-until loop. The values for right and left would be adjusted to satisfy the five tests defined for simple loops.

At this point you're probably saying to yourself, "Wow, I don't conduct even close to the number of tests noted here. And besides, who would have the time?"

To test software completely, a software engineer must be willing to spend more time than has been spent on testing in the past. Of course, not every path or loop test is necessary in every situation. In some cases, it is not practical to force the data to traverse certain paths or loops. In others, combinations of tests can serve dual purposes. In still others, some tests just aren't necessary in the context of the problem. But test we must, and the more thorough the test case design, the higher the quality of software delivered to the customer.

Design test cases using black-box techniques.

Black-box testing methods focus on the functional requirements of the software. That is, black-box testing enables the software engineer to derive sets of input conditions that will fully exercise all functional requirements for a program. Black-box testing is not an alternative to white-box techniques. Rather, it is a complementary approach that is likely to uncover a different class of errors than white-box methods.

Black-box testing attempts to find errors in the following categories: (1) incorrect or missing functions, (2) interface errors, (3) errors in data structures or external data base access, (4) performance errors, and (5) initialization and termination errors.

Unlike white-box testing, which is performed early in the testing process, black-box testing tends to be applied during later stages of testing. Because black-box testing purposely disregards control structure, it focuses attention on the information domain. Tests are designed to answer the following questions:

- How is functional validity tested?
- What classes of input will make good test cases?
- Is the system particularly sensitive to certain input values?
- How are the boundaries of a data class isolated?
- What data rates and data volume can the system tolerate?
- What effect will specific combinations of data have on system operation?

Equivalence partitioning is a black-box testing method that divides the input domain of a program into classes of data from which test cases can be derived. Equivalence partitioning strives to define a test case that uncovers classes of errors (e.g., incorrect processing of all character data), thereby reducing the total number of test cases that must be developed.

Test case design for equivalence partitioning is based on an evaluation of *equivalence classes* for an input condition. An equivalence class represents a set of valid or invalid states for input conditions. Typically, an input condition is either a specific numeric value, a range of values, a set of related values, or a boolean condition (true or false). Equivalence classes can be defined according to the following guidelines:

1. If an input condition specifies a range, one valid and two invalid equivalence classes are defined.
2. If an input condition requires a specific value, one valid and two invalid equivalence classes are defined.
3. If an input condition specifies a member of a set, one valid and one invalid equivalence class are defined.
4. If an input condition is boolean, one valid and one invalid class are defined.

As an example, consider data maintained as part of an automated banking application. The user can "dial" the bank using his or her microcomputer, provide a six-digit password, and follow with a series of keyword commands that trigger various banking functions. The software supplied for the banking application accepts data in the form:

area code—blank or three-digit number
prefix—three-digit number not beginning with 0 or 1
suffix—four-digit number
password—six-digit alphanumeric value
commands—"check," "deposit," "bill pay," ...

The input conditions associated with each data element for the banking application can be specified as:

area code: input condition, boolean—the area code may or may not be present; input condition, range—values defined between 201 and 909, with specific constraints (e.g., all area codes have a 0 or 1 as a second digit).

prefix: input condition, range—specified value > 211 with no 0 digits.

suffix: input condition, value—four-digit length.

password: input condition, boolean—a password may or may not be present; input condition, value—six-character string.

command: input condition, set—contains keyword commands.

Applying the guidelines for the derivation of equivalence classes, test cases for each input domain data item can be developed and executed. Test cases are selected so that the largest number of attributes of an equivalence class are exercised at once.

Three generic equivalence classes are selected for the automated banking software described above:

Class 1.   Telephone number data

Class 2.   Password data

Class 3.   Command data

Telephone number data (class 1) can be further divided into three subclasses:

Class 1.1 area code input

Class 1.2 prefix input

Class 1.3 suffix input

Therefore, five sets of test cases are developed to exercise each of the equivalence classes. Following the guidelines for equivalence partitioning discussed earlier:

Test Case 1 (class 1.1)
Input: a valid area code with the valid number 555-5555
Expected result: valid number is dialed

Test Case 2 (class 1.1)
Input: an invalid area code (e.g., 256) with valid number 555-5555
Expected result: error message indicating invalid area code

Test Case 3 (class 1.1)
Input: no area code and number 555-5555
Expected result: valid number is dialed

Similar tests are designed for the **prefix** and **suffix** values.

Test Case k (class 2)
Input: valid six-digit password
Expected result: accepted password

Test Case k+1 (class 2)
Input: invalid password
Expected result: retry message

Other class 2 tests for invalid characters, etc., would be designed.

Test Case m (class 3)
Input: one example of each valid command
Expected result: proper processing corresponding to command

Test Case m+1 (class 3)
Input: invalid command
Expected result: retry message

Each of the test cases described above exercises one class of data.

For reasons that are not completely clear, more errors tend to occur at the boundaries of the input class than in the "center" of data contained within the class. It is for this reason that *boundary value analysis* (BVA) has been developed. Boundary value analysis is a test case design technique that complements equivalence partitioning. Rather than selecting any element of an equivalence class, BVA leads to the selection of test cases at the "edges" of the class. Rather than focusing solely on input conditions, BVA derives test cases from the output domain as well.

Guidelines for BVA are similar in many respects to those provided for equivalence partitioning:

1. If an input condition specifies a range bounded by values *a* and *b*, test cases that use values *a* and *b* should be designed. In addition, test cases using values just above and just below *a* and *b* should also be designed.

2. If an input condition specifies a number of values, test cases should be developed that exercise the minimum and maximum numbers. Values just above and below minimum and maximum are also tested.

3. Apply guidelines 1 and 2 to output conditions. For example, assume that a temperature vs. pressure table is required as output from an engineering analysis program. Test cases should be designed to

create an output report that produces the maximum (and minimum) allowable number of table entries.

4. If internal program data structures have prescribed boundaries (e.g., an array has a defined limit of 100 entries), be certain to design a test case to exercise the data structure at its boundary.

Most software engineers intuitively perform BVA to some degree. If they apply the guidelines noted above, boundary testing will be more complete, thereby having a higher likelihood for error detection.

As a final comment on test case design, note that black-box testing should always be defined as completely as possible. Equivalence partitioning and BVA should be used to develop as many test cases as required to thoroughly exercise all input classes for a program. Unlike white-box techniques, which are often applied selectively for large programs, black-box testing applies equally to programs of every size.

Review the software testing strategy to ensure that it is complete.

There is an inherent conflict of interest that occurs when a software engineer is responsible for testing software that he or she has developed. Because of the time and energy applied to the analysis, design, and implementation of the computer program, the software engineer tends to treat the program gingerly. That is, tests are conducted, but they may not be as rigorous as those designed by someone who has no vested interest in "showing that the program works" and delivering it on time.

To ensure that the completeness of testing is assessed objectively, a plan for software testing should be documented and reviewed, and the following questions should be answered:

1. Have major test steps been properly identified and sequenced?
2. Will tests demonstrate traceability to validation criteria/ requirements established as part of problem analysis?
3. Are major software functions demonstrated early?
4. Is a test schedule explicitly defined?
5. Have test resources and tools been identified, and are they available?
6. Has a test record-keeping mechanism been established?
7. Have test drivers and stubs been identified and has work to develop them been scheduled?

8. Have both white- and black-box tests been specified?
9. Have all independent logic paths been tested?
10. Are all test cases identified and listed with expected results?
11. Is error handling to be tested?
12. Are boundary values to be tested?
13. Are timing and performance to be tested?

In some large software organizations, an *independent test group* (ITG) is created to perform the final stages of software testing. As its name implies, the ITG is composed of people other than those on the software engineering team. Its main objective is to "break" the software—that is, to uncover defects prior to release. Because the ITG is charged with finding errors, it does not have the "conflict of interest" that sometimes haunts software engineers who must test their own programs.

Recognize that debugging occurs as a consequence of software testing.

Throughout this chapter, we have seen that software testing is a process that can be systematically planned and specified. A strategy can be defined, test case design can be conducted, and results can be evaluated against prescribed expectations.

Debugging occurs as a consequence of successful testing. That is, when a test case uncovers an error, debugging is the process that results in the removal of the error. Although debugging can and should be an orderly process, it is still very much an art. A software engineer evaluating the results of a test is often confronted with a *symptomatic* indication of a software problem. That is, the external manifestation of the error and the internal cause of the error may have no obvious relationship to one another. The poorly understood mental process that connects a symptom to a cause is *debugging*.

Debugging is *not* testing, but it always occurs as a consequence of testing.* Referring to Figure 6.6, we see that the debugging process begins with the execution of a test case. Results are assessed, and a lack of correspondence between expected and actual is encountered. In many cases, the noncorresponding data are a symptom of an underlying cause that is as yet hidden. The debugging process

---

* In making this statement, we take the broadest possible view of testing. Not only does the software engineer test the software prior to release, but the customer "tests" software every time a program is used!

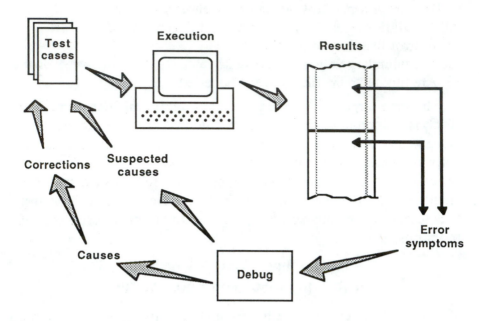

Figure 6.6 The Debugging Process

attempts to match symptom with cause, thereby leading to error correction.

Apply a set of debugging principles when an error or a symptom is encountered.

It is difficult to suggest a set of "cook book" steps for the debugging process. Often, the prompt discovery of the cause of an error is a combination of careful thought, systematic testing, and good fortune (blind luck). However, by following a simple set of debugging principles, we can improve the chances of success during this sometimes frustrating activity.

Debugging Principle 1: Evaluate the symptom carefully, and attempt to develop a reasonable hypothesis for the cause.

The debugging process will always have one of two outcomes: (1) the error (cause of the symptom) will be found, corrected, and removed, or (2) the error will not be found. In the latter case, the person performing debugging may suspect a cause, design a test case to help validate his or her suspicion, and work toward error correction in an iterative fashion.

Why is debugging so difficult? In all likelihood, human psychology has more to do with the answer than software technology. However, a few characteristics of bugs provide some clues:

1. The symptom and the cause may be geographically remote. That is, the symptom may appear in one part of a program, while the cause may actually be located at a site that is far removed. Highly coupled program structures (Chapter 4) exacerbate this situation.

2. The symptom may disappear (temporarily) when another error is corrected.

3. The symptom may actually be caused by non-errors (e.g., round-off inaccuracies).

4. The symptom may be caused by human error that is not easily traced.

5. The symptom may be a result of timing problems rather than processing problems.

6. It may be difficult to accurately reproduce input conditions (e.g., a real-time application in which input ordering is indeterminate).

7. The symptom may be intermittent. This is particularly common in embedded systems that couple hardware and software inextricably.

During debugging, we encounter errors that range from mildly annoying (e.g., an incorrect output format) to catastrophic (e.g., the system fails, causing serious economic or physical damage). As the consequences of an error increase, the amount of pressure to find the cause also increases. Often, pressure forces a software developer to fix one error and at the same time inadvertently introduce two more.

Regardless of the approach that is taken, debugging has one overriding objective: to find and correct the cause of a software error. In general, three categories for debugging approaches may be proposed: brute force, backtracking, and cause elimination.

The *brute force* category of debugging is probably the most common and least efficient method for isolating the cause of a software error. We apply brute force debugging methods when all else fails. Using a "let the computer find the error" philosophy, memory dumps are taken, run-time traces are invoked, and the program is loaded with **writeln** statements. We hope that somewhere in the morass of information that is produced we will find a clue that can lead us to the cause of an error. Although the mass of information produced may ultimately lead to success, it can also lead to wasted effort and time. Thought must be expended first.

Backtracking is a fairly common debugging approach that can be used successfully in small programs. Beginning at the site where a symptom has been uncovered, the source code is traced backward (manually) until the site of the cause is found. Unfortunately, as the number of source lines increases, the number of potential backward paths may become unmanageably large.

The third approach to debugging—*cause elimination*—is manifested by induction or deduction and introduces the concept of binary partitioning. Data related to the error occurrence are organized to isolate potential causes. A "cause hypothesis" is devised, and the above data are used to prove or disprove the hypothesis. Alternatively, a list of all possible causes is developed, and tests are conducted to eliminate each possibility. If initial tests indicate that a particular cause hypothesis shows promise, data are refined in an attempt to isolate the bug.

Debugging Principle 2: Use debugging tools when they are available.

Each of the above debugging approaches can be supplemented with debugging tools. We can apply a wide variety of debugging compilers, dynamic debugging aids ("tracers"), automatic test case generators, memory dumps, and cross reference maps. Many software development environments support dynamic debugging tools that enable a software engineer to set break points within his or her source code and then execute the program statement by statement, examining the contents of memory locations or registers. Such tools are interactive and can provide substantial insight into the cause of a bug. It is important to note, however, that tools are not a substitute for careful evaluation based on a complete software design document and clear source code.

Debugging Principle 3: Get help from a colleague if the cause remains elusive.

Any discussion of debugging approaches and tools is incomplete without mention of a powerful ally: other people! Each of us can recall puzzling for hours or days over a persistent bug. A colleague wanders by and in desperation we explain the problem and throw open the listing. Instantaneously (it seems), the cause of the error is uncovered. With a smug smile, our colleague wanders off. A fresh viewpoint, unclouded by hours of frustration, can do wonders. A final maxim for debugging might be: *"When all else fails, get help!"*

WHAT THIS MEANS TO YOU

Few things are more embarrassing than the following situation: You have spent much time and energy analyzing, designing, and implementing a computer program. You've run a few tests, and everything seems to be working properly. You bring the program to your customer and begin to demonstrate its function, and within the first minute of operation it fails!

You undoubtedly tested the software with a few test cases, but to build high quality software you have to do more. A testing strategy that combines test case execution and program construction must be planned. Test cases should be designed using techniques that focus on processing internals and information domain externals. In essence, we have to test with a single objective in mind: to force the program to fail.

In this chapter, a number of important testing strategies and test case design techniques have been presented. If you follow each of the steps described, and take testing as seriously as you take analysis, design, and implementation, you'll build higher quality programs. Errors will be found early. And that's a cause for rejoicing. You've uncovered defects in the software when they can do no damage—before the software is put into operation. Avoid embarrassment; test thoroughly.

FURTHER READINGS

Beizer, B., *Software Testing Techniques,* Van Nostrand-Reinhold, 1983.

Dunn, R., *Software Defect Removal,* McGraw-Hill, 1984.

Evans, M.W., *Productive Software Test Management,* Wiley, 1984.

Hetzel, W., *The Complete Guide to Software Testing,* QED, 1984.

Howden, W.E., *Functional Program Testing and Analysis,* McGraw-Hill, 1987.

Myers, G., *The Art of Software Testing,* Wiley, 1979.

McCabe, T., *Structured Testing,* IEEE Computer Society, 1982.

PROBLEMS AND POINTS TO PONDER

6.1 A formal outline for a *Software Test Plan* is not presented in this chapter because every software engineering organization tends to develop its own format. Suggest an outline that will accommodate the testing activities suggested by the steps in this chapter.

6.2 Write a set of guidelines for conducting module testing. The guidelines should contain a detailed checklist to help ensure that thorough testing at the module level has been conducted.

6.3 Discuss the advantages of top-down and bottom-up testing in your own words. Are there cases where a breadth-first approach might be better than a depth-first strategy?

6.4 Develop a detailed integration strategy for one or more of the programs that you designed for problem 4.7. Be sure to describe the order of integration, naming specific modules, the tests that you will conduct, and expected results.

6.5 When are you sure that you're finished testing?

6.6 Attempt to categorize the different types of stubs and drivers that you will have to develop during integration testing. For example, some stubs merely return when invoked, others print a message, others ... .

6.7 Regression testing has been mentioned in a number of places in this chapter. Describe what is meant by the term. Develop a set of guidelines for conducting regression tests during integration testing.

6.8 The following specification (adapted from Myers, G., *The Art of Software Testing*, Wiley-Interscience, 1979) has been written for a simple program:

A program called TRIANGLE accepts three integer numbers, A, B, and C, as input. The numbers represent the side dimensions of a triangle and are assumed to be connected end to end (when possible) and are coplanar. TRIANGLE assesses A, B, and C and determines whether or not these dimensions form a triangle and what type of triangle it is. The program produces the following output:

    E, the triangle is equilateral
    I, the triangle is isosceles
    S, the triangle is scalene
    N, no triangle exists
    X, the input data are in error

The program assumes (and does not have to test for) numeric input whose individual values will not cause arithmetic overflow.

Develop a detailed procedural design for TRIANGLE and then implement the program in the programming language of your choice. Then, using basis path testing methods, derive the cyclomatic complexity, the basis set of independent paths, and a series of test cases for the program. Execute these test cases. Are there other tests that should be conducted? Describe and execute them. Note any errors that you uncover.

6.9 Develop requirements for a software tool that will compute cyclomatic complexity for a Pascal or C program. Design and implement the tool. Use the testing techniques described in this chapter to derive a set of test cases to thoroughly test the tool.

6.10 The simplest of all sorting algorithms is the bubble sort. Develop a procedural design for this sort (your instructor will describe the bubble sort for you if you haven't encountered it before) and perform both basis path and loop testing to design test cases. Implement the sort in Pascal or C and execute your tests. Note any errors that you uncover.

6.11 Apply equivalence partitioning and boundary value analysis to derive test cases for one or more of the programs that were designed for problem 4.7.

6.12 Apply equivalence partitioning and boundary value analysis to derive test cases for the triangle program described in problem 6.8.

6.13 Use the debugging techniques described in this chapter to diagnose and correct any errors uncovered as a result of testing for problems 6.8 through 6.12.

CHAPTER 7

MAKING CHANGES

Change is a fact of life for software developers. Change occurs at the inception of a software project, when a customer refines basic objectives and overall software requirements prior to agreement on a software specification. Changes occur throughout the development phase because of the customer's continuing refinement of project requirements and the developer's continuing modification of design and implementation approach. Changes occur as a consequence of testing, when errors uncovered in the software are corrected by making modifications to both the design and programming language source code.

The size of a program, its complexity, and its area of application all contribute to its propensity to change. Yet all programs—big and small—undergo modification while they are being developed and after they are in the hands of users. These "after delivery" changes—often called *software maintenance*—can be attributed to errors encountered by users, adaptations made to enable the software to accommodate changes to its external environment (e.g., new operating systems, computers, peripheral devices), or enhancements requested by old and new customers and users alike.

Because change is inevitable, we must conduct the software engineering process with the expectation that modifications to the software will occur. But, how do we accommodate change? Isn't it possible to "get it right the first time" so that changes will be nonexistent? Sadly, the only reasonable answer to the second question is "no." The remainder of this chapter is dedicated to the principles and steps required to answer the first question.

Understand and apply a set of basic principles for making modifications.

Although there is no way that we can eliminate change during the software engineering process, there is a set of basic principles that enable us to conduct change in a systematic fashion and develop software that is amenable to change. These principles are described in the steps that follow.

Modification Principle 1: Get the customer involved at the earliest possible time.

Most changes occur because the customer changes his or her mind. Therefore, it behooves us to get the customer involved early, when changes in software requirements are relatively easy to accommodate and little effort will be wasted.

We can get the customer involved in two ways. First, the customer and the software engineer should spend substantial time together during early consultative sessions prior to the development of a *Software Specification*. It is the customer who should assist in the development of a statement of scope for the entire computer-based system and for the software in particular. Second, the customer should review the *Software Specification* (in whatever form it takes) in detail and be required to "sign off" to indicate that the specification properly reflects the goals and requirements for the software.

Experienced software engineering veterans recognize that neither of these suggestions is a guarantee that changes will be reduced substantially. However, because the customer is the primary catalyst for change, it is better to "get changes out of the way early" than to wait until late in the project, when every change that is requested can create chaos.

Modification Principle 2: Be sure that the Software Specification contains a bounded statement of scope for software.

Changes are often required because of ambiguity in the perceived requirements for software. When the statement of scope is bounded, the degree of ambiguity is inherently reduced. Bounding implies that the description of the software is characterized in a manner that is measurable; that is, the description can be assessed in some objective, rather than subjective, manner. For example, the following statement of scope appears reasonable at first glance:

The interactive order entry software will accommodate multiple users in a networked environment. System response for any user must be rapid and the overall interface design must be human friendly.

Although this statement of scope appears innocuous, it is dangerously unbounded. How many users will the system accommodate? What kind of network will the system be implemented on? What is a "rapid" response? What does "human friendly" mean? To develop a bounded scope, we must answer each of these questions so that the software that is implemented can be measured in an objective way for its compliance with scope. If we were to leave the scope as stated above, substantial ambiguity would exist . It is more than likely that many changes would occur as the customer and the developer struggle to understand the meaning of each unbounded phrase.

Modification Principle 3: Be sure that the architectural design exhibits good functional independence.

The concept of functional independence, as characterized by *coupling* and *cohesion,* was discussed in Chapter 4. When the modules in a software architecture are decoupled from one another internally and decoupled from the external environment, changes that occur due to the external environment can be more easily accommodated. Consider the following examples:

1. A program reads information from a data base through a single access module. Because access to the data base is limited (the program is decoupled), the software will require far fewer changes when the data base structure is modified. If, on the other hand, access to the

data base occurs in 10 or 20 modules, the amount of modification would be increased substantially when the data base structure changes.

2. A program produces sophisticated computer graphics output using the Acme X-100 display device. Calls to Acme interface software occur throughout the program. The march of technology eventually causes the Acme X-100 to become obsolete, and a new Turbo Z-1000 is purchased to replace it. Unfortunately, the Turbo has entirely different software, requiring major modifications in every program module that originally used the X-100 software. The program was heavily coupled to an external device, resulting in many changes when the device is switched.

3. An inexperienced software engineer designs a program module that (1) performs simple interactive input, (2) does a data base look-up based on the input, (3) performs a statistical analysis, and (4) produces a graph that provides the results of the analysis. All of this work is accomplished in less than 150 lines of Pascal. When a change in the interactive dialogue is requested, the software engineer's modification causes side effects that create problems in the part of the module that produces the graph. This leads to other changes that result in further side effects, which lead to additional changes, *ad nauseum*. The inexperienced software engineer has fallen prey to creating a design that has poor cohesion—that is, the module performs too many functions.

Each of these examples illustrates the negative effects of poor functional independence. The moral: there is much we can do during design to make changes easier during maintenance.

Modification Principle 4: Design a program structure that exhibits a factored hierarchy.

The concept of *factoring*—the top-down distribution of control and work in a modular program structure—was first introduced in Chapter 4. In a factored program structure, "worker" modules reside at the lowest levels of the module hierarchy. If we consider the reasons that programs are likely to change, we inevitably encounter one of three situations:

1. The customer decides that the input approach "just doesn't hack it" and requests that more (fewer) pull-down menus be used, command strings be shortened (lengthened), data be validated when they were

previously accepted as raw input, a mouse be used instead of cursor control keys, ... The list is almost endless.

2. The developer or customer decides that the computational approach currently being used is inefficient, inaccurate, inappropriate, etc. A new algorithm is suggested.

3. The customer requests additional or different or abbreviated output that requires the use of computer graphics when only alphanumeric output was produced, color displays when monochrome used to be sufficient, etc.

Each of these situations is likely to cause changes in "worker" modules—modules that accept input, perform computations or produce output. In a factored architecture, these modules exist low in the program structure, where they can be easily replaced without propagating side effects throughout the entire program. Changes that result in major modifications to overall program control (effected by top-level modules in the program structure) are less likely to occur. For these reasons, a factored structure is easier (and less error prone) to change.

Modification Principle 5: Perform data design with the objective of deriving simple, stable data structures.

When we think about making changes to software, we often limit our concern to the procedural elements of computer programs. That is, we tend to rush to programming language source code and modify a *do-while* or an *if-then-else*. In reality, it is just as likely that a change in requirements will demand modification to a program's data structure. For this reason, the initial data design will have a strong influence on the ease with which changes are made.

Some of the most difficult and expensive modifications to software can occur because of a relatively simple change in a data structure. For example, recent attempts by the U.S. Post Office to extend five-digit zip codes to a nine-digit format (e.g., 06477-0287) require extensive modification in many programs whose data structures cannot be easily expanded to accommodate the additional four digits. The corresponding changes will cost many companies millions of dollars to make.

The underlying concepts of data design were discussed in Chapter 4. The following guidelines are particularly appropriate when considering the ease of modification of data structures:

1. *Use the simplest data structure for the job.* The more complex the data structure the more difficult it is to modify without error. For this reason, we should design simple data structures, recognizing that we often trade complexity in processing algorithms against simplicity in data structures and vice versa. The moral: don't use a linked list with multiple pointers when two scalar values will do the trick!

2. *Design data structures that can be implemented easily in the target programming language.* If a data structure is designed that cannot be directly implemented in a programming language (e.g., a linked list in FORTRAN), the resultant code (required to implement the linked list) will be complex and difficult to modify. A better alternative is to select a programming language that supports data structures that are appropriate for your work.

3. *Keep file structures stable by reducing redundant occurrences of data items.* When the same data item appears in many places throughout a data base, modification of that item may cause instability (and inconsistency) if all occurrences are not found and modified. The *normalization* technique discussed in Chapter 4 helps us to eliminate redundancy.

Modification Principle 6: Develop design documentation that accurately describes the "as built" program, and keep it up to date as changes are made.

Regardless of the programming language that is used, source code describes software at a relatively low level of abstraction. When significant changes are required, a software engineer should first assess the software architecture (program and data structure), design constraints, and system interfaces. Without careful assessment of these high-level characteristics, it is possible for small code changes to propagate serious (and sometimes fatal) side effects that cause major software errors. If only code exists, the assessment of high-level software characteristics is very difficult.

The *Design Document* provides excellent guidance for making changes—but only if it accurately reflects the "as built" program. Too often, changes are made to program source code and are never reflected in design documentation. After a time, the program and its documentation have only a vague relationship to one another. This situation should be avoided at all cost.

It should be noted, however, that keeping design documentation up to date is easier said than done. The design document sits in a different file (or worse, a file cabinet!) than the source code, which is easily accessible on a software engineer's computer terminal. Unless important elements of the design are "connected" to the source code, keeping both current will be difficult.

Some software developers solve this problem by embedding design information directly into a source code file. With modern laser printers and high-resolution display devices, both text (e.g., PDL) and graphics (e.g., structure charts) can be combined with source code output and produced for review by the person responsible for making a change. If all information is readily available to the software engineer, it is far more likely that modifications will be made to both design and source code.

Modification Principle 7:   Use regression tests to validate each change.

If software engineering principles have been applied to the development of a program, a software testing strategy and procedure have been defined and documented, test cases have been designed, and a suite of tests have been conducted and recorded. Whenever a change is made, new tests should be designed to uncover any errors associated with the change, and a subset of all original tests should be reexecuted in an attempt to uncover possible errors introduced by side effects associated with the change. This approach, called *regression testing,* is an important quality assurance mechanism.

Modification Principle 8:   Assess the impact of a change   before it is made.

A seemingly innocuous change can sometimes be fatal to the operation of a large computer-based system. Each of us has heard the lament: "But all I did was change this one statement!" A simple change sometimes sets off a chain of events that propagates side effects throughout the program. Special vigilance is required when changes are made under the following circumstances:

1. The program structure is highly coupled or the module undergoing change does not exhibit high cohesion.
2. A data structure used throughout the program is changed.

3. A new data item is added to an existing file or data base.

4. A module that serves as the interface to the external environment must be changed.

In each of these situations, side effects are likely.

A set of procedures called *software configuration management* (SCM) is often established for large software projects. When SCM is conducted, each change to the software is reviewed by an independent *change control board* (CCB). The CCB reviews the request for a change, evaluates its potential impact on the system, and then decides whether or not the change should be made. In addition, SCM activities include identification and recording of all changes.

For smaller software projects, a formal SCM procedure introduces unnecessary "red tape." However, the underlying objectives of SCM—to assess the impact of change and control the way in which changes are made—should be applied regardless of a program's size.

A software engineer should assess each change by asking: Is this change really necessary? What will happen if the change isn't made? Are there different ways in which the change can be accomplished? Which has the lowest risk? What other modules are affected by the change? What potential problems could be caused if the change isn't made correctly?

Modification Principle 9: When a major change is to be made, apply software engineering recursively.

A major change to the software element of a computer-based system can be viewed as an independent software engineering project that just happens to have an interface that is more complicated than normal. The interface, of course, comprises all the "connections" to the existing program.

Recalling data flow diagrams (DFDs) introduced in Chapter 3, we can represent the overall flow of an existing program as shown in Figure 7.1. When a change to some portion of the program is requested, the *domain of change* can be isolated on the DFD. In many cases (but not all), once the domain of change is isolated (Figure 7.2), it can be treated as a separate program that must maintain the integrity of all data (I_1, I_2, O_1, O_2, O_3) that cross its interface.

We can apply the same problem analysis, design, coding, and testing steps described earlier in this book to the domain of change—

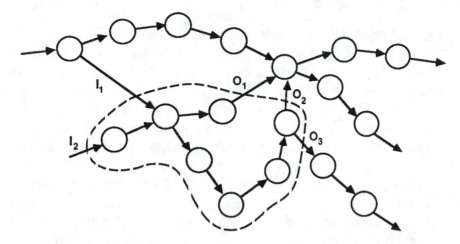

Dashed line identifies the "domain of change"

Figure 7.1   Data Flow Diagrams for Existing Systems

that is, we apply software engineering all over again. For this reason, software engineering steps are as valid during maintenance phase activities as they are during the development of a new program.

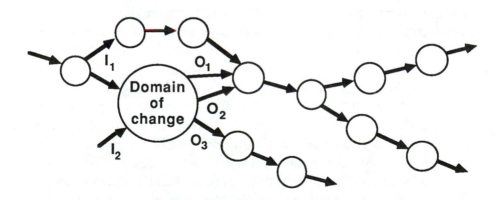

Figure 7.2   Remodel with Domain of Change Isolated

Modification Principle 10: Use formal technical reviews while developing a new program and for all major changes.

At each step in the software engineering process, we have seen that reviews are an effective quality assurance mechanism. The *formal technical review* (FTR), discussed in Appendix B, provides a software engineer with a "filter" that traps defects in the software before it is released to the customer, thereby reducing the number of changes that are required due to correction. In addition, the FTR helps us to develop consistent software, by ensuring that development standards (e.g., that each module have a prologue) have been followed.

During the maintenance phase, the FTR will help to uncover errors in the implementation of a change and errors due to side effects associated with change. In addition, review criteria at all points during the software engineering process can include an assessment of each of the modification principles noted in this chapter.

Create representations of software that are amenable to change.

The analysis, design, coding, and testing methods discussed in this book can be performed in one of two ways: work can be done using a conventional paper, pencil, and computer terminal approach, or work can be accomplished using a computer-aided software engineering (CASE) workstation.

The conventional approach can be effective, but representations of software that are created are often difficult to maintain. In the extreme, data flow diagrams have been placed in a manila folder and stored in a remote file cabinet, the *Design Document* sits in someone else's desk drawer, code is stored in an on-line library, and test data have been "archived" on a diskette. Few people would have the patience to collect all relevant software documentation when it is stored in this way. Managing large volumes of paper, coupled with substantial on-line information, can be a horrendous logistics problem.

Computer-aided software engineering (CASE) is analogous to computer-aided engineering and design (CAE/CAD) that has been applied in older engineering disciplines (e.g., electrical and mechanical engineering) over the past two decades. CASE systems enable the software engineer to create a data base that contains all representations of the software. Once this software engineering data base has been created, it is relatively easy to associate and control all documents for a given software project. Appendix C contains a comprehensive example that focuses on the development of software for a CASE system.

Establish a software maintenance procedure.

Although the technical activities associated with software maintenance can be properly characterized as software engineering, specialized organization, procedures, and controls should be established. The steps associated with software maintenance begin long before a request for maintenance is made. Initially, a maintenance organization (de facto or formal) should be established, reporting and evaluation procedures should be described, and a standardized sequence of events should be defined for each maintenance request. In addition, a record-keeping mechanism for maintenance activities should be established and review and evaluation criteria defined. The steps that follow address each of these activities.

Assign organizational responsibility for software maintenance.

Maintenance for very small one-person projects is almost always the responsibility of the software engineer who analyzed, designed, and implemented the program in the first place. But what happens when this individual is no longer around? Stated another way, how do we maintain programs whose authors are not available to perform modifications or even to answer questions? This is the challenge that is faced by every software development organization.

Although a formal maintenance organization need not be established when relatively small software projects are the norm, an informal delegation of responsibility is essential even for small software developers. One such scheme is illustrated in Figure 7.3. Maintenance requests are channeled through a *maintenance controller* who forwards each request for evaluation to a *system supervisor*. The system supervisor is a member of the technical staff who has spent time becoming familiar with a small subset of production programs. It is the system supervisor's job to assess the potential impact of the requested change and determine the best way to proceed. Once an evaluation is made, a *change control authority* (also called a *change control board*) determines whether action is to be taken.

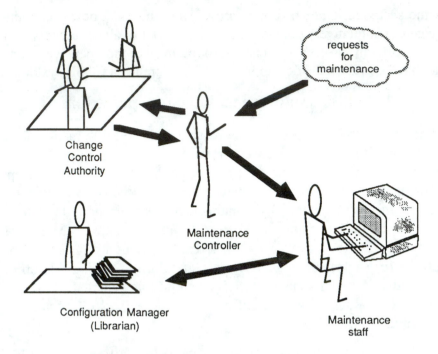

Figure 7.3 Maintenance Organization

The organization suggested above reduces confusion and improves the flow of maintenance activities. Because all maintenance requests are funneled through a single individual (or group), "back door fixes" (i.e., changes that have not been sanctioned and therefore can cause confusion) are less likely to occur. Because at least one individual will always have some familiarity with a production program, requests for changes (maintenance) can be assessed more rapidly. Because specific change control approval is implemented, an organization can avoid making changes that benefit one requester but negatively impact many other users.

Each of the above job titles serves to define an area of responsibility for maintenance. The controller and change control authority may be a single person or (for very large programs) a group of managers and senior technical staff. The system supervisor may have other duties but provides a "contact" with a specific software package.

When responsibilities are assigned prior to the start of maintenance activity, confusion is greatly reduced. More important, an early definition of responsibilities can temper any hard feelings that develop when a person is peremptorily "pulled off" a development effort to conduct maintenance.

Establish a reporting mechanism for all changes.

All requests for software maintenance should be presented in a standardized manner. The software developer normally generates a *maintenance request form* (MRF), sometimes called a *software problem report,* that is completed by the user who desires a maintenance activity. If an error is encountered, a complete description of the circumstances leading to the error (including input data, listings, and other supporting material) must be included. For maintenance that is associated with major enhancements, a brief *change specification* (an abbreviated *Software Specification*) is submitted. The maintenance request form is evaluated as described above.

The MRF is an externally generated document that is used as a basis for planning the maintenance task. Internally, the software organization may develop a *software change report* (SCR) that indicates: (1) the magnitude of effort required to satisfy an MRF, (2) the nature of modifications required, (3) the priority of the request, and (4) after-the-fact data about the modification. The SCR is used to help decide whether or not maintenance should be initiated.

Define the sequence of maintenance events and all important decision points.

The sequence of events that occur as a result of a maintenance request is outlined in the PDL that follows:

```
procedure:  software maintenance;
a maintenance request form is received;
if maintenance type is error
   then begin
   determine the severity of the error;
      if severity is high
         then fix immediately;
         else catalog for later correction;
      endif
   end;
   else begin
      if maintenance type is adaptation
         then begin
```

```
        evaluate scope of change;
        determine impact if adaptation isn't made;
        categorize level of complexity;
        estimate amount of work required;
    end;
    else begin {enhancement has been requested}
        evaluate scope of change;
        determine impact if enhancement isn't made;
        categorize level of complexity;
        estimate amount of work required;
    end;
  prioritize all changes requested;
  do while tasks remain to be done
      select maintenance task from priority queue;
      apply software engineering steps;
  enddo;
```

The first requirement is to determine the type of maintenance that is to be conducted. In many cases, a user may view a request as an indication of software error (corrective maintenance) while a developer may view the same request as adaptation or enhancement. If a difference of opinion exists, a settlement must be negotiated.

Referring to the flow indicated in the PDL, a request for corrective maintenance begins with an evaluation of error severity. If a severe error exists (e.g., a critical system cannot function), personnel are assigned under the direction of the system supervisor and problem analysis begins immediately. For less severe errors, the request for corrective maintenance is evaluated and categorized and then scheduled in conjunction with other tasks requiring software development resources. In some cases, an error may be so severe that normal controls for maintenance must be abandoned temporarily. Code must be modified immediately, without corresponding evaluation for potential side effects and appropriate updating of documentation. This *fire-fighting mode* for corrective maintenance is reserved only for "crisis" situations and should represent a very small percentage of all maintenance activities. It should be noted that fire fighting postpones, but does not eliminate, the need for controls and evaluation. After the crisis has been resolved, these activities must be conducted to ensure that present fixes will not propagate even more severe problems.

Requests for adaptive and perfective maintenance follow a different path. Adaptations are evaluated and categorized (prioritized) prior to being placed on a queue for maintenance action. Enhancements undergo the same evaluation. However, not all requests for enhancement are undertaken. Business strategy, available resources, the direction of current and future software products, and many other issues may cause a request for enhancement to be rejected. Those enhancements that are to be made are also placed on the maintenance queue. The priority of each request is established and the required work is scheduled as if it were another development effort (for all intents and purposes, it is). If extremely high priority is set, work may begin immediately.

Regardless of maintenance type, the same technical tasks are conducted. These maintenance tasks include: modification to software design, review, requisite code modification, module and integration testing (including regression tests using previous test cases), validation tests, and configuration review. The final event in the maintenance flow is a review that revalidates all elements of the software configuration and assures that a specific request for maintenance has, in fact, been fulfilled.

WHAT THIS MEANS TO YOU

Maintainable software is built by analyzing, designing, and implementing it with maintainability in mind. The principles and steps presented in this chapter describe an end game that is much easier to play if we've performed earlier steps well. During the definition and development phases of the software engineering process, we encounter a "pay now or pay much more later" situation. By spending the time and effort to design and build maintainable software, we save time and effort during the maintenance phase.

When you're a student, it's difficult to understand the importance of software maintenance work. The reason for this is simple: you do very little of it at this stage in your development as a software engineer. But rest assured that things will change. Any useful program will undergo maintenance during its lifetime. In fact, the more widely used a program is, the better its overall function, the higher its benefit to users, the more likely it is to undergo change. So if you intend to develop software that has an impact, expect to make changes to it.

By following the principles and steps presented in this chapter, you'll reduce the frustration that often accompanies maintenance tasks, and in so doing, leave yourself more time for creating new programs that challenge your skills and benefit your customers.

FURTHER READINGS

Babich, W.A., *Software Configuration Management,* Addison-Wesley, 1986.

Glass, R. and C. Noiseux, *Software Maintenance Guidebook,* Prentice-Hall, 1981.

Martin, J and C. McClure, *Software Maintenance,* Prentice-Hall, 1983.

Parikh, G., *Handbook of Software Maintenance,* Wiley, 1986.

Parikh, G. and N. Zvegintzov, *Software Maintenance,* IEEE Computer Society Press, 1983.

PROBLEMS AND POINTS TO PONDER

7.1 Your instructor will select one of the programs that you have developed for this course. Exchange your program randomly with that of someone else in the class. Your instructor will specify an enhancement for the program. Implement it within the program obtained from your colleague.

7.2 We indicated that the customer should be involved early in the software engineering process. Should the customer have the same level of involvement throughout? Why?

7.3 Why is functional independence an importance characteristic for achieving maintainable software?

7.4 Does the choice of programming language affect the maintainability of software? Explain your answer with examples.

7.5 Software configuration management is an activity that is generally found only on very large software engineering projects. What elements of SCM are applicable to all software work?

7.6 Get literature from a CASE vendor (your instructor may be able to provide you with company names). Discuss how the vendor's CASE system will help in the maintenance phase.

7.7 Develop an outline for a maintenance request form.

7.8 Review the PDL for the maintenance process flow presented at the end of this chapter. Can you suggest additions or changes to this PDL?

APPENDIX A
SOFTWARE ENGINEERING CHECKLIST

SYSTEM ENGINEERING

Develop or acquire a statement of system scope ____
    Ask questions to understand overall system function ____
    Describe the overall system function ____
    Identify key inputs and outputs ____
    List all constraints that affect the system ____
    Write a plain language paragraph ____
Isolate top-level processes and entities ____
    Examine the statement of scope and select entities ____
    Examine the statement of scope and select processes ____
Allocate processes and entities to physical system elements ____
    Develop a criterion list for allocation and prioritize ____
    Propose at least two alternative allocations ____
    Apply criteria to assess viability of each allocation alternative ____
    Select an allocation ____
Develop a refined statement of scope for each allocated system element ____
Meet with the customer to review the allocation ____
Recognize that iteration is likely ____

ANALYZING A PROBLEM

Refine and clarify software scope ____
Identify objects and operations ____

Identify objects and operations using the statement of software scope as a guide ____

Use objects to identify information originators and receivers ____

Use objects to identify data stores ____

Use objects to identify data and control items ____

Use operations to identify data and control transformations ____

Recognize and apply three fundamental analysis principles ____

When things are uncertain, develop a prototype to help clarify requirements ____

Evaluate the software scope and determine whether the software to be developed is a good candidate for prototyping ____

Develop an abbreviated representation of requirements using an object-oriented approach ____

Create a paper prototype ____

Create an abbreviated design for the prototype ____

Create, test, and refine the prototype software ____

Present the prototype to the customer, who "test drives" the application and suggests modifications ____

Repeat prototyping steps iteratively until all requirements are formalized or until the prototype has evolved into a production system ____

Develop a flow model for the software ____

Use data flow diagrams to indicate how data move through the software ____

Use control flow diagrams to indicate how control influences the software ____

Apply flow model assessment rules ____

Develop a data dictionary to represent object content ____

Write processing narratives for both data and control transforms ____

Begin thinking about software validation ____

Put it all together to form a *Software Specification* ____

Review the specification for correctness, consistency, and completeness ____

Expect to iterate; avoid the temptation to rush into design or coding ____

DESIGNING THE SOLUTION

Refine the *Software Specification* in preparation for design ____

Recognize and apply fundamental design concepts ____

Begin data design by extending work done during problem analysis ____

Review the data dictionary, and select candidate data structures ____

If complex data structures are to be created, simplify their organization ____

Select appropriate internal data structures ____

If a data base management system is appropriate, acquire one! ____

Derive the architectural design ____

Refine the flow model in preparation for design ____

Determine whether the flow model has transform or transaction characteristics ____

Derive program structure using transform mapping when transform flow is present ____

> Isolate the transform center by specifying incoming and outgoing flow boundaries ____
> Perform "first-level factoring" ____
> Perform second-level factoring to derive a preliminary program structure ____
> Refine processing narratives for each module in the program structure ____
> Refine the "first-cut" program structure using fundamental design concepts ____

Derive program structure using transaction mapping when transaction flow is present ____

> Identify the transaction center and the flow characteristics of each action path ____
> Map the DFD into a program structure amenable to transaction processing ____
> Factor and refine the transaction structure and the structure of each action path ____

Derive a procedural design for each module depicted in the program structure ____

> Apply the structured programming philosophy when deriving the procedural design ____
> Refine the processing narratives for each module ____
> Use program design language (PDL) to represent data structures and procedural logic ____

Develop a preliminary test strategy to accommodate the data and program structure ____

Put it all together to create a *Design Document* ____

Review the design document for conformance to software requirements and technical quality ____

PROGRAMMING THE SOLUTION

Use the design document as a guide ____

Use the program structure to determine the order in which modules will be coded ____

> Begin coding modules that reside at low levels in the program structure ____
> Develop code for global data structures ____
> Examine internal data structures and determine how they can be implemented using programming language constructs ____
> Define all data files using programming language conventions ____

Generate programming language source code using the procedural design as a guide ____

Learn the elements of good coding style and apply them ____

Review the resultant code for correctness and readability ____

TESTING THE RESULT

Develop a test plan that describes both strategy and specifics ____
    Define an approach for testing each module in the program structure ____
    Develop an integration strategy for constructing the program structure ____
    Integrate modules using both top-down and bottom-up testing ____
    Define a validation testing strategy to be conducted prior to release ____
Recognize and apply fundamental testing principles ____
Design tests using white-box techniques ____
    Derive test cases using the basis path technique ____
    Draw a flow chart using the design or code as a guide ____
    Determine the cyclomatic complexity of the resultant flow chart ____
    Determine the basis set of linearly independent paths ____
    Prepare test cases that will force execution of each path in the basis set ____
Use loop testing techniques to uncover errors in loops ____
Design test cases using black-box techniques ____
Review the software testing strategy to ensure that it is complete ____
Recognize that debugging occurs as a natural consequence of testing ____
Apply a set of debugging principles when an error or a symptom is encountered ____

MAKING CHANGES

Understand and apply a set of basic principles for making modifications ____
Create representations of software that are amenable to change ____
Establish a software maintenance procedure ____
    Assign organizational responsibility for software maintenance ____
    Establish a reporting mechanism for all changes ____
    Define a sequence of maintenance events and all important decision points ____

SOFTWARE QUALITY ASSURANCE

This appendix contains an overview of software quality assurance with specific emphasis on formal technical reviews (FTRs). Reviews have been recommended as important steps in the software engineering process. Their description here applies to all references to reviews throughout this book.

Even the most jaded software developers will agree that high quality software is an important goal. But how do we define quality? A wag once said, "Every program does something right; it just may not be the thing that we want it to do."

Many definitions of software quality have been proposed in the literature. For our purposes, software quality is defined as: *conformance to explicitly stated functional and performance requirements, explicitly documented development standards, and implicit characteristics that are expected of all professionally developed software.*

There is little question that the above definition could be modified or extended. If fact, a comprehensive definition of software quality could be debated endlessly. For the purposes of this appendix, the above definition serves to emphasize three important points:

1. Software requirements are the foundation from which quality is measured. Lack of conformance to requirements is lack of quality.
2. Specified standards define a set of development criteria that guide the manner in which software is engineered. If the criteria are not met, lack of quality will almost surely result.
3. There are *implicit requirements* that often go unmentioned (e.g., the desire for good maintainability). If software conforms to its ex-plicit requirements but fails to meet implicit requirements, software quality is suspect.

Software quality is a complex mix of factors that will vary across different applications. In the sections that follow, software quality assurance is discussed and the human activities required to achieve quality are described.

SOFTWARE QUALITY ASSURANCE

Quality assurance is an essential activity for any business that produces products to be used by others. Prior to the twentieth century, quality assurance was the sole responsibility of the craftsperson who built a product. Today, every company has mechanisms to ensure quality in its products. In fact, explicit statements of a company's concern for quality (didn't they care before the statement?) have become a marketing ploy during the past decade.

Software quality assurance (SQA) is composed of a variety of tasks associated with seven major activities: (1) application of technical methods, (2) conduct of formal technical reviews, (3) software testing, (4) enforcement of standards, (5) control of change, (6) measurement, and (7) record keeping and reporting.

Software quality is designed into a product or system. It is not imposed after the fact. For this reason, SQA actually begins with the set of technical methods and tools that help the software engineer to achieve a high quality specification and the design to develop a high quality system. Guidelines for achieving specification and design quality have already been discussed in this book (e.g., see Chapters 3 and 4).

Once a specification (or prototype) and design have been created, each must be assessed for quality. The central activity that accomplishes quality assessment is the *formal technical review*. The formal technical review (FTR) is a stylized meeting conducted by technical staff with the sole purpose of uncovering quality problems. In many situations, reviews have been found to be as effective as testing in uncovering defects in software. Reviews are discussed later in this appendix.

Software testing combines a multistep strategy with a series of test case design methods that help ensure effective error detection. Many software developers use software testing as a quality assurance "safety net." That is, developers often assume that thorough testing will uncover most errors, thereby mitigating the need for other SQA activities. Unfortunately, testing, even when performed well, is not as effective as we might like for all classes of errors.

The degree to which formal *standards and procedures* are applied to the software engineering process varies from company to company. In many cases, standards are dictated by customers or regulatory mandate. In other situations standards are self-imposed. If formal (written) standards do exist, an SQA activity must be established to assure that they are being followed. An assessment of compliance to standards may be conducted by software developers as part of a formal technical review, or, in situations where independent verification of compliance is required, the SQA group may conduct its own audit.

A major threat to software quality comes from a seemingly benign source: *changes*. Every change to software has the potential for introducing error or creating side effects that propagate errors. The change control process, a task that is part of software configuration management, handles requests for change, evaluates the nature of change, and controls its impact. Change control is applied during software development and also later during the software maintenance phase.

Measurement is an activity that is integral to any engineering discipline. An important objective of SQA is to track software quality and assess the impact of methodological and procedural changes on improved software quality. To accomplish this, software metrics must be collected. Software metrics encompass a broad array of technical and management-oriented measures of software and the process through which software is developed.

Record keeping and reporting for software quality assurance provide procedures for the collection and dissemination of SQA information. The results of reviews, audits, change control, testing, and other SQA activities must become part of the historical record for a project and should be disseminated to development staff on a need-to-know basis. For example, the results of each formal technical review for a procedural design are recorded and can be placed in a "folder" that contains all technical and SQA information about a module.

The scope of quality assurance responsibility might best be characterized by paraphrasing a popular automobile commercial: "Quality is Job #1." The implication for software is that many different constituencies in an organization—software engineers, project managers, customers, salespeople, and the individuals who serve within the SQA group— have software quality assurance responsibility.

The SQA group serves as the customer's in-house representative. That is, the people who perform SQA must look at the software from the customer's point of view. Does the software adequately meet the quality factors defined for a specific application? Has software development been conducted according to preestablished standards? Have technical disciplines properly performed their roles as part of the SQA activity? The SQA group attempts to answer these and other questions to ensure that software quality is maintained.

SOFTWARE REVIEWS

Software reviews are a "filter" for the software engineering process. That is, reviews are applied at various points during software development and serve to uncover defects that can then be removed. Software reviews serve to "purify" the software engineering steps that we have called analysis, design, and coding.

There are many different types of reviews that can be conducted as part of software engineering. Each has its place. An informal meeting around the coffee machine is a form of review, if technical problems are discussed. A formal presentation of software design to an audience of customers, management, and technical staff is a form of review. In this appendix, however, we focus on the *formal technical review* (FTR)—often called a *walkthrough*. A formal technical review is the most effective filter from a quality assurance standpoint. Conducted by software engineers (and others) for software engineers, the FTR is an effective means for improving software quality.

A formal technical review (FTR) is a software quality assurance activity that is performed by software engineers. The objectives of the FTR are: (1) to uncover errors in function, logic, or implementation for any representation of the software; (2) to verify that the software under review meets its requirements; (3) to assure that the software has been represented according to predefined standards; (4) to achieve software that is developed in a uniform manner; and (5) to make projects more manageable. In addition, the FTR serves as a training ground, enabling junior engineers to observe different approaches to software analysis, design, and coding. The FTR also serves to promote backup and continuity because a number of different people become familiar with parts of the software that they may not have otherwise seen.

Each FTR is conducted as a meeting and will be successful only if it is properly planned, controlled, and attended. In the paragraphs that follow, guidelines are presented for formal technical reviews.

The Review Meeting

Regardless of the FTR format that is chosen, every review meeting should abide by the following constraints:

- Between three and five people should be involved in the review
- Advance preparation should occur; this generally requires one to two hours of work for each person
- The duration of the review meeting should be less than two hours

Given these constraints, it should be obvious that an FTR focuses on a specific (and small) part of the overall software. For example, rather than attempting to review an entire design, walkthroughs are conducted for each module or small group of modules. By narrowing focus, the FTR has a higher likelihood of uncovering errors.

The focus of the FTR is on a *product*—a component of the software (e.g., a portion of a *Software Specification*, a detailed module design, a source code listing for a module). The individual who has developed the product—the *producer*—informs the project leader that the product is complete and that a review is required. The project leader contacts a *review leader* who evaluates the product for readiness, generates copies of product materials, and distributes them to two or three *reviewers* for advance preparation. Each reviewer is expected to spend between one and two hours reviewing the product, making notes and otherwise becoming familiar with the work. Concurrently, the review leader also reviews the product and establishes an agenda for the review meeting, which is typically scheduled for the next day.

The review meeting is attended by the review leader, all

reviewers, and the producer. One of the reviewers takes on the role of a *recorder,* that is, the individual who records (in writing) all important issues raised during the review. The FTR begins with an introduction of the agenda and a brief introduction by the producer. The producer then proceeds to "walk through" the product, explaining the material, while reviewers raise issues based on their advance preparation. When valid problems or errors are discovered, the recorder notes each.

At the end of the review, all attendees of the FTR must decide whether to (1) accept the product without further modification, (2) reject the product due to severe errors (once corrected, another review must be performed), or (3) accept the product provisionally (minor errors have been encountered and must be corrected, but no additional review will be required). The decision made, all FTR attendees "sign-off," indicating their participation in the review and their concurrence with the review team's findings.

Review Reporting and Record Keeping

During the FTR, a reviewer (the recorder) actively records all issues that have been raised. These are summarized at the end of the review meeting, and a review issues list is produced. In addition, a simple review summary report is completed. A review summary report answers three questions:

1. What was reviewed?
2. Who reviewed it?
3. What were the findings and conclusions?

The review *summary report* is a single-page form (with possible attachments) that becomes part of the project historical record and may be distributed to the project leader and other interested parties. A review *issues list* is attached to the summary report and serves two purposes: (1) to identify problem areas within the product and (2) to serve as an action item checklist that guides the producer as corrections are made.

It is important to establish a follow-up procedure to assure that items on the issues list have been properly corrected. Unless this is done, it is possible that issues raised can "fall between the cracks."

Review Guidelines

Guidelines for the conduct of formal technical reviews must be established in advance, distributed to all reviewers, agreed upon, and then followed! A review that is uncontrolled can often be worse than no review at all.

The following guidelines are a minimum set for formal technical reviews:

1. *Review the product, not the producer.* An FTR involves people and egos. Conducted properly, the FTR should leave all participants with a warm feeling of accomplishment. Conducted improperly, the FTR can take on the aura of an inquisition. Errors should be pointed out gently; the tone of the meeting should be loose and constructive; the intent should not be to embarrass or belittle. The review leader should control the review meeting to ensure that the proper tone and attitude are maintained and should immediately halt a review that has gotten out of control.

2. *Set an agenda and maintain it.* One of the key maladies of meetings of all types is drift. Since an FTR is really nothing more than a stylized meeting, it must be kept on track and on schedule. The review leader is charged with the responsibility for maintaining the review schedule and should not be afraid to nudge people when drift sets in.

3. *Limit debate and rebuttal.* When an issue is raised by a reviewer, there may not be universal agreement on its impact. Rather than spending time debating the question, the issue should be recorded for further discussion off-line.

4. *Enunciate problem areas, but don't attempt to solve every problem that is noted.* A review is not a problem-solving session. The solution of a problem can often be accomplished by the producer alone or with the help of only one other individual. Problem solving should be postponed until after the review meeting.

5. *Take written notes.* It is sometimes a good idea for the recorder to make notes on a chalk board, so that wording and prioritization can be assessed by other reviewers as information is recorded.

6. *Limit the number of participants and insist upon advance preparation.* Two heads are better than one, but 14 are not necessarily better than four. Keep the number of people involved to the necessary minimum. However, all review team members must prepare in advance.

Written comments should be solicited by the review leader (providing an indication that the reviewer has reviewed the material).

7. *Develop a checklist for each product that is likely to be reviewed.* A checklist helps the review leader to structure the FTR and helps each reviewer to focus on important issues. Checklists should be developed for analysis, design, code, and even test documents.

8. *Allocate resources, and schedule time for FTRs.* For reviews to be effective, they should be scheduled as a task during the software engineering process. In addition, time should be scheduled for the inevitable modifications that will occur as the result of an FTR.

APPENDIX **C**

A COMPREHENSIVE EXAMPLE

This appendix contains a comprehensive example that illustrates the application of each of the software engineering steps presented in this book.

The example presented in this appendix is used to illustrate the application of each software engineering step for system engineering, problem analysis, software design, coding, and testing. The example is presented in the following manner:

1. Background information is presented to establish the context for the computer-based system to be developed.

2. Each software engineering step (as it appears in Appendix A) is listed in sequence. Major steps are noted in **boldface** type font. In some cases, substeps are not specifically noted but are implied by the example that is presented.

3. Following each checklist entry, work associated with the example problem is presented to illustrate the application of the step. All work that would be produced by a software engineer is presented in smaller type font.

4. General comments about the example are presented in *italics*.

It is important to note that our focus will narrow as we move into the example problem. That is, all elements of the example system will be considered during system engineering. Problem analysis will focus on only one software component of the example system, and design, coding, and testing will narrow the focus even further. Finally, a change to one module of the implemented software will be tracked.

Background for the Example

CaseTools Corporation [a hypothetical company] has recently acquired venture capital funding with the intent of developing a computer-aided software engineering (CASE) workstation. The founders of CaseTools Corp. have convinced their backers that the CASE market will grow to over $1 billion per year by the mid-1990s.

CaseTools Corp. has assessed current products in the CASE market and has found that no company has developed workstation software that encompasses all necessary steps for conducting software engineering in an automated and semiautomated fashion. They see this as an opportunity that will enable CaseTools Corp. to capture substantial market share. Because it will take approximately two years to bring their product to market (an optimistic estimate), CaseTools Corp. has decided to develop their system with minimum hardware dependence, assuming that new and more powerful microcomputer-based workstations will be available in the short term.

CaseTools Corp. has identified the fundamental objective for their product: To create a product, called CT/9000, that assists software developers to describe and build systems. The CT/9000 product will assist the software developer by establishing an interactive dialogue that combines software-based intelligence with human input and guidance. Systems are described through a series of documentation activities that combine notation for information domain modeling, problem partitioning, data content representation, functional representation, and control/procedural representation with a method for developing these representations. Finally, software is built using a series of construction steps that transform design representations into programs through a process that includes automatic or semiautomatic code generation; transmittal for compilation, assistance for program testing, and techniques for conducting and controlling changes.

* * * * * *

The remainder of this appendix depicts the application of software engineering steps to the CT/9000 system.

Develop or acquire a statement of system scope ___ .
    Ask questions to understand overall system function ___
    Describe the overall system function ___
    Identify key inputs and outputs ___
    List all constraints that affect the system ___
    Write a plain language paragraph ___

CT/9000 Computer-Aided Software Engineering System.

The CT/9000 CASE system is a microcomputer-based workstation environment for the development of computer software. CT/9000 conducts an interactive dialogue with the software engineer using a variety of interactive devices that include keyboard, mouse, function keys. Work is conducted through a display screen using windows and pull-down menus. Using the CT/9000, the software engineer can describe software and systems through a series of documentation activities that combine notation for information domain modeling, problem partitioning, data content representation, functional representation, and control/procedural representation. In addition, CT/9000 supports procedures for project planning and control. Finally, software is built using a series of construction steps that transform design representations into programs through a process that includes automatic or semiautomatic code generation, transmittal for compilation, assistance for program testing, and techniques for conducting and controlling changes.

    CT/9000 creates a comprehensive data base for software engineering that includes all documents and representations developed as part of the software engineering process. All information in the data base is identified in a manner that enables cross reference and the ability to associate data from one document with data in another document. Both graphical and textual information are supported.

    CT/9000 produces hardcopy documentation using laser printer output so that both text and graphics can be merged with equal facility. All information maintained by the CT/9000 system can be transmitted via network links to mainframe computers or other CT/9000 workstations.

Isolate top-level processes and entities ___

Using the statement of scope for CT/9000, we apply the substeps described in Chapter 2 to perform an object-oriented analysis of the system.

Examine the statement of scope and select entities _____

Entities are defined by selecting all nouns in the statement of scope.
The CT/9000 entity table presented below is the result of this work.

CT/9000 Entity Table

Entity Name	Allocation
CT/9000 CASE Workstation	
. alias: workstation environment, CT/9000	
computer software	
alias: programs	
systems	
dialogue	
software engineer	
interactive devices	
alias: mouse	
keyboard	
function keys	
display screen	
windows	
pull-down menus	
documentation activities	
notation	
information domain modeling	
problem partitioning	
data content representation	
control/procedural representation	
procedures	
project planning and control	
construction steps	
design representations	
code generation	
program testing	
changes	
data base	
documents	
alias: representations, information, text, graphics	
software engineering process	
hardcopy	
alias: output	
laser printer	
network links	
mainframe computers	

Examine the statement of scope, and select processes _____

Processes are defined by selecting all verbs in the statement of scope. The CT/9000 process table presented below is the result of this work.

CT/9000 Process Table

Process	Actor	Object
conducts	CT/9000	dialogue
using	software engineer	devices
accomplished	interaction	display screen
		windows
		pull-down menus
describe	software engineer	software
combine	activities	notation
		modeling
		partitioning
		representation
supports	CT/9000	procedures
		project planning
		control
is built	software	construction steps
transform	construct. steps	design representation
includes	process	code generation
		program testing
		changes
	data base	documents
		representations
enables	data base	cross reference
to associate	data	document
supported	information	
	text	
	graphics	
produces	CT/9000	hardcopy
	laser printer	hardcopy
merged	text, graphics	hardcopy
transmitted	information	network links
	information	mainframe computers
	information	other workstations

Allocate processes and entities to physical system elements ____
  Develop a criterion list for allocation and prioritize ____

Criteria for Allocation of CT/9000 System

1.   Overall system price (quantity one) must be less than $10,000 including hardware.
2.   Hardware must be standard and need not be purchased with CT/9000 software.
3.   Software should be hardware independent; any hardware linkage should be isolated.
4.   Software should be operating system independent; any OS linkage should be isolated.
5.   Human-machine interaction must accommodate the "third-generation" interface approach, making use of windows and mouse interaction.
6.   Each step of the software engineering process must be supported using automatic, semiautomatic, or manual procedures.
7.   The use of manual procedures for document preparation is to be discouraged.
8.   An off-the-shelf data base management system should be used; ideally, more than one DBMS should be supported.
9.   Information generated during one step must be cataloged in a data base and transferred to other steps in a simple manner.
10.   The system must be designed to be evolutionary, that is, the basic architecture must support the addition of new features with minimum integration time.
11.   Interactive displays should be high resolution and exhibit advanced drawing and interaction capability.
12.   Hardcopy output should be publication quality.
13.   The system should support change control and other configuration management features.
14.   CT/9000 should be more than a glorified drafting tool; it should apply "intelligence" to information created by the user.
15.   System performance must be consistent with typical engineering application of workstations [specific performance data to be specified].

  Propose at least two alternative allocations ____
  Apply criteria to assess viability of each allocation alternative____

The nature of the CT/9000 product precludes dramatically different system alternatives. However, it is possible to suggest a number of different allocations within the context of the CASE application.

The CT/9000 workstation is composed of hardware, software, people, data base, document, and procedural system elements that are allocated in the following manner:

Allocation Alternative 1

Hardware: The workstation will be implemented on a 32-bit microcomputer workstation that supports the UNIX operating system.

Software: Engineering analysis and design representation capability will be supported; however, the software will use greatly simplified user interaction and relatively primitive display representations; hardcopy output will be produced on low-resolution devices. Project planning, implementation, and testing activities will not have software support. Sophisticated analysis of representations is not available.

People: The software engineer will use the hardware/software elements as a drawing tool. All evaluation capability will be applied external to the system, i.e., all intelligence is supplied by the user.

Data base: The XYZ DBMS will be used to store representations created through application of the software.

Procedural: CT/9000 will be used solely for the creation of software engineering representations. It will not be used for project planning and control, nor will it enforce documentation and/or change control.

Assessing the viability of alternative 1 against the stated assessment criteria:

Allocation 1 has been proposed as a "quick release" product that will enable Case-Tools Corp. to get to market within 12 months. Although the allocation does meet criteria 1 through 4, 8, and possibly 15, it fails to meet all remaining criteria and is therefore considered deficient.

Allocation Alternative 2

Hardware: The workstation will be implemented on a 32-bit microcomputer workstation that supports the UNIX operating system.

Software: Engineering analysis and design representation capability will be supported; a third-generation interface capability is supported and includes requirements for windows and mouse. Limited rule-based evaluation of software engineering representations are implemented by the software. Hardcopy output is generated to a laser printer. Project planning, implementation, and testing activities will not have software support. Sophisticated analysis of representations is not available.

People: The software engineer will use the hardware/software elements as a drawing tool. Some evaluation capability will be automated but the majority will be applied external to the system.

Data base: The XYZ DBMS will be used to store representations created through application of the software.

Procedural: CT/9000 will be used solely for the creation of software engineering representations. It will not be used for project planning and control, nor will it enforce documentation and/or change control.

Assessing the viability of Alternative 2 against the stated assessment criteria:

Allocation 2 has been proposed as a "middle ground" product that will enable Case-Tools Corp. to get to market within 18 months. The allocation does meet criteria 1 through 5, 8 through 11, and possibly 15. The criteria that are not met are relatively low priority. This alternative will be considered as a possible contender.

Allocation Alternative 3

Hardware: The workstation will be implemented on a 32-bit microcomputer workstation that supports the UNIX operating system.

Software: Engineering analysis and design representation capability will be supported; a third-generation interface capability is supported and includes requirements for windows and mouse. Expanded rule-based evaluation of software engineering representations is implemented by the software and provides data on inconsistencies, omissions, and requirements traceability. Software support (coupled with DBMS) for documentation and change control is available. Hardcopy output is generated to a laser printer. Project planning, implementation, and testing activities will have software support.

People: The software engineer will use the hardware/software elements as a drawing tool. Substantial evaluation capability will be automated.

Data base: The XYZ DBMS or the ABC DBMS or the PQR DBMS will each be supported to store representations created through application of the software.

Procedural: CT/9000 will be used for all steps in the software engineering process. It will support both documentation and change control.

Assessing the viability of alternative 3 against the stated assessment criteria:

Allocation 3 has been proposed as an "ultimate" product that will enable Case-Tools Corp. to get to market within 24 months. The allocation meets all criteria but is deemed impractical from a business and economic point of view.

Conclusion: Allocation 2 is selected. The following entity table shows allocations for specific CT/9000 entities:

CT/9000 Entity Table for Allocation 2

Entity Name	Allocation
CT/9000 CASE Workstation	32-bit micro software, Unix XYZ DBMS
alias: workstation environment CT/9000.	
computer software	analysis, design representations including DFDs, data dictionary, PDL, source code, standard text, and graphics

CT/9000 Entity Table for Allocation 2 (continued)

Entity Name	Allocation
alias: programs	
systems	
dialogue	human-machine
	interface
software engineer	user
interactive devices	hardware
	compatible with micro
alias: mouse	
keyboard	
function keys	
display screen	hardware
	compatible with micro
windows	software
pull-down menus	software
documentation activities	procedural
notation	software, procedural
information domain modeling	software, procedural
problem partitioning	software, procedural
data content representation	software, procedural
control/procedural representation	not supported
procedures	procedural
project planning and control	not supported
construction steps	procedural
design representations	software
code generation	not supported
program testing	software
changes	not supported
data base	XYZ DBMS
documents	software, XYZ DBMS
alias: representations	
information	
text	
graphics	
hardcopy	laser printer
alias: output	
laser printer	IJK printer
network links	not supported
mainframe computers	not supported

Develop a refined statement of scope for each allocated system element _____
Meet with the customer to review the allocation _____
Recognize that iteration is likely _____

The refined statement of scope for each of the system elements described in allocation 2 would have to be developed at this time. Because our focus is software, a refined statement of scope for the CT/9000 software element is presented below.

CT/9000—Statement of Scope

CT/9000 software encompasses support software for generic computer graphics, text manipulation, human-interface management, data base interface, and output management. In addition, CT/9000 software includes analysis/design application software for creation/analysis of software engineering documentation components and automated evaluation of limited analysis and design representations.

CT/9000 software supports an interactive dialogue between the user and the workstation, enabling the user to describe programs and data. In addition, CT/9000 software produces hardcopy documentation from the software engineering information stored in the CT/9000 data base.

An interactive dialogue between user and CT/9000 has the following characteristics: All interaction occurs in an "activity context" that is known to CT/9000, and only those commands relevant to the activity context are available to the user at any given time. Commands may be selected by pull-down menu or through keyboard codes. Commands are categorized by major CT/9000 function and should be organized hierarchically. The type and labeling of commands should imply function. At any given time, those commands relevant to a specific context should be highlighted. "Help" facilities are available for each command. Common commands should be grouped into "command macros" so that context-directed activities can be expedited for the user. In all cases, the user should be protected from disasters resulting from the selection of an incorrect command. The user should observe system function through one or more windows that appear and disappear as a consequence of commands.

System documentation is created by developing an information hierarchy that includes both text and graphics. Pictorial representations include notation and a symbol grammar that depicts information flow, information content, information structure, program structure, and control structure. Generation and analysis functions are used to create pictorial documentation components. Some documentation components will consist of natural language (English) text or artificial language text such as programming language or PDL. Documentation components are arranged hierarchically, representing progressively more refined detail. Each level of the documentation hierarchy should be accessible from another level. Information at one level can be "exploded" into more detailed information at a lower level. All documentation can be printed at publication quality resolution to hardcopy or display and represented in whole or in part. Documentation components should be identified so that all components related to a project or subproject can be referenced as a group.

Within the context of CT/9000, the term "system" is used to characterize a set of documentation components that include the following generic types: (1) descriptive text, (2) pictorial representations using specific notation and symbology, (3) tabular and textual representations of information domain items and structures, and (4) programming language source code. Each documentation component must be connected to other related components. A system element consists of a set of documentation components that are organized hierarchically.

The customer—in this case the CaseTools marketing group—has reviewed the statement of scope for CT/9000 software and has made the following comments:

Comments on the CT/9000 Statement of Scope

1. Statement should indicate that software is to be decoupled from operation system and data base manager to the greatest extent possible.
2. Statement should indicate that software should be hardware decoupled.
3. Be more specific with regard to the meaning of "creation/analysis of software engineering documentation."
4. We'd like to see an example of this "activity context" that you have alluded to in the second paragraph.
5. What kinds of "commands" are involved in the dialogue? Examples?
6. Can "help" be switched on and off? How much help is available?
7. What is the preliminary notation to be implemented? Is it open-ended?
8. How are different types of documentation related to one another?
9. What about performance issues and design constraints?

Each of the above questions would have to be addressed as part of the iteration on this system-level statement of scope for software. It is likely that many questions would be answered during software problem analysis—the next software engineering activity to be applied to CT/9000.

Refine and clarify software scope ____

The CT/9000 software engineering group has noted all review comments and will attempt to clarify each as object-oriented analysis is undertaken in the next steps. The basic statement of scope for CT/9000 software remains unchanged.

Identify objects and operations ____

Identify objects and operations using the statement of software scope as a guide ____

Use objects to identify information originators and receivers ____

Use objects to identify data stores ____

Use objects to identify data and control items ____

Use operations to identify data and control transformations ____

An object table is created from the statement of scope. A description of each object is presented in italics below the object.

Object Table

Object Name	Type
support software	abstract

software that is used in the support of all application functions and serves as the interface to hardware and operating system.

alias: generic computer graphics
            text manipulation
            human-interface management
            data base interface
            output management

applications software	abstract

software that performs analysis/design functions that are of direct interest to the user.

documentation components (DC)	data item

basic unit of information representation; described in detail later.

alias: programs
            data
            hardcopy documentation

representations	data item

graphical and text notation that describes analysis or design.

dialogue	abstract

the set of commands, prompts, and responses conducted between the user and the CT/9000 software. Input devices for dialogue are mouse and KB. In all cases, command, prompt interaction should be consistent and simple.

user	originator

each user develops documentation components on an individual workstation.

workstation	abstract

incorporates hardware and software.

CT/9000 data base	data store

on-line repository for all documentation components and other software representations.

Object Table (continued)

Object Name	Type
activity context	abstract

the set of symbols, rules, and analysis features that are relevant for a particular CT/9000 function.

commands	data item

any action selected by the user that will result in CT/9000 input, processing, or output.

type	data item

a number of command types are defined. These correspond to major and second-level functions and include document management, drawing, text management and word processing, analysis, hierarchy management, change.

command macros	data item

a sequence of commands that are stored and may be selected with a single command by the user.

pull-down menu	data item

a window that contains commands associated with a major function. Invoked via mouse or KB select.

KB codes	data item

keyboard commands that correspond to mouse picks. In addition, all input text arrives through the KB.

help facilities	data store

a special file of explanatory instructions, guidelines, and prompts that are displayed when the help function is selected.

system documentation	data item

a collection of documentation components that are developed using major functions. System documentation is organized hierarchically, and each component can be traced from other related components.

The object table is continued for all objects noted in the CT/9000 statement of software scope. Each object is classified and described as shown above.

Next, an Object-Operation Table is created.

Object-Operation Table

Operation	Objects	Type
describe	programs	data trans.
	data	
stored	information	data trans.
	data base	
produces	hardcopy doc.	data trans.
selected	commands	control trans.
organized	commands	data trans.
highlighted	commands	data trans.
	function	
grouped	commands	data trans.
	command macros	
protected	user	
	disaster	
appear	windows	control trans.
disappear	windows	control trans.
created	system doc.	data trans.
	doc. components	
includes	hierarchy	data trans.
	text	
	graphics	
depicts	notation	data trans.
	flow	
	content	
	structure	
consist	components	data trans.
	structured English	
	PDL	

The object-operation table is continued for all operations noted in the CT/9000 statement of software scope.

When things are uncertain, develop a prototype to help clarify requirements ____

> Evaluate the software scope and determine whether the software to be developed is a good candidate for prototyping ____
> Develop an abbreviated representation of requirements using an object-oriented approach ____
> Create a paper prototype ____
> Create an abbreviated design for the prototype ____
> Create, test, and refine the prototype software ____

Present the prototype to the customer, who "test drives" the application and suggests modifications ____
Repeat prototyping steps iteratively until all requirements are formalized or until the prototype has evolved into a production system ____

A prototype for the CT/9000 user interface is to be created so that the CaseTools Corp. marketing group (the customer) can assess the "human friendliness" of the design. Figures C.1 and C.2 represent some of the many "screen frames" created to depict the mode of interaction with the CT/9000 workstation software. In actuality, a working prototype of the user interface would be created using a prototyping tool. For obvious reasons, the working prototype cannot be included in this example.

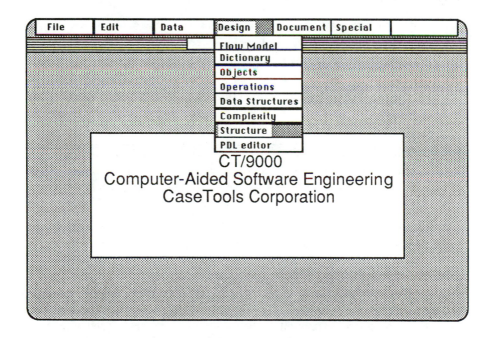

Figure C.1 Prototype Screen Frame for CT/9000

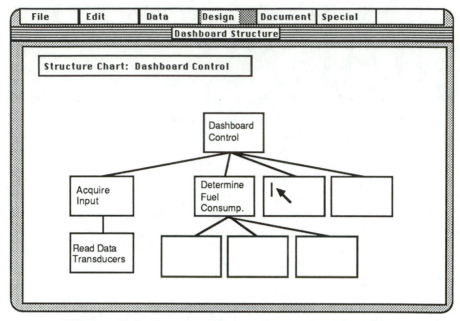

Figure C.2   Prototype Screen Frame for CT/9000

Develop a flow model for the software ____
   Use data flow diagrams to indicate how data move through the
   software ____
   Use control flow diagrams to indicate how control influences the
   software ____
   Apply flow model assessment rules ____

---

*At this point the scope of the example narrows. One element of the
CT/9000 software is a **PDL Stepwise Refinement Editor** (PDLSRE)
that enables the designer to create detail designs in PDL using software support. A refined statement of scope for PDLSRE is developed
and a flow model is created.*

PDL Stepwise Refinement Editor

The CT/9000 PDL Stepwise Refinement Editor (PDLSRE) enables the user to
create detail design representations of program modules using PDL [*as described in
Chapter 4 of this book*]. The design is created through a process of stepwise refinement in which each statement at any level of detail can be expanded (elaborated
upon) into more detailed PDL statements. Different levels of the procedural design
may be stored in the same module file and recalled by level number.
   The user interacts with the editor through standard pull-down menu selections

and keyboard entry. The PDL representation for each module becomes a documentation component that is stored in a module file of the CT/9000 software engineering data base.

Figure C.3 shows a level 01 data flow diagram for the PDLSRE. Three classes of commands may be selected by the user: PDL input commands, file processing commands, and PDL statement expansion commands. PDL is input in an interpretive mode so that correct syntax can be maintained. In addition, the user can select "PDL macros" for common procedural activities (e.g., if-then-else, case) as well as user-defined functions. All PDL is stored in a module file that can be read by PDLSRE and other CT/9000 functions (e.g., hardcopy production) that are outside the scope of this function.

Figure C.4 depicts a level 02 DFD for the PDL Stepwise Refinement Editor. PDLSRE is initiated through one or more mouse picks on menu commands that lead to information flow along one of three major paths shown. The information flow paths correspond to the command categories noted above.

Conceptually, the data structure that is created by PDLSRE takes the form illustrated in Figure C.5. A module is described with a set of level 1 PDL statements. Some subset of these statements is expanded to level 2 to provide greater elaboration of detail. The process of "stepwise refinement" continues until sufficient detail is developed. Expansion can occur either depth first or breadth first, as illustrated in the figure.

Develop a data dictionary to represent object content ____

Data Dictionary for PDLSRE

commands = generic.commands + PDLSRE.commands
gereric.commands = * acquired from the system support software for menu servicing *
PDLSRE.commands = [input.commands | file.commands | expansion.commands]
PDL = * a combination of syntax and pseudocode to be defined *
input.commands = [select.macro | indent | underline.keywords]
file.commands = [open | close | save | save as | delete | print]
expansion.commands = [expand.statement | include.file | define.level]
module.file =header information + PDL + pointers
select.macro =   [condition | loop.while | loop.until | case | macro.name]
indent = * this command implies that automatic indenting will be used to represent module control structure *
underline.keywords = * this command will cause all PDL keywords to be underlined on the display screen *

The data dictionary is continued until all data items at DFD level 01 and 02 are defined and expanded.

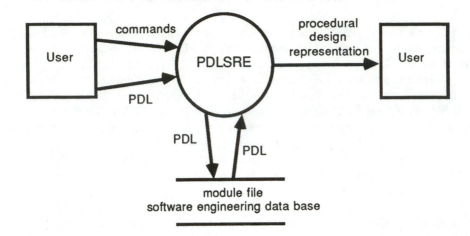

Figure C.3 Level 01 DFD for PDL Stepwise Refinement Editor

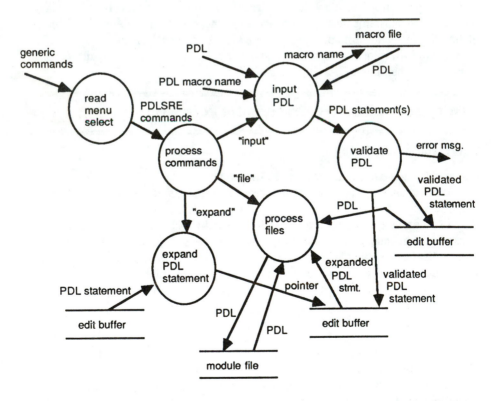

Figure C.4 Level 02 DFD for PDL Stepwise Refinement Editor

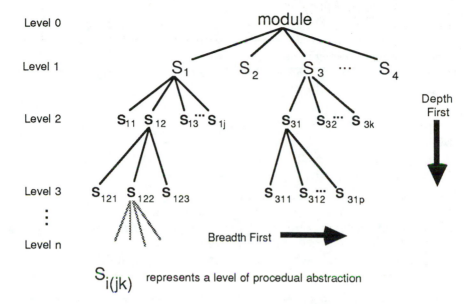

Figure C.5 Conceptual Data Structure for PDLSRE

Write processing narratives for both data and control transforms ___

Referring to Figure C.4:

Process Name: **Read Menu Select**
This process interfaces with system support functions for general processing of mouse picks associated with any pull-down menu. The system support functions provide this process with generic pick information (generic commands) that is translated (via table-driven algorithm) into the appropriate command selected by the user (PDLSRE commands). Command information is passed to a transaction processor.

Process Name: **Process Commands**
This transaction process accepts information passed from the PDLSRE process that interfaces with system support functions for general menu processing. It determines the command type and passes control to the appropriate command processing function.

Process Name: **Input PDL**
This process accepts PDL entered via the keyboard. In addition, it processes requests for PDL macros by accessing the macro from a macro file and embeds the PDL associated with the macro into the input text stream of PDL statements.

Process name: **Validate PDL**
This process validates all PDL input by the user by parsing to determine correct use of keywords, delimiters, and special characters. Validation occurs interpretively as each statement is entered. The process produces error messages below any PDL statement that is incorrect. Validated PDL statements are stored in an edit buffer for further processing and/or display.

Process Name: **Process Files**
This process handles all file processing functions for PDLSRE. All open, close, save, etc. commands are processed through this function. In addition, this process merges information in the edit buffer to create various levels of refinement for a module. This process interfaces directly with the module file.

Process Name: **Expand PDL Statement**
This process enables a user to select a PDL statement for expansion. It establishes pointers within a data structure so that various levels of procedural detail can be maintained within one module file. It stores information in the edit buffer that is ultimately merged to create the PDL description of a module contained in the module file.

Begin thinking about software validation ____

Requirements for Software Validation

Validation of PDLSRE must encompass a testing strategy that will ensure proper processing of all PDLSRE commands and proper input of PDL. In addition, the integrity of the module file must be assured and subsequent modifications to the file must be performed correctly. The following classes of tests are to be conducted once PDLSRE is implemented.

Class 1:   Tests to validate proper acquisition of generic menu picks and translation to specific PDLSRE commands.

Class 2:   Tests to ensure that PDL text can be properly input, that PDL macros can be properly referenced, generated, and embedded in PDL text.

Class 3:   Tests to validate the expansion capability for PDL at any level of detail.

Class 4:   Tests to validate proper representation of various levels of procedural design within a single module file.

Class 5:   Tests to validate proper creation and access to the module file.

Class 6:   Tests to ensure that modifications to an existing module file have been properly stored and can be recalled correctly.

Class 7:   Tests to ensure that other CT/9000 functions can properly access information contained within the module file.

The testing classes described above become an "outline" for test planning. For large projects, the development of a testing strategy can begin at this time. However, detailed test case design is postponed until after design is complete.

Put it all together to form a *Software Specification* ____
**Review the specification for correctness, consistency,
and completeness** ____
**Expect to iterate; avoid the temptation to rush into
design or coding** ____

The Software Specification for CT/9000 software includes all information developed in the preceding Problem Analysis steps, organized as discussed in Chapter 3, as well as additional information concerning each major software function (not presented here).

Refine the *Software Specification* **in preparation for design** ____

The steps associated with software design will focus on the PDL Stepwise Refinement Editor that has been specified in the preceding Problem Analysis steps.

Refining the Flow Model

Further refinement of the level 02 DFD (Figure C.4) leads to the development of a level 03 DFD for PDLSRE shown in Figure C.6. The data flow diagram has transaction characteristics (transaction center at **process commands**) and makes use of a single file access process (**read/write module file**).

**Begin data design by extending work done during problem
analysis** ____
    Review the data dictionary and select candidate data
    structures ____
    If complex data structures are to be created, simplify their
    organization ____
    Select appropriate internal data structures ____
    If a data base management system is appropriate,
    acquire one! ____

Data Design for PDLSRE

The data dictionary and corresponding data flow diagrams indicate that the following data structures should be considered:
    module file
    edit buffer
    macro file

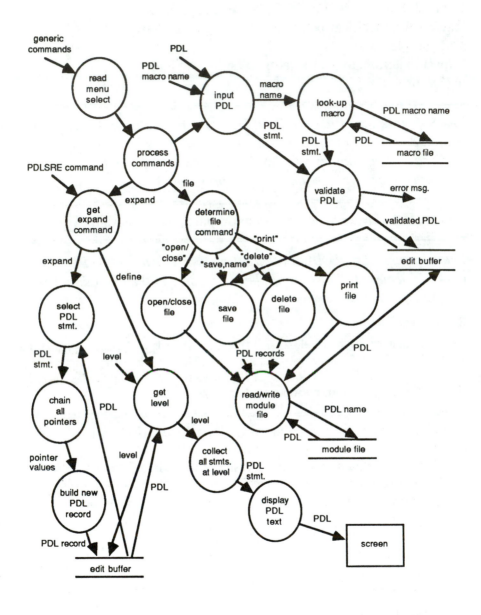

Figure C.6 Level 03 DFD for PDL Stepwise Refinement Editor

Data structure name: **module file**

Each module file contains header information, PDL statement records, and supplementary descriptive information. The data dictionary is expanded to accommodate a detailed description.

module.file = header information + {PDL statement record}^{n} + supplementary descriptive information

header.information = file name + module name/descriptor + document component identifier + version identifier + creation.date + last modification date + author name + project identifier

PDL statement records = statement level indicator + statement text + next pointer + depth pointer + back pointer

supplementary descriptive information = processing narrative pointer + restrictions text pointer + constraints pointer + graphics pointer

file.name = *eight character ID* + . + MOD

module.name/descriptor = *up to 32 alphanumeric characters*

.

.

.

statement level indicator = [1|2|...|8]

statement text = valid PDL statement

next pointer = * address of next PDL statement at the same level *

depth pointer = * address of the PDL statement that begins an expansion of the PDL statement that contains the pointer *

back pointer = *address of the statement that was expanded; occurs only at last statement of expansion*

Expansion continues for all data objects.

Data structure name: **edit buffer**

The edit buffer is a memory-resident image of the current PDL representation of a module. The data structure implementation is a multiple linked list sometimes called a ring structure.

PDL statements at a given level of detail are appended directly to the edit buffer using **next pointer**. However, when a new level of detail is to be added (i.e., a PDL statement is to be expanded) a **depth pointer** address is added to the PDL statement record in the edit buffer and all PDL statements at the new level of detail are then appended to the edit buffer. This approach is illustrated graphically in Figure C.7.

edit buffer = {PDL statement record}^{n}

PDL statement record = statement level indicator + statement text + next pointer + depth pointer + back pointer

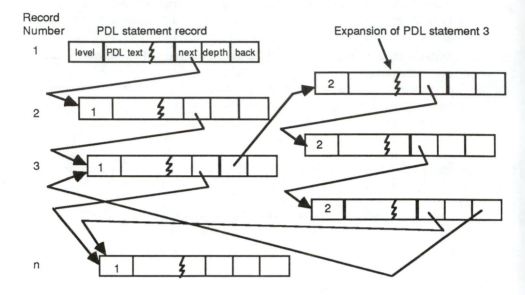

Figure C.7   List Structures for Edit Buffer

Data structure name: **macro file**

The macro file contains named PDL macros that can be referenced by name and em-bedded into the module PDL text.

macro file = name + {PDL statement record}^{n} + eom
name = NAME = + * macro name, up to 32 alphanumeric characters *
eom = * end of macro indicator *

Derive the architectural design ____
　　　Refine the flow model in preparation for design ____
　　　Determine whether the flow model has transform or transaction
　　　characteristics ____
Derive program structure using transform mapping when transform flow is present ____
　　　Isolate the transform center by specifying incoming and outgoing
　　　flow boundaries____

Perform "first-level factoring" ____
Perform second-level factoring to derive a preliminary program structure ____
Refine processing narratives for each module in the program structure ____
Refine the "first-cut" program structure using fundamental design concepts____

Derive program structure using transaction mapping when transaction flow is present____

Identify the transaction center and the flow characteristics of each action path ____
Map the DFD into a program structure amenable to transaction processing____
Factor and refine the transaction structure and the structure of each action path ____

Evaluation of the level 03 DFD for CT/9000 PDLSRE software (Figure C.6) indicates that most transforms (bubbles) show good functional independence and need no further refinement. However, the transform **validate PDL** is not cohesive and must be further refined before architectural mapping commences. Figure C.8 presents the level 03 DFD with further elaboration of the **validate PDL** transform.

The level 03 DFD shown in Figure C.8 has an overall transaction flow characteristic. Flow emanating from the transaction center (**process commands**) can be divided into three regions as shown in Figure C.8. Flow in region I is transform. Flow in region II is another transaction flow. Flow in region III has a minor transaction characteristic and two transform action flows.

A first-level factoring of the DFD shown in Figure C.8 is illustrated in the program substructure shown in Figure C.9. A transaction mapping was applied to derive this structure. Each of the regions (Figure C.8) is mapped into program substructures shown in Figures C.10, 11, and 12. The program substructure for region I is derived using a transform mapping. The role of the **file processing controller** is taken by **determine file command** transform (and corresponding module) shown in Figure C.11. The module **expansion processing controller** serves as both the transaction controller and the dispatcher for the transaction substructure shown in Figure C.12.

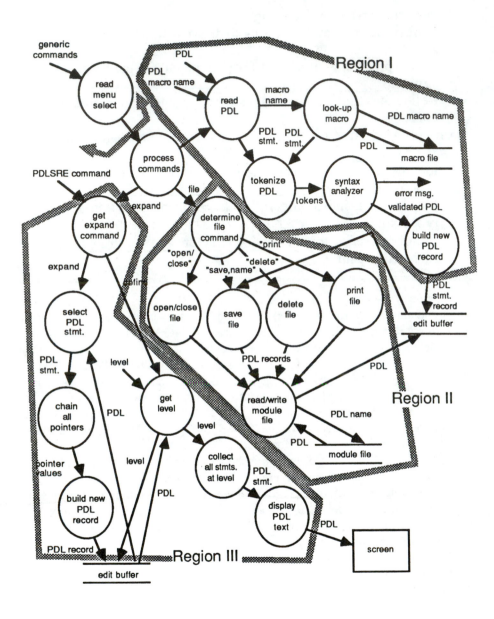

Figure C.8 Refined Level 03 DFD for PDLSRE

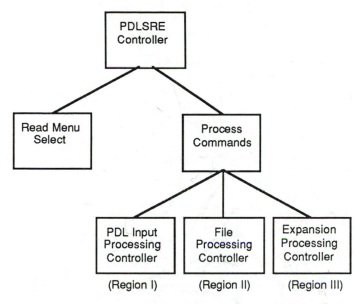

Figure C.9 First-Level Factoring for PDLSRE Mapping

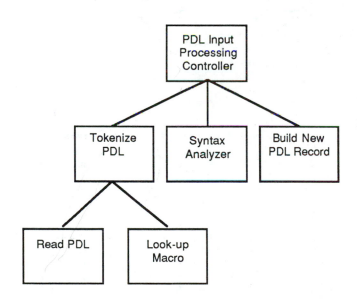

Figure C.10 Second-Level Factoring for Region I

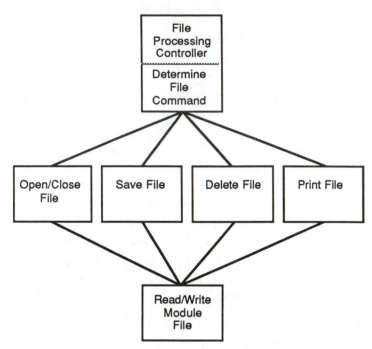

Figure C.11   Second-Level Factoring for Region II

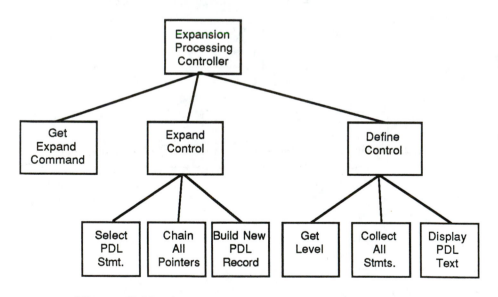

Figure C.12   Second-Level Factoring for Region III

down from the **PDLInputProcessingController**. The integration of the **Synt**
Analyzer module may be delayed if time pressure necessitates moving on to oth
more pressing work.

3. Modules for Region II (Figure C.11) will be integrated as a cluster working
top down from the **FileProcessingController**. Integration will be performed in a
depth-first manner working left to right in the program substructure (Figure C.11).
It is important to test the module **Read/WriteModuleFile** as early as possible to ensure integrity of the Module File data structure.

4. Modules for Region III (Figure C.12) will be integrated as a cluster working
bottom-up beginning with a subcluster of modules that includes **ExpandControl**
and those modules subordinate to it (Figure C.12). The **GetExpandCommand** and
ExpansionProcessingController modules will be integrated next. Finally, the **De-**
fineControl subcluster will be integrated.

In all cases, module tests designed for each module should be conducted and used regressively for integration.

Put it all together to create a *Design Document* ____
Review the design document for conformance to software require-
ments and technical quality ____

The Design Document for PDLSRE software would include all infor-
mation developed in the preceding design steps, organized as dis-
cussed in Chapter 4.

   Design reviews would be conducted on the preliminary design
developed and represented in Figures C.9 through C.12. Design
walkthroughs would be conducted for each procedural design descrip-
tion for all modules in the PDLSRE program structure.

Use the design document as a guide ____
Use the program structure to determine the order in which modules
will be coded ____

   ⌄ Begin coding modules that reside at low levels in the program
      structure ____
   ⌄ Develop code for global data structures ____
      Examine internal data structures and determine how they can be
      implemented using programming language constructs ____
      Define all data files using programming language
      conventions ____

Generate programming language source code using the procedural de-
sign as a guide ____

Derive a procedural design for each module depicted in the program structure ____

   Apply the structured programming philosophy when deriving the
   procedural design ____
   Refine the processing narratives for each module ____
   Use program design language (PDL) to represent data structures
   and procedural logic ____

A procedural design would have to be developed for each module de-
scribed in Figures C.9 through C.12. However, for the purposes of
this example we consider a complete procedural design for a single
module, **ProcessCommands**, *shown in Figure C.9.* **ProcessCom-**
mands *is a dispatcher for the overall transaction architecture.*

Procedural Design Description

Module Name: **ProcessCommands**

Processing Narrative: This module receives PDLSRE commands from the pull-
down menu system support interface and determines the command category so that
control and the command ID can be passed to the appropriate command controller.

Interface Description:
   input: pdlsre command (see data dictionary)
   output:
   1.   Command identifier that is associated with a particular PDLSRE
        command and passed to a subordinate module
   2.   Error indicator if the pdlsre command received is not recognized.

Modules called: PDL input processing controller, File processing controller, Expansion processing controller

Data Structures: This module makes use of an internal table that contains each
valid PDLSRE command, an associated category listing in the range 1 to 3, and a
numeric command id that is used to identify the command in all subsequent processing. The table contains up to 64 commands and takes the form shown in Table
C.1.

Table C.1 PDLSRE COMMAND TABLE

PSRE.command	Command Category (Code)	Command ID
select.macro	1	1
indent	1	2
underline.keywords	1	3
open	2	4
close	2	5
{... other commands not shown}		
command n	1, 2, or 3	n
eot {end of table}	0	0

*A procedural design for the module **ProcessCommands** is defined using PDL described in Chapter 4.*

```
procedure ProcessCommands (input: pdlsre command,
      command table; output: error indicator);
type
    command table [1..n] = record
        command name: char;
        category code: integer;
        command id: integer;
    end;
type cmd category, cmd id, cmd counter:integer;
type pdlsre command: char;
type cmd found flag, error indicator: boolean;
cmd counter:= 0;
cmd found flag:= false;
do while command table entries remain
increment cmd counter by 1;
if psre command = command.name
    then begin
        cmd category := category code   [cmd counter];
        cmd.id := command id [cmd counter];
        cmd found flag := true;
    else error indicator := true;
endif
enddo
if cmd found flag = true
    then
        case of cmd category:
          when cmd category = 1 select
            PdlInputProcessingController(cmd id);
          when cmd category = 2 select
            FileProcessingController(cmd id);
```

```
          when cmd category = 3 select
            ExpansionProcessingController(cmd id);
        endcase
    else return error.indicator;
endif
end;
```

Develop a preliminary test strategy to accommodate the data and program structure

The focus at this stage is twofold: (1) to develop the module test strategy for each PDLSRE module individually, and (2) to develop an integration approach for all modules in the PDLSRE program structure.

*For the purposes of this example, we develop a module test strategy for the **ProcessCommands** module (a similar module test strategy would be developed for each module in the program structure) and an integration approach for all PDLSRE software.*

Module Test Strategy for Module ProcessCommands

1. Develop a test driver that will feed **ProcessCommands** all valid (and one or two invalid) PDLSRE commands. Also, develop stubs for each of the command controllers called by **ProcessCommands**. Each stub should report entry and provide an echo of those values passed to it.

2. Execute all statements in the module by designing test cases using the basis path technique.

3. Perform loop testing on the simple *do while* loop contained in the module.

4. Evaluate error processing by passing a "bad" command to the module and checking the error.indicator (see PDL) value returned to the module test driver.

5. Evaluate the bounds of the command.table data structure (see PDL) by testing correspondence to first and last entry. Check validity of 64-entry limit.

Preliminary Integration Testing Strategy

The overall integration testing strategy for PDLSRE software will take a "sandwich" approach. The following phases are recommended:

1. The top-level program control and input substructure (Figure C.9) will be integrated first using a top-down strategy. Initially, module **ReadMenuSelect** will be integrated with **PDLSRE Controller,** and acquisition of command information will be validated. Next, module **ProcessCommands** will be integrated and all module tests will be performed to ensure proper command processing. Each of the three command controllers will be integrated next beginning with the **PDLInput–ProcessingController** and working left to right (Figure C.9).

2. Modules for Region I (Figure C.10) will be integrated as a cluster working top

Learn the elements of good coding style and apply them ____
Review the resultant code for correctness and readability ____

For the purposes of this example, Pascal source code for the module
ProcessCommands *is developed. It should be noted that code would*
be generated for each of the modules in PDLSRE, using the procedu-
ral design as a guide. All "coding rules" presented in Chapter 5 apply.

```
const MaxCommands = 64;
type
    n = 1..MaxCommands;
    CommandRec = record
        Name:   char;
        CategoryCode = 1..3;
        Id:   integer;
    end;
    CommandTable = array [1..MaxCommands] of
    CommandRec;

procedure ProcessCommands (var PDLSRECommand: char; var
CmdTbl: CommandTable; var ErrorIndicator: boolean; var
CommandId:   integer);
{
-------------------- PROLOGUE --------------------
Processing Narrative: This module receives PDLSRE
commands from the pull-down menu system support
interface and determines the command category.
CommandId is passed to the appropriate command
controller.
Interface description:
Input: pdlsre command (see data dictionary)
        CommandTable
Output:CommandId, associated with a particular command
        and passed to a subordinate module.
        ErrorIndicator, PDLSRE command received cannot
        be identified.
Data Structures: This module makes use of an internal
table that contains each valid PDLSRE command, an
associated category listing in the range 1 to 3, and a
numeric command id that is used to identify the command
in all subsequent processing. The table contains up to
64 commands and takes the form shown in Table C.1 of
the design document.
Author:   Scott McMahon
Date:   1 May 88
```

```
Reviewers: A. Frederick, L. Shapiro
Modifications: none
---------------------------END PROLOGUE
}
var CmdCategory, CmdId, CmdCounter: integer;
var CmdFoundFlag, ErrorIndicator: boolean;
Begin
CmdCounter:= 1;
CmdFoundFlag:= false;
while CmdTbl[CmdCounter].name <> "eot" and
      CmdFoundFlag = false
   do begin
   if PDLSRECommand = CmdTbl[CmdCounter].name
      then begin
      CmdCategory:=CmdTbl[CmdCounter].category.code;
      CmdID:=CmdTbl[CmdCounter].Id;
      CmdFoundFlag:=true
      end;
   CmdCounter := CmdCounter + 1; end;
if CmdFoundFlag = true
   then begin
      case CmdCategory of
      1: PDLInputProcessingController (CmdId);
      2: FileProcessingController (CmdId);
      3: ExpansionProcessingController (CmdId);
      otherwise ErrorIndicator:= true
      end;
   end;
   else ErrorIndicator:= true
end;
```

*Pascal source code for the **ProcessCommands** module undergoes a formal technical review (also called a "code walkthrough"). The code walkthrough is conducted to assess correctness, readability, and consistency with design. Why not conduct your own walkthrough on the above code?*

Develop a test plan that describes both strategy and specifics ____
Define an approach for testing each module in the program structure ____

A preliminary module test strategy was completed at the conclusion of procedural design. The module test strategy is reassessed and refined

once coding is completed. Once again, we focus on the module
ProcessCommands, *refining the original test strategy to accommodate
the Pascal implementation.*

Module Test Strategy for ProcessCommands

1. Develop a test driver that will feed **ProcessCommands** all valid (and one or two invalid) PDLSRE commands. The driver must contain the CommandTable data structure that is terminated with an "eot" character. Further, the driver must echo the ErrorIndicator value at the conclusion of the test.

2. Three stubs must be developed for each command controller called by **Process-Commands**. Each stub should report entry and provide an echo of those values passed to it.

3. Execute all statements in the module by designing test cases using the basis path technique. Caution: be certain to properly account for the compound condition contained in the while-do statement and the conditions implied by the case statement.

4. Perform loop testing on the simple while-do loop contained in the module. Test for 0, 1, 2, m, n-1, n passes through the loop, where n is the number of CommandTable entries and $2 < m < (n-1)$.

5. Evaluate error processing by passing a "bad" command to the module and checking the ErrorIndicator value returned to the module test driver.

6. Evaluate the bounds of the CommandTable data structure by testing correspondence to first and last entry. Check validity of 64-entry limit.

Develop an integration strategy for constructing the program structure _____

Integrate modules using both top-down and bottom-up testing _____

Integration Test Strategy

The overall integration testing strategy for PDLSRE will take a "sandwich" approach. The following phases are recommended:

1. The top-level program control and input substructure (Figure C.9) will be integrated first using a top-down strategy. Initially, module **ReadMenuSelect** will be integrated with **PDLSREController** and acquisition of command information will be validated. Next, module **ProcessCommands** will be integrated and all module tests will be performed to validate proper command processing. Each of the command controllers will be integrated next starting with the **PDLInputProcessing–Controller** and working left to right (Figure C.9).

Test cases for phase 1 will be designed using equivalence partitioning and boundary value analysis.

Test Suite 1: Values of PDLSRECommand from each of the command categories

1, 2, and 3 will be executed. In all cases, branching to the appropriate command controller should be validated.

Test Suite 2: The PDLSRECommand corresponding to the first and last CommandTable entries are input. Branching to the appropriate command controller should be validated.

Test Suite 3: All module tests associated with **ReadMenuSelect** and **ProcessCommands** are re-executed.

2. Modules for Region I (Figure C.10) will be integrated as a cluster working top down from **PDLInputProcessingController**. The integration of the **Syntax–Analyzer** module may be delayed if other more pressing work must be conducted first.

Test suites, similar in form to those defined for phase 1, are specified for phase 2.

3. Modules for Region II (Figure C.11) will be integrated as a cluster working top down from **FileProcessingController**. Integration will be performed in a depth-first manner working left to right in the program substructure. It is important to test the module **ReadWriteModuleFile** as early as possible to ensure the integrity of the Module File data structure.

Test suites, similar in form to those defined for phase 1, are specified for phase 3.

4. Modules for Region III (Figure C.12) will be integrated as a cluster working bottom up beginning with a subcluster of modules that includes **ExpandControl** and those modules subordinate to it. The **GetExpandCommand** and **Expansion–ProcessingController** modules are integrated next. Finally, the **DefineControl** subcluster will be integrated.

Test suites, similar in form to those defined for phase 1, are specified for phase 4.

Define a validation testing strategy to be conducted prior to release ____

Validation Test Strategy

Validation of the PDLSRE must encompass a strategy that will ensure proper testing of all PDLSRE commands and proper input of PDL. In addition, the integrity of the module file must be assured and subsequent modifications to the file must be performed correctly. The following classes of tests are to be conducted once PDLSRE is implemented.

Class 1: Tests to validate proper acquisition of generic menu picks and translation to specific PDLSRE commands

Class 2: Tests to ensure that PDL text can be properly input; that PDL macros can be properly referenced, generated, and embedded in PDL text

Class 3: Tests to validate the expansion capability for PDL at any level of detail

Class 4: Tests to validate proper representation of various levels of procedural design within a single module file

Class 5: Tests to validate proper creation of and access to the module file

Class 6: Tests to ensure that modifications to an existing module file have been properly stored and can be recalled correctly

Class 7: Tests to ensure that other CT/9000 functions can properly access information contained within the module file

Design tests using white-box techniques ____

Derive test cases using the basis path technique ____

Draw a flow chart using the design or code as a guide ____

Determine the cyclomatic complexity of the resultant flow chart ____

Determine the basis set of linearly independent paths ____

Prepare test cases that will force execution of each path in the basis set ____

*For the purposes of this example, we again focus on the **Process-Commands** module represented in PDL and implemented in Pascal. Each of the above steps is applied to other selected PDLSRE modules.*

Using Pascal source code for **ProcessCommands** as a guide, the flow chart shown in Figure C.13 is developed. The cyclomatic complexity may be computed using either of the two algorithms:

$V(G)$ = number of enclosed areas + 1

= 7 + 1

= 8

or

$V(G)$ = number of simple conditions + 1

= 8

Therefore, the basis set for the **ProcessCommands** module contains eight independent paths. A set of basis paths is given below:

Path 1:   1-2-8-14-15
Path 2:   1-2-3-8-9-9a-15
Path 3:   1-2-3-8-9-10-10a-15
Path 4:   1-2-3-8-9-10-11-11a-15
Path 5:   1-2-3-8-9-10-11-12-15
Path 6:   1-2-3-4-5-6-7-2-...-8-...
Path 7:   1-2-3-4-6-7-8-2-...
Path 8:   1-2-3-4-6-7-8-2-3-8-...

Test cases to exercise each of the basis paths are given in Table C.2.

```
1:      CmdCounter:= 1;
1:      CmdFoundFlag:= false;
2,3:    while CmdTbl[CmdCounter].name <> "eot" and
            CmdFoundFlag = false
        do begin
4:      if PDLSRECommand = CmdTbl[CmdCounter].name
            then begin
5:          CmdCategory:=CmdTbl[CmdCounter].category.code;
5:          CmdID:=CmdTbl[CmdCounter].Id;
5:          CmdFoundFlag:=true;
            end;
6:      CmdCounter:= CmdCounter + 1;
7:      end;
8:      if CmdFoundFlag = true
        then begin
            case CmdCategory of
9, 9a       1: PDLInputProcessingController (CmdId);
10,10a      2: FileProcessingController (CmdId);
11,11a      3: ExpansionProcessingController (CmdId);
12          otherwise ErrorIndicator:= true;
            end;
13      end;
14      else ErrorIndicator:= true;
15      end;
```

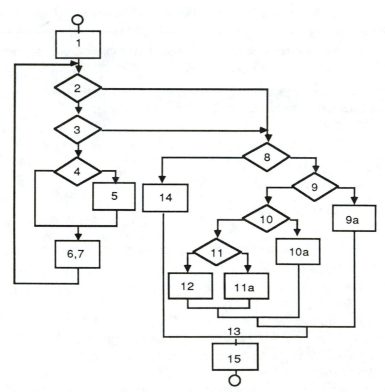

Figure C.13 Flow Chart Corresponding to PDL Above

Table C.2 TEST CASES—Statement Coverage for ProcessCommands

Path	Input PDLSRE Command	Expected Results CmdId	ErrorIndicator
1	invalid command	undefined	true
2	valid command, cat. 1	corresponding CmdId	false
3	valid command, cat. 2	corresponding CmdId	false
4	valid command, cat. 3	corresponding CmdId	false

Note: Tests for the paths 2, 3, and 4 will require a reorganization of records in the CommandTable so that the first entry provides a match.

5	valid command, table error	1, 2, or 3	true

Note: Test for path 5 requires first entry in table to have invalid CmdCategory.

6	valid commands, cat.1, 2, 3	corresponding CmdId	false
7	invalid command	undefined	true

Note: This test implies a situation in which no match occurs and the end of the table is reached.

8	invalid command	undefined	true

Note: In actuality, this test is identical to the path 7 test.

Use loop testing techniques to uncover errors in loops____

The only loop in the **ProcessCommands** module is the following code segment:

```
while CmdTbl[CmdCounter].name <> "eot" and
      CmdFoundFlag = false
do begin
if PDLSRECommand = CmdTbl[CmdCounter].name
      then begin
      CmdCategory:=CmdTbl[CmdCounter].category.code;
      CmdID:=CmdTbl[CmdCounter].Id;
      CmdFoundFlag:=true;
      end;
   CmdCounter := CmdCounter + 1; end;
```

Loop testing requires a set of test cases for 0, 1, 2, m, n-1 and n passes through the loop where n is the number of CommandTable entries and $2<m<(n-1)$.

Passes through the loop = 0

To achieve this loop, the first entry in the CommandTable must be set to "eot." However, this makes the table null and is meaningless in the context of this procedure.

Passes through the loop = 1

To achieve this loop, the first entry in the CommandTable must be set to match the PDLSRECommand value passed to the **ProcessCommands** module.

Passes through the loop = 2

To achieve this loop, the second entry in the CommandTable must be set to match the PDLSRECommand value passed to the **ProcessCommands** module.

Passes through the loop = *m*

To achieve this loop, the *m*th entry in the CommandTable must be set to match the PDLSRECommand value passed to the **ProcessCommands** module.

Passes through the loop = *n*-1

To achieve this loop, the *(n-1)*st entry in the CommandTable must be set to match the PDLSRECommand value passed to the **ProcessCommands** module.

Passes through the loop = *n*

To achieve this loop, the *n*th entry in the CommandTable must be set to match the PDLSRECommand value passed to the **ProcessCommands** module.

An alternative test that will achieve *n* passes through the loop is to pass a PDLSRECommand value that is invalid.

Design test cases using black-box techniques ___

Equivalence Partitioning

The input domain for the PDLSRE software may be divided into the following equivalence classes:

Class 1:   PDLSRE commands that are input using menu picks or the keyboard.
Class 2:   PDL statements input via the keyboard.
Class 3:   PDL records obtained from the module file.
Class 4:   Information contained in the edit buffer used as input to a variety of
           program functions.

Test cases can be designed to reflect both valid and invalid inputs for each class. For example, the specific test cases for equivalence class 1 would be:

Class 1, Test 1

Test data: The valid PDLSRE command **open**

Expected results: The system should prompt for a module file name. Once the appropriate file name is provided or "new" is chosen, the system should load the file, providing an indication of success by displaying level 1 PDL. If new is chosen, the system should create an untitled file and display a blank window for PDL input.

Class 1, Test 2

Test data: An invalid PDLSRE command **opin**

Expected results: The system should respond with an error message indicating that an invalid command "opin" has been specified. The tester should verify that no damage to files or process sequence has occurred.

Review the software testing strategy to ensure that it is complete ____
Recognize that debugging occurs as a natural consequence of testing ____
Apply a set of debugging principles when an error or a symptom is encountered ____

A walkthrough of the PDLSRE test strategy and test procedure would be conducted to ensure that tests are complete at both the module and integration levels and that all system requirements have been met. The conduct of the walkthrough and any necessary corrections or additions are left to the reader as an exercise.

Derive a procedural design for each module depicted in the program structure ____

Apply the structured programming philosophy when deriving the procedural design____

Refine the processing narratives for each module ____

Use program design language (PDL) to represent data structures and procedural logic ____

*A procedural design would have to be developed for each module described in Figures C.9 through C.12. However, for the purposes of this example we consider a complete procedural design for a single module, **ProcessCommands**, shown in Figure C.9. **ProcessCommands** is a dispatcher for the overall transaction architecture.*

Procedural Design Description

Module Name: **ProcessCommands**

Processing Narrative: This module receives PDLSRE commands from the pull-down menu system support interface and determines the command category so that control and the command ID can be passed to the appropriate command controller.

Interface Description:

input: pdlsre command (see data dictionary)

output:

1. Command identifier that is associated with a particular PDLSRE command and passed to a subordinate module
2. Error indicator if the pdlsre command received is not recognized.

Modules called: PDL input processing controller, File processing controller, Expansion processing controller

Data Structures: This module makes use of an internal table that contains each valid PDLSRE command, an associated category listing in the range 1 to 3, and a numeric command id that is used to identify the command in all subsequent processing. The table contains up to 64 commands and takes the form shown in Table C.1.

Table C.1 PDLSRE COMMAND TABLE

PSRE.command	Command Category (Code)	Command ID
select.macro	1	1
indent	1	2
underline.keywords	1	3
open	2	4
close	2	5
{... other commands not shown}		
command n	1, 2, or 3	n
eot {end of table}	0	0

*A procedural design for the module **ProcessCommands** is defined using PDL described in Chapter 4.*

```
procedure ProcessCommands (input: pdlsre command,
      command table; output: error indicator);
type
    command table [1..n] = record
        command name: char;
        category code: integer;
        command id: integer;
    end;
type cmd category, cmd id, cmd counter:integer;
type pdlsre command: char;
type cmd found flag, error indicator: boolean;
cmd counter:= 0;
cmd found flag:= false;
do while command table entries remain
increment cmd counter by 1;
if psre command = command.name
    then begin
        cmd category := category code   [cmd counter];
        cmd.id := command id [cmd counter];
        cmd found flag := true;
    else error indicator := true;
endif
enddo
if cmd found flag = true
    then
        case of cmd category:
          when cmd category = 1 select
            PdlInputProcessingController(cmd id);
          when cmd category = 2 select
            FileProcessingController(cmd id);
```

```
        when cmd category = 3 select
          ExpansionProcessingController(cmd id);
        endcase
      else return error.indicator;
endif
end;
```

Develop a preliminary test strategy to accommodate the data and program structure____

The focus at this stage is twofold: (1) to develop the module test strategy for each PDLSRE module individually, and (2) to develop an integration approach for all modules in the PDLSRE program structure.

*For the purposes of this example, we develop a module test strategy for the **ProcessCommands** module (a similar module test strategy would be developed for each module in the program structure) and an integration approach for all PDLSRE software.*

Module Test Strategy for Module ProcessCommands

1. Develop a test driver that will feed **ProcessCommands** all valid (and one or two invalid) PDLSRE commands. Also, develop stubs for each of the command controllers called by **ProcessCommands**. Each stub should report entry and provide an echo of those values passed to it.
2. Execute all statements in the module by designing test cases using the basis path technique.
3. Perform loop testing on the simple *do while* loop contained in the module.
4. Evaluate error processing by passing a "bad" command to the module and checking the error.indicator (see PDL) value returned to the module test driver.
5. Evaluate the bounds of the command.table data structure (see PDL) by testing correspondence to first and last entry. Check validity of 64-entry limit.

Preliminary Integration Testing Strategy

The overall integration testing strategy for PDLSRE software will take a "sandwich" approach. The following phases are recommended:

1. The top-level program control and input substructure (Figure C.9) will be integrated first using a top-down strategy. Initially, module **ReadMenuSelect** will be integrated with **PDLSRE Controller,** and acquisition of command information will be validated. Next, module **ProcessCommands** will be integrated and all module tests will be performed to ensure proper command processing. Each of the three command controllers will be integrated next beginning with the **PDLInput–ProcessingController** and working left to right (Figure C.9).
2. Modules for Region I (Figure C.10) will be integrated as a cluster working top

down from the **PDLInputProcessingController**. The integration of the **Syntax–Analyzer** module may be delayed if time pressure necessitates moving on to other more pressing work.

3. Modules for Region II (Figure C.11) will be integrated as a cluster working top down from the **FileProcessingController**. Integration will be performed in a depth-first manner working left to right in the program substructure (Figure C.11). It is important to test the module **Read/WriteModuleFile** as early as possible to ensure integrity of the Module File data structure.

4. Modules for Region III (Figure C.12) will be integrated as a cluster working bottom-up beginning with a subcluster of modules that includes **ExpandControl** and those modules subordinate to it (Figure C.12). The **GetExpandCommand** and **ExpansionProcessingController** modules will be integrated next. Finally, the **DefineControl** subcluster will be integrated.

In all cases, module tests designed for each module should be conducted and used regressively for integration.

Put it all together to create a *Design Document* ____
Review the design document for conformance to software requirements and technical quality ____

The Design Document for PDLSRE software would include all information developed in the preceding design steps, organized as discussed in Chapter 4.

Design reviews would be conducted on the preliminary design developed and represented in Figures C.9 through C.12. Design walkthroughs would be conducted for each procedural design description for all modules in the PDLSRE program structure.

Use the design document as a guide ____
Use the program structure to determine the order in which modules will be coded ____
  - Begin coding modules that reside at low levels in the program structure ____
  - Develop code for global data structures ____
  Examine internal data structures and determine how they can be implemented using programming language constructs ____
  Define all data files using programming language conventions ____
Generate programming language source code using the procedural design as a guide ____

Learn the elements of good coding style and apply them ____
Review the resultant code for correctness and readability ____

For the purposes of this example, Pascal source code for the module ***ProcessCommands*** *is developed. It should be noted that code would be generated for each of the modules in PDLSRE, using the procedural design as a guide. All "coding rules" presented in Chapter 5 apply.*

```
const MaxCommands = 64;
type
    n = 1..MaxCommands;
    CommandRec = record
        Name:   char;
        CategoryCode = 1..3;
        Id:   integer;
    end;
    CommandTable = array [1..MaxCommands] of
    CommandRec;

procedure ProcessCommands (var PDLSRECommand: char; var
CmdTbl: CommandTable; var ErrorIndicator: boolean; var
CommandId: integer);
{
-------------------- PROLOGUE --------------------------
Processing Narrative: This module receives PDLSRE
commands from the pull-down menu system support
interface and determines the command category.
CommandId is passed to the appropriate command
controller.
Interface description:
Input: pdlsre command (see data dictionary)
        CommandTable
Output:CommandId, associated with a particular command
        and passed to a subordinate module.
        ErrorIndicator, PDLSRE command received cannot
        be identified.
Data Structures: This module makes use of an internal
table that contains each valid PDLSRE command, an
associated category listing in the range 1 to 3, and a
numeric command id that is used to identify the command
in all subsequent processing. The table contains up to
64 commands and takes the form shown in Table C.1 of
the design document.
Author:  Scott McMahon
Date:  1 May 88
```

```
Reviewers: A. Frederick, L. Shapiro
Modifications: none
---------------------------END PROLOGUE
}
var CmdCategory, CmdId, CmdCounter: integer;
var CmdFoundFlag, ErrorIndicator: boolean;
Begin
CmdCounter:= 1;
CmdFoundFlag:= false;
while CmdTbl[CmdCounter].name <> "eot" and
      CmdFoundFlag = false
   do  begin
   if PDLSRECommand = CmdTbl[CmdCounter].name
      then begin
      CmdCategory:=CmdTbl[CmdCounter].category.code;
      CmdID:=CmdTbl[CmdCounter].Id;
      CmdFoundFlag:=true
      end;
   CmdCounter := CmdCounter + 1; end;
if CmdFoundFlag = true
   then begin
      case CmdCategory of
      1: PDLInputProcessingController (CmdId);
      2: FileProcessingController (CmdId);
      3: ExpansionProcessingController (CmdId);
      otherwise ErrorIndicator:= true
      end;
   end;
   else ErrorIndicator:= true
end;
```

*Pascal source code for the **ProcessCommands** module undergoes a formal technical review (also called a "code walkthrough"). The code walkthrough is conducted to assess correctness, readability, and consistency with design. Why not conduct your own walkthrough on the above code?*

===

Develop a test plan that describes both strategy and specifics ____
   Define an approach for testing each module in the program
   structure ____

===

A preliminary module test strategy was completed at the conclusion of procedural design. The module test strategy is reassessed and refined once coding is completed. Once again, we focus on the module **ProcessCommands**, *refining the original test strategy to accommodate the Pascal implementation.*

Module Test Strategy for ProcessCommands

1. Develop a test driver that will feed **ProcessCommands** all valid (and one or two invalid) PDLSRE commands. The driver must contain the CommandTable data structure that is terminated with an "eot" character. Further, the driver must echo the ErrorIndicator value at the conclusion of the test.

2. Three stubs must be developed for each command controller called by **Process-Commands**. Each stub should report entry and provide an echo of those values passed to it.

3. Execute all statements in the module by designing test cases using the basis path technique. Caution: be certain to properly account for the compound condition contained in the while-do statement and the conditions implied by the case statement.

4. Perform loop testing on the simple while-do loop contained in the module. Test for 0, 1, 2, m, n-1, n passes through the loop, where n is the number of CommandTable entries and $2<m<(n-1)$.

5. Evaluate error processing by passing a "bad" command to the module and checking the ErrorIndicator value returned to the module test driver.

6. Evaluate the bounds of the CommandTable data structure by testing correspondence to first and last entry. Check validity of 64-entry limit.

Develop an integration strategy for constructing the program structure _____

Integrate modules using both top-down and bottom-up testing _____

Integration Test Strategy

The overall integration testing strategy for PDLSRE will take a "sandwich" approach. The following phases are recommended:

1. The top-level program control and input substructure (Figure C.9) will be integrated first using a top-down strategy. Initially, module **ReadMenuSelect** will be integrated with **PDLSREController** and acquisition of command information will be validated. Next, module **ProcessCommands** will be integrated and all module tests will be performed to validate proper command processing. Each of the command controllers will be integrated next starting with the **PDLInputProcessing-Controller** and working left to right (Figure C.9).

Test cases for phase 1 will be designed using equivalence partitioning and boundary value analysis.

Test Suite 1: Values of PDLSRECommand from each of the command categories

1, 2, and 3 will be executed. In all cases, branching to the appropriate command controller should be validated.

Test Suite 2: The PDLSRECommand corresponding to the first and last CommandTable entries are input. Branching to the appropriate command controller should be validated.

Test Suite 3: All module tests associated with **ReadMenuSelect** and **ProcessCommands** are re-executed.

2. Modules for Region I (Figure C.10) will be integrated as a cluster working top down from **PDLInputProcessingController**. The integration of the **Syntax--Analyzer** module may be delayed if other more pressing work must be conducted first.

Test suites, similar in form to those defined for phase 1, are specified for phase 2.

3. Modules for Region II (Figure C.11) will be integrated as a cluster working top down from **FileProcessingController**. Integration will be performed in a depth-first manner working left to right in the program substructure. It is important to test the module **ReadWriteModuleFile** as early as possible to ensure the integrity of the Module File data structure.

Test suites, similar in form to those defined for phase 1, are specified for phase 3.

4. Modules for Region III (Figure C.12) will be integrated as a cluster working bottom up beginning with a subcluster of modules that includes **ExpandControl** and those modules subordinate to it. The **GetExpandCommand** and **Expansion-ProcessingController** modules are integrated next. Finally, the **DefineControl** subcluster will be integrated.

Test suites, similar in form to those defined for phase 1, are specified for phase 4.

Define a validation testing strategy to be conducted prior to release ____

Validation Test Strategy

Validation of the PDLSRE must encompass a strategy that will ensure proper testing of all PDLSRE commands and proper input of PDL. In addition, the integrity of the module file must be assured and subsequent modifications to the file must be performed correctly. The following classes of tests are to be conducted once PDLSRE is implemented.

Class 1: Tests to validate proper acquisition of generic menu picks and translation to specific PDLSRE commands

Class 2: Tests to ensure that PDL text can be properly input; that PDL macros can be properly referenced, generated, and embedded in PDL text

Class 3: Tests to validate the expansion capability for PDL at any level of detail

Class 4: Tests to validate proper representation of various levels of procedural design within a single module file

Class 5: Tests to validate proper creation of and access to the module file

Class 6: Tests to ensure that modifications to an existing module file have been properly stored and can be recalled correctly

Class 7: Tests to ensure that other CT/9000 functions can properly access information contained within the module file

---

Design tests using white-box techniques ____

Derive test cases using the basis path technique ____

Draw a flow chart using the design or code as a guide ____

Determine the cyclomatic complexity of the resultant flow chart ____

Determine the basis set of linearly independent paths ____

Prepare test cases that will force execution of each path in the basis set ____

---

*For the purposes of this example, we again focus on the **Process-Commands** module represented in PDL and implemented in Pascal. Each of the above steps is applied to other selected PDLSRE modules.*

Using Pascal source code for **ProcessCommands** as a guide, the flow chart shown in Figure C.13 is developed. The cyclomatic complexity may be computed using either of the two algorithms:

$V(G)$ = number of enclosed areas + 1

   = 7 + 1

   = 8

or

$V(G)$ = number of simple conditions + 1

   = 8

Therefore, the basis set for the **ProcessCommands** module contains eight independent paths. A set of basis paths is given below:

Path 1:   1-2-8-14-15
Path 2:   1-2-3-8-9-9a-15
Path 3:   1-2-3-8-9-10-10a-15
Path 4:   1-2-3-8-9-10-11-11a-15
Path 5:   1-2-3-8-9-10-11-12-15
Path 6:   1-2-3-4-5-6-7-2-...-8-...
Path 7:   1-2-3-4-6-7-8-2-...
Path 8:   1-2-3-4-6-7-8-2-3-8-...

Test cases to exercise each of the basis paths are given in Table C.2.

```
1:      CmdCounter:= 1;
1:      CmdFoundFlag:= false;
2,3:    while CmdTbl[CmdCounter].name <> "eot" and
            CmdFoundFlag = false
        do begin
4:      if PDLSRECommand = CmdTbl[CmdCounter].name
            then begin
5:          CmdCategory:=CmdTbl[CmdCounter].category.code;
5:          CmdID:=CmdTbl[CmdCounter].Id;
5:          CmdFoundFlag:=true;
            end;
6:      CmdCounter:= CmdCounter + 1;
7:      end;
8:      if CmdFoundFlag = true
        then begin
            case CmdCategory of
9, 9a       1: PDLInputProcessingController (CmdId);
10,10a      2: FileProcessingController (CmdId);
11,11a      3: ExpansionProcessingController (CmdId);
12          otherwise ErrorIndicator:= true;
            end;
13      end;
14      else ErrorIndicator:= true;
15      end;
```

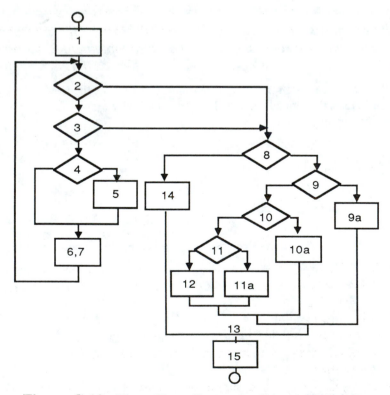

Figure C.13 Flow Chart Corresponding to PDL Above

Table C.2 TEST CASES—Statement Coverage for ProcessCommands

	Input	Expected Results	
Path	PDLSRE Command	CmdId	ErrorIndicator
1	invalid command	undefined	true
2	valid command, cat. 1	corresponding CmdId	false
3	valid command, cat. 2	corresponding CmdId	false
4	valid command, cat. 3	corresponding CmdId	false

Note: Tests for the paths 2, 3, and 4 will require a reorganization of records in the CommandTable so that the first entry provides a match.

5	valid command, table error	1, 2, or 3	true

Note: Test for path 5 requires first entry in table to have invalid CmdCategory.

6	valid commands, cat.1, 2, 3	corresponding CmdId	false
7	invalid command	undefined	true

Note: This test implies a situation in which no match occurs and the end of the table is reached.

8	invalid command	undefined	true

Note: In actuality, this test is identical to the path 7 test.

Use loop testing techniques to uncover errors in loops____

The only loop in the **ProcessCommands** module is the following code segment:

```
while CmdTbl[CmdCounter].name <> "eot" and
     CmdFoundFlag = false
do  begin
if PDLSRECommand = CmdTbl[CmdCounter].name
    then begin
    CmdCategory:=CmdTbl[CmdCounter].category.code;
    CmdID:=CmdTbl[CmdCounter].Id;
    CmdFoundFlag:=true;
    end;
  CmdCounter := CmdCounter + 1; end;
```

Loop testing requires a set of test cases for 0, 1, 2, m, n-1 and n passes through the loop where n is the number of CommandTable entries and $2<m<(n-1)$.

Passes through the loop = 0
To achieve this loop, the first entry in the CommandTable must be set to "eot." However, this makes the table null and is meaningless in the context of this procedure.

Passes through the loop = 1
To achieve this loop, the first entry in the CommandTable must be set to match the PDLSRECommand value passed to the **ProcessCommands** module.

Passes through the loop = 2
To achieve this loop, the second entry in the CommandTable must be set to match the PDLSRECommand value passed to the **ProcessCommands** module.

Passes through the loop = *m*

To achieve this loop, the *m*th entry in the CommandTable must be set to match the PDLSRECommand value passed to the **ProcessCommands** module.

Passes through the loop = *n*-1

To achieve this loop, the *(n-1)*st entry in the CommandTable must be set to match the PDLSRECommand value passed to the **ProcessCommands** module.

Passes through the loop = *n*

To achieve this loop, the *n*th entry in the CommandTable must be set to match the PDLSRECommand value passed to the **ProcessCommands** module.

An alternative test that will achieve *n* passes through the loop is to pass a PDLSRECommand value that is invalid.

Design test cases using black-box techniques ____

Equivalence Partitioning

The input domain for the PDLSRE software may be divided into the following equivalence classes:

Class 1: PDLSRE commands that are input using menu picks or the keyboard.
Class 2: PDL statements input via the keyboard.
Class 3: PDL records obtained from the module file.
Class 4: Information contained in the edit buffer used as input to a variety of program functions.

Test cases can be designed to reflect both valid and invalid inputs for each class. For example, the specific test cases for equivalence class 1 would be:

Class 1, Test 1

Test data: The valid PDLSRE command **open**

Expected results: The system should prompt for a module file name. Once the appropriate file name is provided or "new" is chosen, the system should load the file, providing an indication of success by displaying level 1 PDL. If new is chosen, the system should create an untitled file and display a blank window for PDL input.

Class 1, Test 2

Test data: An invalid PDLSRE command **opin**

Expected results: The system should respond with an error message indicating that an invalid command "opin" has been specified. The tester should verify that no damage to files or process sequence has occurred.

Review the software testing strategy to ensure that it is complete ____
Recognize that debugging occurs as a natural consequence of testing ____
Apply a set of debugging principles when an error or a symptom is encountered ____

A walkthrough of the PDLSRE test strategy and test procedure would be conducted to ensure that tests are complete at both the module and integration levels and that all system requirements have been met. The conduct of the walkthrough and any necessary corrections or additions are left to the reader as an exercise.

INDEX

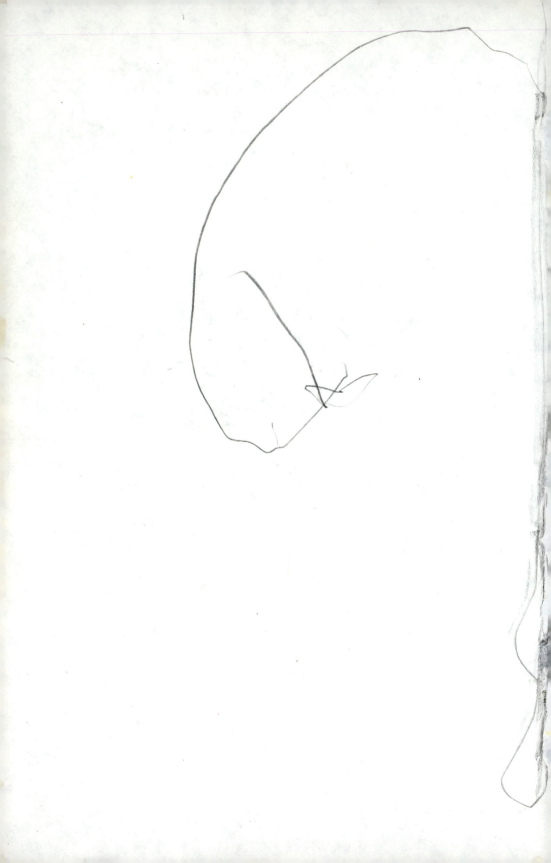